VERSIFICATION AND SYNTAX
IN JEREMIAH 2-25
Syntactical Constraints in Hebrew Colometry

SOCIETY
OF BIBLICAL
LITERATURE

DISSERTATION SERIES
J. J. M. Roberts, Old Testament Editor
Charles Talbert, New Testament Editor

Number 117

VERSIFICATION AND SYNTAX IN JEREMIAH 2-25
Syntactical Constraints in Hebrew Colometry

by
Walter Theophilus Woldemar Cloete

Walter Theophilus Woldemar Cloete

VERSIFICATION AND SYNTAX IN JEREMIAH 2-25
Syntactical Constraints in Hebrew Colometry

Scholars Press
Atlanta, Georgia

VERSIFICATION AND SYNTAX IN JEREMIAH 2-25

Walter Theophilus Woldemar Cloete

© 1989
The Society of Biblical Literature

Library of Congress Cataloging in Publication Data

Cloete, W.T. Woldemar (Walter Theophilus Woldemar)
   Versification and syntax in Jeremiah 2-25 : syntactical
constraints in Hebrew colometry / W.T. Woldemar Cloete.
    p.   cm. -- (Dissertation series / Society of Biblical literature : no. 117)
   Includes bibliographical references.
   ISBN 1-55540-389-1 (alk. paper). -- ISBN 1-55540-390-5 (pbk. :
alk. paper)
    1. Bible. O.T. Jeremiah II-XV--Language, style. 2. Hebrew poetry, Biblical--
History and criticism. I. Title. II. Series:
Dissertation series (Society of Biblical literature) : no. 117.
BS1525.5.C56 1989
224'.2066--dc20
                                          89-10726
                                          CIP

Printed in the United States of America
on acid-free paper

Contents

Foreword

This study was accepted as the author's dissertation for D. Litt. at the University of Stellenbosch during 1987. For its inclusion in this series I sincerely thank Prof J.J.M. Roberts.

It is again my pleasant duty to express my heartfelt thanks to all among my friends, family and colleagues who have in some way contributed to its completion, especially those who helped to improve the grammar and style of my English. They are, of course, not to be held responsible for the views expressed or any errors remaining.

I thank the University of the Western Cape for granting me a year of study leave in the early stages of the research, the Eberhard-Karls-Universität of Tübingen for the use of their research facilities, and the University of Stellenbosch for financial support and for permission to publish the dissertation. The kind help of library staff in Bellville, Stellenbosch, Tübingen and Pretoria is gratefully acknowledged.

Special words of thanks are due to my promoters and examiners, namely Prof F.C. Fensham, Prof Walter Claassen, Prof Walter Gross and Dr Paul Kruger, for their encouragement, patience and guidance in this area of Old Testament study which Budde (1882, 2) aptly called "das gefährliche Glatteis".

Although only a few minor corrections have been made to the dissertation since its completion, it has received a completely new format. For help in this respect I gladly express my sincere appreciation to Walter Claassen, Emil Jung and especially Niël van der Merwe.

Lastly, I thank my wife Relna and our children, Rachel, Helene and Walter, for bearing with me again the tensions of the preparation of a manuscript.

May this study and its publication in some way contribute to a better understanding of the Bible and to the glory of God.

Bellville
May 1989

Chapter 1

Introduction

1.1 Poetry in the Old Testament?

Scholars usually distinguish prose and poetry in the Old Testament, and Watson (1984) even used the term *poetry* in the title of his recent book. The existence of poetry in the Old Testament was, however, called into question by Kugel who wrote (1981, 69):

> There is no word for 'poetry' in biblical Hebrew. There are a great number of genre classifications in the Bible ... but nowhere is any word used to group individual genres into larger blocs corresponding to 'poetry' and 'prose' .... Thus, to speak of 'poetry' at all in the Bible will be in some measure to impose a concept foreign to the biblical world.

Further on Kugel stated (1981, 85): "To see biblical style through the split lens of prose or poetry is to distort the view ..." A discussion of his view here can serve to clarify some concepts basic to the work presented here. What did Kugel mean by the above statements?

Upon a closer examination of Kugel's book it becomes clear that he was not so much reacting against the application of the term *poetry* to parts of biblical literature, but was rather warning

1. that it would not be possible to sharply differentiate poetry from prose, and
2. that our western concept of poetry might not correspond to that which is poetic in the Old Testament.

To the differentiation of prose from poetry we can return. Kugel's second warning was aimed mainly at the assumption that parts of the Old Testament were *metrical*, as is clear from his writing (1981, 85):

> For the distinction between 'poetry' and 'prose' is as noted not native to the texts: it is a Hellenistic imposition based, at least originally, on the faulty assumption that parts of the Bible were metrical ...

1

Kugel was very explicit on the faultiness of the notion of Biblical metre (1981, 301):

> no meter has been found, because none exists. Or, as others have urged, *parallelism is the only meter of biblical poetry* - but even for this statement to be correct, each of these terms must be understood in a nontraditional manner.

Kugel did distinguish "biblical Hebrew's 'high' or 'rhetorical' style" from its more ordinary counterpart (1981, 302). To him what is called biblical *poetry* was "a complex of heightening effects used in combinations and intensities that vary widely" (1981, 94), and so he stated: " 'Prose' and 'poetry' are a matter of degree" (1981, 302).

In a way this is correct, as long as the attention is focused on what makes poetry poetic, but then there may be, and in the Old Testament there is, poetic prose, which itself is sometimes loosely called poetry; cf. Budde (1902, 3) and Freedman (1977, 22 = 1980, 18). This practice is not limited to biblical studies; cf. Stutterheim (1961, 225-226). The confusion arises from the use of the terms *prose* and *poetry* as if they were opposites, which they are not (Alonso-Schökel, 1971, 99). The proper opposite of prose is *verse* (cf. Lotz, 1972, 1; Hartman, 1980, 11, 52), for which unfortunately the word *poetry* is often used as a synonym. The word *poetry*, properly used, implies some judgement of *quality* and/or *substance*, whereas the terms *prose* and *verse* do not, but refer only to *form*. If one would refute the existence of the two forms or modes, as Kugel tried to do, the use of the term *verse* would be advisable. It would also avoid a constant switching between the two meanings of *poetry*. Admittedly, in biblical studies the term *verse* is already being used (1) for the numbered verses and (2) sometimes for small sections of verse (e.g. by Budde, 1902, 4; De Moor, 1978b, 188), for which the use of terms like *bicolon* and *tricolon* is preferable. The possibility of ambiguity is nevertheless very limited, as the context will in almost all cases indicate which meaning is intended. With the term *poetry* the ambiguity is not avoidable. Since this study is concerned with *form* and not with quality, the term *verse* will be used.

The question to be answered, then, is whether there is verse in the Old Testament. To this question we answer in the affirmative, as would nearly all Old Testament scholars.

1.2 Verse and prose in the Old Testament

In spite of the near unanimity among scholars about the existence of verse in the Old Testament there is very little clarity as to its exact *extent* and as to the basis on which it *distinguishes* itself from prose. The textual tradition of the Old Testament does not provide us with an accurate distinction between verse and prose. Within the tradition some books are regarded as poetical, and correctly so. However, verse in the Old Testament is not limited to those books and, especially in the prophetical books, verse and prose alternate. Apparently, the sections of each which are interspersed in this way can be quite small. Moreover, the verse was generally not recorded and copied colographically, i.e. no indication of the ends of cola were given and the lines on the writing material were simply filled out. In those exceptional cases where an effort was made to copy some verse sections colographically, the delimitation is unreliable and most of Old Testament verse was excluded from this practice (Kugel, 1981, 119-127; Watson, 1984, 15). The Massoretic accent signs are of a very late origin, and were not intended to indicate colon boundaries, although some of them often coincide with colon boundaries. The use of a slightly different version of the Massoretic accent sign system for the poetical books is hardly an aid in distinguishing verse from prose, because it was not applied to all sections of verse in the Old Testament. The presence of parallelism has often been regarded as the distinguishing characteristic of Hebrew verse. However, parallelism is sometimes present in prose and sometimes absent in verse and the very concept of parallelism is notoriously difficult to define. A more detailed discussion is offered in paragraph **2.1**. Suffice it here to state that the presence of parallelism is not a reliable criterion by which to distinguish Hebrew verse from prose. Our distinguishing of verse from prose in the Old Testament is further complicated by a lack of knowledge as to the versification system employed by the Old Testament poets. In all probability the versification system was such that cola of various lengths occurred, without strict regulation on the phonological level. Thus the very nature of the versification system does not contribute to an easy distinction of the verse from the prose.

1.3   Verse: general characterisation

As to the differentiation between prose and verse it will be useful here to summarise those characteristics which are usually regarded as distinctive. In verse one usually finds:

1.   Special use made of the sounds of the language.
2.   Preference for certain words which seldom occur in normal speech and for unusual combinations of words.
3.   Extensive use of metaphor and picturesque speech.
4.   Rhythmical structuring of the text.
5.   Unusual syntactical features. (Cf. Mukarovsky, 1964, 17, 20, 27; Zhirmunsky, 1966a, 15-18; Leech, 1969, 42-53.)

The list of characteristics could be enlarged or made more precise. Some overlapping between them in their purposely broad formulation shown above, need in the present context be no problem.

It will, of course, be clear that the presence of any one of these characteristics is no absolute proof as to whether a given text should be regarded as verse or as prose. Their usefulness, for this differentiation, depends on the measure and intensity to which, if not all, at least several of them are employed in the given text.

The same characteristics function in ancient Hebrew literature and can there, as elsewhere, be regarded as indicators that a specific portion of text is verse:

1.   Special use of the sounds of the language is sometimes made in stylised prose texts, for instance in Num 22:4-5 (cf. Gross, 1974, 189). However, such use of the sounds of the language clearly has more structural aim and effect in verse texts, for example in Pr 22:10, 7:20, 1:15, 5:7-13, 31:17, 18 and 31 (cf. Thompson, 1973, 116-120; his sequence), Jer 18:13-17 (cf. Collins, 1978a, 260-261) and Nah 1:10 (cf. Cooper, 1976, 86-93).
2.   Preference for unusual words and unusual combinations of words in Hebrew verse is not limited to the use of word pairs but is perhaps clearest when word pairs are employed. These

have been studied repeatedly and from various angles in the past three decades. It will here suffice to refer to the study of Watters (1976), the broad discussion by O'Connor (1980a, 96-109) and the excellent study of Berlin (1985, especially 65-80).

3. Metaphor and picturesque speech are used in prose texts, but much more extensively and intensively in verse texts, for example in Is 5:1-7 and various parts of Genesis 49.

4. The exact nature and functioning of the versification system in the verse of the Old Testament is still unclear today, in spite of intensive study by many scholars from various scholarly backgrounds. However, it is possible to slightly anticipate here - referring to paragraph 1.4 - by saying that some kind of rhythmical structuring has to be reckoned with in certain parts of Old Testament literature, namely the verse parts.

5. That there are syntactical differences between Hebrew prose and Hebrew verse has long been known. Until fairly recently, however, no systematic study of these differences had been undertaken. Even today an overall view of the differences is difficult to obtain and there remains much to be studied. Nevertheless, it can confidently be stated that there are marked differences between the syntax of Hebrew prose and that of Hebrew verse; cf. e.g. the studies of Bloch (1946), Thompson (1973), Sappan (1981) and Hoftijzer (1981).

But there is something more basic that distinguishes verse from prose. It was almost bluntly stated by Hartman (1980, 11): *"Verse is language in lines.* This distinguishes it from prose". In other words: "There is a dichotomy - not a spectrum - between verse and prose. Lineation distinguishes them" (Hartman, 1980, 52). This remains true, even if the verse is oral or is written down without indications of the line or colon boundaries, i.e. in a non-colographical way, as is generally the case with Old Testament verse. The *lines* will be in the verse, whether they are visible or audible. This is no new insight. It was stated as follows by De Groot (1964, 299): "Continuous correspondence of successive segments, called 'lines', is the only constant feature which distinguishes verse from prose." At least some Old Testament scholars also realised this, as is clear from a careful reading of Gray (1915, 54-55, 126-127) and from Budde's (1902, 4) stating:

> It is the fundamental rule of all metrical composition, the one indispensable condition, that the continuous flow of the discourse should be divided into short word-groups, which, as far as the sense is concerned, have a certain independence.

For these short word-groups Budde used the terms *stichos* and *line*, referring to what is here called a colon, and he claimed that their boundaries were quite clear, a conviction which we do not share.

Watson (1984, 46) for his discussion of the distinction between prose and poetry (i.e. verse) took as point of departure a statement of Fraser which can be quoted in a slightly fuller form:

> The difference between verse and prose or speech is not that verse has rhythm and prose and speech have not, but that in verse a rhythmical unit, the line, is superimposed upon the grammatical unit of all discourse, the sentence. Prose is written in sentences. Verse is written in sentences and also in lines (Fraser, 1970, 1-2; cf. Cunningham, 1976, 267).

However, exactly because this basic difference between verse and prose was not easily obtainable from the Old Testament text, as has been explained above, Watson (1984, 46-60) listed and discussed 19 indicators by means of which Hebrew verse can be distinguished from prose.

The lines or cola, then, are the distinguishing characteristic of verse, and they in turn are describable in terms of a *versification system*. The versification system may be a metre, which is why it is often stated that metre constitutes verse; cf. e.g. Lotz (1972, 2 and *passim*) and Cunningham (1976, 256, but cf. 267).

In view of the above remarks one can assert that the distinction between verse and prose can with good grounds be applied to Old Testament literature, in spite of the difficulty of distinguishing them in practice.

1.4   Metre and rhythm

Amongst Old Testament scholars there are various conflicting theories as to the metrical or rhythmical structure of Hebrew verse;

cf. chapter 2 below. These theories were conveniently summarised very briefly by De Moor (1978a, 121-122), referring also to Eissfeldt (1964, 75-86 and 988-989). The conflicting opinions are due to a number of factors:

1. The fact that the exact pronunciation of the Hebrew text is unknown. This mainly concerns the position of stress, the presence or absence of final vowels and the articulation of shortened vowels.
2. The possibility that the Hebrew versification system underwent changes during the period in which the texts originated.
3. The problem of colon delimitation and the question whether a single colon or a longer line with one caesura (or more) should be regarded as the basic structural element in the versification.
4. The presence of not always easily identifiable later additions to or alterations in the text.
5. The difficulty in certain cases of distinguishing between prose and verse.
6. The variety of backgrounds in scholarly training from which the researchers come.

It has been noted that there are even scholars who claim that Old Testament verse has no metre, at least not in the usual sense. In his recent description of Ugaritic and Israelite versification De Moor (1978a), following the example of Young (1950), also argued for the absence of metre in these poetic systems. As was done in 1.1, De Moor's view will be examined here in order to clarify the basic concepts concerned. A careful reading of his article reveals serious defects in his argument.

One can agree with De Moor's (1978a, 122) statement that "if there existed a metre, it was somehow connected with the word accent". From the fact that apparently no major structural difference between the verse of Ugarit and that of Israel resulted from the dropping of final short vowels, he concluded (1978a, 123) "that if there existed a metre, it could only have been a so-called 'free' metre, i.e. a metre in which the number of unstressed syllables was of secondary importance". This conclusion seems to be quite correct.

De Moor (1978a, 123-128) then adduced examples from which it is clear that the number of unstressed syllables vary, as do also the number of letters (consonants) and the number of syllables, but "the number of main stresses within each distichon is fairly balanced", from which facts he concluded that the verse had no metre at all. Next he proceeded to argue (1978a, 128-138) that the verse had a free rhythm.

To evaluate rightly his argument and conclusions, one needs a clear conception of *rhythm* and *metre* and of the relationship between the two, as well as between them and the verbal material on the one hand, and any individual performance of the poem on the other hand. The latter distinction was emphasised by Zhirmunsky (1966a, 19):

> ... the study of a work of poetry or music must be strictly separated from the study of the devices used in its *performance*. In dealing with a poem we distinguish its metrical characteristics, as such, from the various devices employed in its declamation, which may depend to a considerable extent on the completely separate *art of the performer*. (Cf. also Wimsatt and Beardsley, 1959, 587-588; Lotz, 1972, 3).

De Moor (1978a, 127, 129, 132), however, explicitly related his theory to the performing of the text by singers, to chanting and to devices employed in reciting. His argument thus brings no proof as to the metrical or rhythmical structure of the verse. This is also true of his effort to deduce the type of rhythm of the poetry from the probable type of rhythm of the music (1978a, 129-132). De Moor referred to Wohlenberg in this respect, but apparently did not observe the latter's warning (1967, 562): "Andererseits kann man aber auch der metrischen Forschung noch nicht empfehlen, sich um nähere Auskunft an die Musik zu wenden." Wohlenberg seems to have thought that, given more detail as to the music, one should be able to deduce the metre of the verse from such knowledge of the music. Research on poetic metre has shown that this is not possible *in principle* (cf. Zhirmunsky, 1966a, 23-27; Wimsatt and Beardsley, 1959, 588-590; Lotz, 1972, 3; Beardsley, 1972, especially 245-248; Chisholm, 1977, 117).

As to the other distinctions mentioned above, Zhirmunsky can again be quoted. He summarised his own discussion of them as follows (1966a, 23):

Hence, in the study of metrics, it is essential to distinguish between three basic concepts: 1) the natural *phonetic characteristics* of the given *linguistic material* ('the material to be rhythmicized' in the terminology of the classical theorists: *to rhythmizomenon*); 2) *meter*, the ideal law governing the alternation of strong and weak sounds in the verse; 3) *rhythm*, as the actual alternation of strong and weak sounds, resulting from the interaction between the natural characteristics of the linguistic material and the metrical law. (Cf. also Chisholm, 1975, 36-42; Bjorklund, 1978, *Preface* and 7).

De Moor's concept of metre was something quite different from that of the metricists. He wrote (1978, 127-128): "Is it still possible to speak of a free metre? In my opinion it is not. Metre implies a more or less fixed, measurable length of time between one arsis and another."

That is not the case in all kinds of metre, for as Zhirmunsky wrote (1966a, 171):

Pure tonic verse is based on a count of the stressed syllables; the number of unstressed syllables is a variable quantity. The general pattern of such verse is $x \stackrel{\prime}{-} x \stackrel{\prime}{-} x \stackrel{\prime}{-} \dot{x}$ where $x = 0, 1, 2, 3 \ldots$
. . . When attention is focused on the stressed syllables, groups of unstressed syllables - even though they contain varying numbers of syllables - may be perceived as equivalent to each other.

Of course, the number of unstressed syllables between stresses is of essential importance in shaping the rhythm of individual lines or of the poem as a whole: since, however, such syllables form no part of the compositional structure, they belong to the area of rhythm, not meter.

Wimsatt and Beardsley also took this view (1959, 590):

Meter involves measurement, no doubt, or it can hardly with meaning be called 'meter'. But all measurement is not necessarily temporal measurement - even when the things measured occur in a temporal succession. (Cf. also Beardsley, 1972, 247-248; Mukarovsky, 1977, 32, 116-117.)

Thus what plays the decisive role here, is not at all "a more or less fixed measurable length of time", but our *perception* of the recurrence of a group of unstressed syllables followed by one stressed syllable as being equal.

It has been shown that for instance in some of the pure tonic verse of the Russian poet Mayakovsky even the number of stressed syllables per line can vary from one to six although lines with three or four occur most often (Zhirmunsky, 1966a, 236-241; 1966b, 213, cf. also 216-218; Gasparov, 1980, 12). According to Brown (1973, 171-172) the number of unaccented syllables between the accents in Mayakovsky's pure tonic verse may vary from none to six, whereas the number of accents per line varies from one to nine. "The mere fact that the number of stresses per line varies means neither that it becomes 'free verse' nor that it loses its structure as purely tonic meter" (Zhirmunsky, 1966b, 218). Once this is understood, the efforts of researchers like Kurylowicz (1972, 166-178; 1975, 215-225) and Cooper (1976, 119-121) to find rules which would make equal the number of stressed syllables per colon become unnecessary.

This lack of clarity as to the concept of metre is specifically related to pure tonic metre, in De Moor's terminology "free metre". A more basic deficiency in his concept of metre, and for that matter also in that of many other writers on Hebrew metrics, is a lack of appreciation for the *abstractness* of metre and as a result a confusion of metre and rhythm; cf. Alonso-Schökel (1971, 102-104). On the abstractness of metre Stankiewicz (1960, 77-78) wrote: "Meter itself is only a theoretical construct, an abstract scheme that is never fully implemented . . ."; cf. also Hrushovski (1960, 178-179). Outside the field of Hebrew studies the abstractness of metre was emphasised in various recent studies on the nature of metre and its functioning in English verse, but according to Tarlinskaya (1980, 46-47) even in those, with one exception, no clear distinction between metre and rhythm was maintained. It also became clear that various degrees of abstraction can be and probably should be distinguished if our aim is to have a clear concept of metre (Tarlinskaja and Teterina, 1974, 63-65; Tarlinskaya, 1980, 48-51).

In any case it can safely be said that, whereas progress in recent general linguistics is slowly influencing the study of the Hebrew language, recent developments in general metrics have had no similar fertilising effect on the study of Hebrew verse, either as to basic concepts or as to methodology. Whereas, at some earlier stages in the study of Hebrew metrics, the metrical theories were directly influenced by developments outside of Semitic and Old Testament studies, it seems as if in recent years Hebrew metrics has isolated itself from such influence and continued along the lines drawn before the progress in general metrics made in this century. A clear example of this can be seen in the work of Segert (1953; 1958; 1960; 1969) who, in spite of his intention and effort to incorporate newer methods, ended up with the hypothesis that all three of the previously advocated metrical systems were used by the Hebrew poets consecutively.

Zhirmunsky's definitions of *metre* and *rhythm* have been quoted above. It should be added that metre is a certain type of versification system or prosody, namely one "whose mode of organization is numerical" (Hartman, 1980, 17), i.e. metre "is the numerical regulation of certain properties of the linguistic form" (Lotz, 1972, 2).

Now that a clear concept of metre and rhythm and an impression of the uncertainty on these matters among Old Testament scholars have been obtained, it should be considered whether these concepts are applicable to the verse of the Hebrew Old Testament. It will be clear that rhythm is applicable, seeing that both prose and verse partake of rhythm. Moreover, the verse sections are rhythmically structured by the use of lines. As was stated above, such lines or cola are describable in terms of a versification system. Whether the specific system should be called a metre is at this stage still unclear, because it depends on the nature of the system, but it may well be that the concept of metre as defined here will be applicable to the versification system of Old Testament verse.

1.5 Importance of colometry

Thus far the terms *line* and *colon* have been used interchangeably. It will be necessary to clarify the concepts indicated by these terms as well. The term *line* usually indicates a visual concept and thus relates easily to written or printed verse. That is not to say that it cannot be applied to verse of oral origin which was transmitted in written form without lineation, for, as has been stated above, lineation is the distinguishing characteristic of verse and is not necessarily destroyed when such verse is reduced to writing, even if the written form is without visible lineation. The term *colon* indicates "a cohesive, sequential stretch of the verse line characterized by syntactic affinity or connectedness utilized for metric purposes", and although this concept "is related to the notion of caesura", in some verse each line can be a colon (Lotz, 1972, 11). Of course the word *colon* also has other meanings, but when applied to verse it is unambiguous, whereas *line* in discussions of Hebrew verse sometimes indicates the colon (e.g. Budde, 1902, 4; O'Connor, 1980a) and sometimes the bicolon and tricolon (e.g. Collins, 1978a; Alter, 1983).

Another very widely used term is *stichos* or *stich*, which unfortunately is as ambiguous in studies of Hebrew verse as is *line* (Mowinckel, 1967, 159), for it is sometimes used for the colon (e.g. Budde, 1902, 4; Mowinckel, 1950, 380; Loretz, 1975, 267; Van der Lugt, 1980, 148), but otherwise for the bicolon and tricolon. In the latter case the colon is called hemistichos, hemistich or hemistichium (Segert, 1953, 527; Hrushovski, 1965, 211; Alonso-Schökel, 1971, 101). On the other hand Watson (1984, 12, 14) distinguished approximately half of a single colon on account of its recurrence, which he then called hemistich. It is extremely doubtful, however, whether such a recurrent part of a colon really is a "metrico-structural unit" as Watson described it. It should perhaps rather be called a formula, following Loewenstamm (1980, 282 and *passim*).

The ambiguity of the term *stichos* is well exemplified in a recent description of Hebrew verse in which it is sometimes used for the bi- or tricolon (Burden, 1986, 49, 58) but otherwise for the colon (1986, 48). The same author also used *line* in both senses (1986, 51-52). The use of the term *colon* avoids ambiguity and is consistent with the well established use of the terms *bicolon* and *tricolon* (Loretz, 1979, 10). Therefore, it is preferred to use the term *colon* for the smallest structured metrical unity in Old Testament Hebrew verse. Other terms that have been used for it include *verset* (Hrushovski), *Reihe* (Sievers) and *membrum* (Lowth), the latter being "the standard Latin translation" of the Greek term κωλον (Kugel, 1981, 2; cf. Baker, 1973, 430).

Parallel to the duplication of terms for the colon there are other terms for *colometry*. The most widely used in studies of Hebrew and Ugaritic verse is *stichometry*, derived from *stichos* and therefore sharing its ambiguity. The term *lineation* derived from *line* has the same problem when applied to Hebrew verse. Loretz, who had formerly used the term *Stichometrie*, later preferred *Kolometrie* in order to have a consistent terminology and to avoid ambiguity (Loretz, 1979, 10). This is not a new term, seeing that Buber (1964, 1176) had already used it, and it might even be older. For the reasons given by Loretz, we prefer *colometry* to its possible alternatives.

A related concept is that of *stichography*, used by Kugel (1981, 119) to indicate the "spacing of verses or verse-halves", i.e. the arrangement of verse text on writing material in such a way that the colon boundaries are made visible, in some cases with indication as to which cola belong closer together than others. Watson (1984, 15) equated ancient scribal practice with stichography and modern analysis with stichometry, but surely the ancient scribe would have had to practice the latter to produce the former, which is exactly what the modern interpreter also has to do. So Watson's distinction is not the correct one. If there has to be distinguished between the act of delimiting or measuring of the cola on the one hand and the written or printed representation of delimited cola on the other, the latter could be called stichography or, as we would prefer, *colography*. However, this fine distinction between the action and its result, which imply each other, is in practice seldom necessary. It will then be possible to use the term *colometry* for both, as has generally been the case with the term stichometry.

There is a tendency among many Old Testament scholars to assume that the colometry of Hebrew verse is known. This is no doubt partly due to the "authoritative" editions of the Hebrew text providing their readers with colometrically arranged text, i.e. with a colography, for those parts which the scholar specifically responsible regarded as verse. Translations and even commentaries sometimes simply follow BHK or BHS as the case may be. Of this many examples can be found in **4.2.2**. Generally there is a large measure of certainty as to the boundaries of small groups of cola, e.g. of bicola or tricola, especially where a bicolonic structure is used consistently. However, this is often enough not the case. Moreover, within these small groups of cola the individual colon boundaries are often in doubt due to uncertainty about the exact nature of the versification system, about the text critical integrity of the text, and sometimes about the syntactical relation between the words. It was seen above that the type of versification system which most probably has to be

reckoned with, as far as its phonological component is concerned, is a
pure tonic metre, i.e. one in which neither the number of unstressed
syllables between the stressed ones nor the number of stresses per
colon is fixed. This implies, generally speaking, that there seldom can
be any "metrical" grounds for changing the text. It further implies,
again generally speaking, that no phonological features of the colon -
concretely the number of syllables per colon, the number of
unstressed syllables between the stressed ones and the number of
stressed syllables per colon - can be used in arguments concerning
colon delimitation, unless these clearly exceed the maximal or
minimal limits, about which scholars still differ strongly.

Some scholars realised that many of the colon boundaries were as
yet uncertain. Alonso-Schökel (1971, 124) wrote: ". . . in einigen
Versen ist die Zäsur nicht auszumachen . . .", and in his study of
Psalms 1-41 Ridderbos stated: "Es steht häufig nicht fest, wie die
Stichen abgegrenzt werden müssen" (1972, 12; cf. also 14). That the
scholars responsible for the preparation of the editions were not
always so sure of the correct colon delimitation, is illustrated by the
differences between the colometry presented in BHK and BHS, even
in the case of Jeremiah where the same scholar was responsible for
both editions.

The uncertainty concerning colon boundaries is aggravated by the
lack of concensus on the nature of *enjambement* and its relative
presence or absence in Hebrew verse. According to Robinson (1947,
22) and Alonso-Schökel (1971, 187) it did not occur in Hebrew verse,
whereas Mowinckel (1967, 170) stated that it occurred "rather
seldom". Ridderbos (1972, 14) suggested that the word "rather"
should be deleted from Mowinckel's statement. According to Loretz
(1979, 478) enjambement was more frequent in later texts than in
earlier ones. In contrast with biblical Hebrew verse ancient Greek
verse - both originally oral in nature - was characterised by a strict
phonological metre and abundant enjambement. As a result
enjambement in Greek verse has received much attention from
scholars, including Parry, Lord, Peabody (1975, 125-143) and Kirk
(1976), in whose studies various types, degrees and categories of
enjambement were distinguished. To the best of our knowledge no
similar study of either Ugaritic or Hebrew verse has been
undertaken; cf. Loretz (1979, 478 n.1). However, some scholars found

fairly large numbers of occurrences of enjambement in Hebrew verse, e.g. Dahood (1976, 671), Van der Lugt (1980, 192-194) and Althann (1983, 35, 40, etc.). That the relation between colon and clause was not simple was emphasised by O'Connor (1980a, 49, 67-68); cf. also Yoder (1972, 52).

Exactly *what* should be called enjambement in Hebrew verse is uncertain. The term was used by Begrich (1934, 178 = 1964, 141) to refer to the reversal of the length relation of two clauses in a *Fünfer*, but Alonso-Schökel (1971, 187) denied the applicability of the term to such cases. If the colon boundary in such bicola could be proven to occur after the middle of the bicolon, i.e. not to coincide with the most prominent syntactical boundary, such cases should in terms of the definitions given by Link (1979, 197) be described with reference to two factors, namely enjambement *and* caesura. According to Heller (1977, 18) enjambement "is an artificial interruption of continuous syntax by means of line division", and she significantly added: "A more precise definition is difficult because so many kinds of word boundary are utilized". Cf. also Abbott (1974). The kinds of boundary associated with enjambement differ from one verse system to the other. It can also be noted beforehand that in verse systems where parallelism on the semantic and syntactic levels play a large role and where the versification system is not a strict phonological metre, enjambement is rare. Nevertheless, the possibility of enjambement has to be reckoned with in the search for the correct colometry. Perhaps one could try to determine which syntactic boundaries are seldom used as colon boundaries, and regard those cases where they are so utilised as enjambement.

The uncertainty among scholars as to the correct colometry should not mislead us to think that there is no correct colometry. According to Loretz (1979, 7) the colometry of Canaanite verse is subject to *Gesetzmässigkeiten*, and even though these can at present not be formulated in rules, the cola vary within certain margins, and there is no possibility of the absence of rules. Similarly Gordon, whilst agreeing with Young (1950) and Pardee (1981) that Ugaritic and Hebrew verse had no metre, recognised in it "a metric approxima-tion", a factor of "bulk", to which he also referred as "a bag of tricks" on which the poet could draw (Gordon, 1981, 186). It should be noted that these views were uttered without any reference to, and probably without any knowledge of the research of Collins (1978a) and O'Connor (1980a). Indeed, the crucial importance of lineation for verse to be verse implies that there must be a correct colometry.

Although it may be doubted by some whether there can be any hope of establishing the correct colometry of Hebrew verse to the exclusion of arbitrariness, the fact *that* the correct colometry is important should not be doubted. Referring to the interpretation of Ugaritic mythological texts Pope (1966, 231) stated:

> ... stichometry is of crucial importance. If a bicolon or tricolon be wrongly divided, or the parallelism misapprehended, no depth or breadth of erudition is likely to redeem the situation. Thus it happens that many of the misinterpretations of Ugaritic passages start with faulty stichometry or failure to divine the structure of the poetic parallelism.

The truth of this statement was illustrated by Pope in the same review (1966, 232-236). With the added uncertainties as to the history of the text the quoted statement is equally applicable to Old Testament verse. At least some scholars have indicated their awareness of the problem. One example is Loretz, who wrote:

> Ein poetischer Text sollte auch ohne Kenntnisse metrischer Gesetzmässigkeiten für den Leser zugänglich und verständlich sein. Dennoch ist auf dem Gebiet der he[bräischen] Poesie die Lage so, dass ein Eindringen in die Texte erst nach einer Vorentscheidung über die Möglichkeiten und Grenzen all dessen, was in der sogen[annten] Metrik erlaubt und nachweisbar ist, erfolgreich wird (Loretz, 1975, 265; cf. 267).

It is for that reason that he could describe his approach to the Psalms:

> ... von der Kolometrie her die Probleme der kleinsten Einheiten der Psalmen an der Wurzel zu fassen. Die wichtigste Stelle nimmt deshalb die Aufarbeitung der Kolometrie ein (Loretz, 1979, 10).

There should also be clarity on the reasons *why* the correct colometry is so important.

In verse the versification system, and the lineation which it describes, controls the reader's or listener's temporal experience of the poem (Hartman, 1980, 13-15, 52). Lineation, therefore, has *aesthetic* as well as *communicative* value. For that reason one must agree with Hartman's (1980, 60) statement: "Lineation can be well or poorly used, but it can never be immaterial". In Hebrew verse lineation, i.e. colometry, also indicates the syntactical relationships between the constituents within the colon. Loretz hinted at this when he stated that the aim of colometry is "jeweils eine sinnvolle poetische Einheit, also nicht eine mechanische Texteinteilung" (1975, 267). Similarly Buber defined colometry as "die Gliederung in Einheiten die *zugleich* Atemeinheiten und Sinneinheiten sind" (1964, 1176). The identity of the colon with a meaningful syntactical unity was stated also by Mowinckel (1950, 380). Furthermore, seeing that the order of constituents in Old Testament Hebrew, especially the position of the verb at or near the beginning of the clause, contributes to the meaning of the clause (Gross, 1982, 62-68), the determining of the beginning of the colon is definitive for the correct understanding of the combination of word order and word form, at least as far as the verbs are concerned. There are also other syntactical consequences of the colon boundaries which cannot be properly studied as long as the exact positions of the colon boundaries are unknown; cf. the criticisms by Gross (1976, 54) of Michel's (1960) work on this point.

In spite of the importance of the colon boundaries for the correct understanding and full appreciation of Hebrew verse many Old Testament scholars seem to treat the delimitation of cola with the lack of scientific precision which Wahl described:

> From examples of perfect or almost-perfect parallelism we note the tendency of words to group themselves in sets of approximately two to four words with some sort of syntactic unity (cola), which sets tend to coalesce in groups of two or three parallel sets (the line). Now when we have two larger sets of about five to eight words which are mutually parallel we are inclined to see whether these sets cannot each be divided into smaller units closer to the size of a normal colon. Usually we find that this is possible syntactically (e.g. we do not have to break up a construct series) and stylistically (one colon corresponds to another [though not necessarily successive] colon, . . .) (Wahl, 1976, 20-21).

1.6   Aims and method of the present study

Given the importance of the correct colometry and the uncertainty
among scholars as to the position of the colon boundaries, it is
necessary that more research be done in this field. Two aspects
should be distinguished, namely the colometric analysis, i.e. the
delimitation of cola in specific Hebrew verse texts, and the
formulation of a description of the colometric system.

It should be pointed out that the colometric system to be described
is part of a more comprehensive whole, namely the versification
system, which would include *inter alia* specifications for the
combination of cola, for the form and nature of strophic structures
and for methods of closure in Hebrew verse. Attempts to describe
Hebrew versification usually cover all these aspects, although some
recent studies have either concentrated on or limited themselves to
one of the aspects, e.g. line-forms (Collins, 1978a) or strophic
structures (Van der Lugt, 1980). Because of the need for a new
description of the colometric system based on motivated colometric
analysis of an extensive body of verse text, it has been decided to limit
this study to the colometric system.

It is preferred to take the colon as the basic structural unit to be
described within a description of Hebrew versification. This was the
view of O'Connor (1980a, 52-53) - cf. our discussion in **3.3.5.2** - and
of Cross who referred to the cola as "the basic units" (1983a, 129; cf.
131) or "the fundamental units or building blocks of Hebrew poetry"
(1983b, 159). Most scholars would prefer the bicolon or tricolon, e.g.
Freedman stated: ". . . the basic unit was the full line (distich or
bicolon) . . ." (1972, xxxiv = 1980, 44). Alonso-Schökel (1971, 124)
also took the latter view, but he admitted that the question was
"weithin nur nominell". Although we recognise the bicolon as an
often preferred *target form* of Hebrew verse it would be both imprac-
tical and a prejudgement of the material to take the bicolon as point
of departure. The bicolon, tricolon, etc. are of too large a variety, and
would contain the uncertain colon boundaries, which as has been
pointed out in **1.5** it is essential to determine. The colon is taken as
the basic unit which is used to build longer sequences, whether these
consist of two, three or more such cola.

The new description needed must be both valid and adequate, but
should not contain any superfluous specifications of elements which

are merely the result of the essential components of the system described. In a number of fairly recent studies the Hebrew versification system, and more specifically that component of it which determines colometry, was described as being of a syntactic nature. There are important differences between the descriptions given in these studies, e.g. between the descriptions given by Collins (1978a) and by O'Connor (1980a). Therefore, it has become necessary to compare and evaluate the various descriptions, if this approach is to be to the advantage of Old Testament studies. If an analysis of Hebrew verse indicates the existence of syntactical constraints within the colometric system, it will also be necessary to establish the exact relation between these and possible other constraints within that system. So, for instance, the possible role of regulation of the phonological features of the text and the possible existence of enjambement has to be considered.

To many scholars, however, the idea of a versification system of a syntactic nature, or even of a partly syntactic nature, is a contradiction in terms. Thus there is more than the practical applicability of the approach to be considered. The theoretical status of the approach and of the descriptions produced by it has to be clarified. It will have to be asked *inter alia* whether such descriptions do describe the versification system or merely the products of the system, and if they do describe the system whether such a system should be called a type of metre.

In order to achieve these aims this study must begin by surveying the various descriptions of the Hebrew versification system presently applied. In chapter 2 the non-syntactical systems presently in use are surveyed, to identify their deficiencies, especially as to the reliable delimitation of cola, and to note references made to the role of syntax. In chapter 3 the various descriptions devised by exponents of the syntactical approach are examined and evaluated. The insights obtained from chapters 2 and 3 are then applied in establishing the colometry of the verse sections in Jeremiah chapters 2 - 25. This is presented in chapter 4, of which the scope and method are stated in 4.1, followed by the delimited Hebrew cola in 4.2.1, the grounds for our delimitation in 4.2.2, and a description of the Hebrew colometric system as we understand it in 4.3. The latter is an integration of insights from chapters 2 and 3 and 4.1 - 4.2.2. In chapter 5 the study is summarised and the conclusions are offerred. These include the advantages of our description of the colometric system over previous descriptions. The relation of the colometric system to the versification system as a whole as well as the theoretical status of the system is also discussed.

Because of the circularity of the argument involved, a study of this type can easily be criticised and its results discounted. But such a view of it would be erroneous in at least two respects. Firstly, if somewhere along the circle a fixed point can be found, then the circle should no longer cause any doubt about the validity of the description given. The circularity of the argument would then rather serve to show how well the different parts of the system function together. Moreover, the circularity of the argument is inevitable, as Cross stated:

> ... the interdependence of the tasks of analysis and recon-
> struction, prosodic, textual, and historico-linguistic, involves the
> student of Hebrew poetry in the circular reasoning inevitable in
> all complex inductive research (Cross, 1983a, 133).

All studies of the Hebrew versification system inevitably make use of circular argumentation, not only between the different levels to be analysed and reconstructed, but also between the structural analysis of the verse text and the versification system reconstructed.

Chapter 2

Versification Systems presently applied to Hebrew Verse: Non-syntactical Approaches

The discussion of these systems must in this context necessarily be brief. The main aim here is to point out their inability to provide a reliable and valid delimitation of cola. It will also be noted whether exponents of these systems take syntax into account, and if they do, how they do so.

2.1 Parallelism

Since the 18th century when Robert Lowth presented his insights into Hebrew poetry and stressed the importance of what he termed *parallelismus membrorum* the factor of parallelism has played a varying but always important role in the description of Hebrew versification. Lowth was not the first to recognise the phenomenon. Because of probable differences between discovery date and publication date it is impossible to determine whether his contemporaries Mazzocchi, Schoettgen or Michaelis anticipated his discovery. Be that as it may, Lowth obtained his insights partly from Azariah de Rossi and David Kimchi and via them probably from earlier Jewish commentators (Baker, 1973, 433-435; cf. also Gordis, 1971, 63, 90 n.2; Segert, 1953, 500-502). It was, however, through the work of Lowth that the phenomenon of *parallelismus membrorum* received its classical formulation and enough attention for the term to become established.

Already in his earlier work on the poetry of the Hebrews, delivered as lectures in the 1740s and published in 1753, Lowth referred to Hebrew verse as mostly arranged in "distichs" which "in some measure consist of versicles or parallelisms corresponding to each other", and also to "that poetical and artificial conformation of the sentences, which we observe in the poetry of the Hebrews" (Lowth, 1787, II, 32-33). Then, before dividing parallelism into the three well-known types or "species", he gave the following description which takes the *syntactical* aspect as basis:

> The poetical conformation of sentences, which has often been
> alluded to as characteristic of the Hebrew poetry, consists chiefly
> in a certain equality, resemblance, or parallelism between the
> members of each period; so that in two lines (or members of the
> same period) things for the most part shall answer to things, and
> words to words, as if fitted to each other by a kind of rule or
> measure. This parallelism has much variety and many gradations;
> it is sometimes more accurate and manifest, sometimes more
> vague and obscure . . . (Lowth, 1787, II, 34).

Later, in his commentary on Isaiah (first published in 1778), Lowth
gave his definition of parallelism, in which he distinguished basically
between semantic and syntactic parallelism:

> The correspondence of one verse, or line, with another, I call
> *parallelism*. When a proposition is delivered, and a second is
> subjoined to it, or drawn under it, equivalent, or contrasted with
> it, in sense; or similar to it in the form of grammatical
> construction; these I call parallel lines; and the words or phrases,
> answering one to another in the corresponding lines, parallel
> terms (Lowth, 1787, II, 32 n.10 = 1848, viii).

Lowth also stated his view on the relationship between parallelism
and metre:

> In this peculiar conformation, or parallelism of the sentences, I
> apprehend a considerable part of the Hebrew metre to consist;
> though it is not improbable that some regard was also paid to the
> numbers and feet. But of this particular we have at present so
> little information, that it is utterly impossible to determine,
> whether it were modulated by the ear alone, or according to any
> settled or definite rules of prosody (Lowth, 1787, II, 53-54).

It is clear, then, that Lowth was sceptical as to the possibility of
determining the phonological aspects of Hebrew metre, and that for
colon delimitation he relied instead on parallelism, which he
understood to be syntactical to a fairly large extent.

Parallelism is perhaps the factor that has been used most often to
establish the lineation of Hebrew (and Ugaritic) poetry. Although it
is a useful concept one has to bear in mind some severe difficulties
pertaining to it.

From scholarly writings in which the term is used it is clear that various meanings are attached to it, a confusion partially due to the inaccurate use made of Lowth's term and partially due to the *variety of parallelistic phenomena in language and literature*. Parallelism is not limited to verse. Parallelism of action is employed in literary narrative (Todorov, 1972) and syntactical parallelism occurs in prose, for instance in G.B. Shaw's prose (Ohmann, 1970, 216-218), in Ugaritic prose (Segert, 1979, 730) as well as in Old Testament prose. Some parallelisms belong to syntax, others to style (Matthews, 1981, 34). It is, however, in poetic language that parallelism abounds and where often more than one of the variety of parallelistic phenomena occur together. Von Herder (1833, I, 39-42) pointed out that parallelism is a characteristic of all poetry. Its variety is illustrated by general discussions of its use in poetry (Austerlitz, 1961; Jakobson, 1966; 1972, 170-171) and its diffuseness is clear from discussions of oral traditional poetry (Finnegan, 1977, 98-102). It is even possible, though not scientifically very accurate, to speak of metre as rhythmic parallelism (Leech, 1969, 111; Van der Westhuizen, 1973, 45), though this was surely not what Lowth had intended. Neither did he have in mind phonological parallelism, such as discussed by Cooper (1976, 86-93), Schramm (1976) and Berlin (1985, 103-126). From her discussion of morphological and syntactic parallelism in the Old Testament Berlin concluded: "Parallelism is an extremely complex device" (Berlin, 1979, 43; cf. 1985, 141). This is no new discovery, for Gray already wrote: ". . . the really important question . . . is how far the phenomena covered by the term parallelism can be classified, and how far they conform to laws that can be defined" (Gray, 1915, 4; cf. also Muilenburg, 1953, 97-98). Also aware of this complexity was Pardee (1981, 128-130), who called for

> an extensive set of criteria for determining when parallelism is
> present or not which would solve problems . . . and which would
> provide a reasoned categorization of types of parallelism.

Some of the complexity is reflected in the studies of Geller (1979; 1982b) and Berlin (1979; 1985), but so much of it remains that it is difficult to share the confidence of Geller (1982a, 66, 70) who maintained that parallelism in biblical verse "is definitely describable". The most consistent application of parallelism in all of

Ancient Near Eastern literature is to be found in Ugaritic verse
(Segert, 1979, 731; cf. already 1953, 509), yet even with regard to
Ugaritic verse Margalit (1980, 3-4) pointed out that the approach via
"sense-functional" parallelism had severe limitations and proposed a
structuralist theory of prosodic analysis which would "separate out its
form-relevant aspects".

Lowth referred to the "conformation of sentences" (i.e. lines of
verse, or cola) as *parallelismus membrorum*. Writers on general
poetic theory differ as to what should be called parallelism. Kayser
(1948, 115) defined parallelism as "eine... Gleichordnung von
Satzteilen bzw. von ganzen Sätzen...", a repetition of the construction. Such "Satzparallelismus", however, Arbusow (1963, 32) called
parisosis, and he distinguished it from *parallelismus membrorum*,
which he described as "Gedankenparallelismus, 'Tautologie des
Gedankens'", i.e. semantic parallelism. Again, similar to Lowth,
Hammond (1961, 475) described "syntactic parallelism between
successive lines" as "systematic concordance of juxtaposed equivalent
syntactic structures with metrical units".

A new application of the term parallelism within the field of Old
Testament studies is that of Berlin, who maintained a strict distinction between repetition and parallelism and preferred to apply the
term parallelism not to the aspect *repeated* in the successive cola, but
to the aspect which is *altered* from the one colon to the next. Thus she
defined grammatical parallelism as: "The alteration of grammatical
structure in parallel stichs, or, better, the pairing of two different
grammatical structures in parallel stichs..." (Berlin, 1979, 20).

Objections against the term parallelism have been raised by Geller
(1982b, 35 n.1), who would prefer the term *binarism*. However, the
latter term would stress exactly that facet which Fohrer, to our mind
correctly, regarded as having been overemphasised by the use of the
term *parallelismus membrorum*. "Es gibt kein 'Gesetz' des
Parallelismus oder der Zweiheit der Versglieder..." (1967, 68; cf.
also 64). He preferred to speak of repetitive style (1967, 70) and
stated, "dass man statt von einer Zweiheit der Versglieder richtiger
von einer möglichen Mehrgliedrigkeit sprechen solle, neben der auch
die Eingliedrigkeit zu beobachten sei" (1962, 38). In our view
parallelismus membrorum - along with other kinds of parallelism -

is a reality in Hebrew verse, but it should not be understood necessarily to imply binarism.

In his recent discussion Watson (1984, 114-122) indicated his
awareness of the problems which the parallelistic approach faces, and
he explained that what is usually called parallelism in biblical studies
is a group of four mathematical analogues, namely

a. proper congruence, i.e. the same sequence of the same signs
    (parallelism in a restricted sense of the word)
b. reflexive congruence, i.e. the reversed sequence of the same
    signs (chiasmus or mirror symmetry)
c. proper anti-congruence, i.e. the same sequence of the opposite
    signs
d. reflexive anti-congruence, i.e. the reversed sequence of the
    opposite signs (Watson, 1984, 117-119).

There is thus an urgent need for terminological clarity, which can be
achieved either by

1. doing away with the concept of parallelism altogether and using
    other, more precise, terms from the fields of semantics, syntax,
    etc. in its stead (so O'Connor, 1980a, 87-88; Margalit, 1980, 4),
    or by
2. qualifying the term every time in order to express on which level
    of language the parallelism occurs, keeping in mind that
    parallelism may be present on more than one level in a single
    example (so Berlin 1979; 1985).

This is not the end of the problem, however, as there still is a lack of
clarity as to *when* successive cola should be called parallel, especially
when one or more elements of either colon have no counterpart in
the other. These relationships, it seems can best be described in
syntactical terms. To this, again, is related the question of the so-
called double-duty modifier: Should the modifier which does double
duty be reckoned as part of the first colon (Watson, 1984, 214), or as
a separate colon between the two parallel cola - so Dahood (1967),
who named it in syntactical terms, but nevertheless called it a
"metrical pattern" - or should it perhaps even be taken as part of

the last colon? The latter possibility is rather improbable from a syntactical point of view, but the first two must seriously be taken into account.

Besides parallelism between cola, there is also parallelism between bicola (Begrich, 1934, 184-197; cf. the Finnish example quoted by O'Connor, 1980a, 92-93). Possibly parallelism can also occur within a single colon. The latter would mostly involve parallelism between two very brief phrases or clauses, but could also involve more than two. The question here is, of course, whether such brief parallel phrases or clauses occurring in direct succession should be regarded as separate cola or as one. One way of answering this question is by accepting, in addition to the breaks at the ends of cola, the existence of minor caesurae in such cola. The obscurity contained in this problem is reflected by the difference between the descriptions which, for example, Watson and O'Connor gave in such cases. Watson (1975) regarded three successive verbs with suffixes as a three-word tricolon, whereas O'Connor (1980a, 75, 86-87), not counting suffixes as units, would regard such a case as one line, i.e. in Watson's terms, a single colon.

Popper (1925) argued that in the study of Hebrew verse the principle of parallelism should be applied to the delimitation of cola with the utmost rigour. In this he believed to be in agreement with the fundamental conclusions reached by Smith (1912) and Gray (1915) as to the predominance of parallelism. Popper proved, however, that both Smith and Gray had let themselves be influenced by factors other than parallelism only (1925, 75-78, 80-83). On this account Popper severely criticised them, but he failed to provide proof that delimitation of cola could be undertaken on grounds of parallelism alone. Indeed, Popper knew that there were other factors involved, for in the same sentence where he called for a rigorous application of the "parallelistic test" he referred to "parallelism, which is *a* characteristic feature in *much* Hebrew poetry and prophecy" (Popper, 1925, 65; emphases added; cf. also 67, 84).

The strongest opposition to regarding parallelism as the basis of Hebrew metrics was expressed by Mowinckel (1950, 391):

> Das ist ein Irrtum; der parallelismus membrorum, oder richtiger: der 'Gedankenreim', ist keine metrische, sondern eine stilistische Erscheinung; über Metrik hat man damit nichts gesagt.

Later he apparently realised that this was an overstatement, for he
wrote:

> Die grundlegende Bedeutung des Gedankenreims für das
> Verständnis auch der metrischen Probleme der hebr. Poesie ist
> sowohl von G.B. Gray ... als von Th.H. Robinson ... stark
> betont worden (Mowinckel, 1956, 100 n.3).

This role of parallelism is generally accepted today (cf. Nelis, 1982,
1393), which does not mean, however, that cola can always be
delimited by relying on parallelism, for even Mowinckel who made
much of "die prinzipielle Zweiheit der hebräischen Verszeile" (1956,
101) was well aware of

1. the so-called synthetic parallelism (1956, 100-101),
2. the existence of tricola (1956, 103-104),
3. parallelism between bicola or tricola (1956, 103), and
4. the existence of monocola (1956, 106).

In addition to these factors some mentioned earlier should also be
taken into account, namely

1. incomplete parallelism,
2. parallelism within the colon,
3. the extreme complexity of parallelism, and
4. the resultant terminological obscurity.

All these factors make it impossible to rely on parallelism alone in
the search for the system of Hebrew versification. In addition it is still
uncertain whether a number of monocola can occur *consecutively* as
claimed by Fohrer (1967) for Hebrew verse - and recently by
Margalit (1980, 143-144) for Ugaritic verse - but denied by
Mowinckel (1967, 265) and more tentatively by Alonso-Schökel
(1971, 119-125).

In conclusion we must return to Lowth and point out two inter-related facts:

1. Lowth was not concerned with parallelism as such, but with *parallelismus membrorum*, the word *membrum* referring to the single line or colon (Baker, 1973, 430). He focused his attention on parallel cola.

2. In Lowth's descriptions and definitions, especially the earlier ones, *syntax* played a large role, not only as to some successive cola having identical or similar syntax, but - of more import - also as to the *delimitation of cola*.

Other writers on parallelism were also aware of the role of syntax in Hebrew versification. This definitely was so in the case of Gray (1915, 54-55, 126-127) and Hrushovski, from whose definition of parallelism can be quoted here: "A 'verse' consists of 2 (or 3 or 4) parts or hemistichs. Each such part is a phrase, a basic rhythmical and logical unit . . ." (Hrushovski, 1965, 211).

It would seem, therefore, both from Lowth's formulations and from the shortcomings of the approach to Hebrew versification on the basis of parallelism that more attention should be given to the fact that it is *members* or *cola* which are parallel, instead of to the *parallelism* of the members, i.e. we should concentrate on the ends of cola and their syntactical status.

2.2 Accent count

Making use of Lowth's discovery of *parallelismus membrorum* and taking into account the important role played by stress in biblical Hebrew grammar, Julius Ley in the 1870s counted the number of *Begriffsworte* or *concept-words* per colon and established that Hebrew metre was based on the stressed syllable of each such meaningful word (cf. Segert, 1953, 483-484; Margalit, 1975, 289-290). Interestingly Parker (1974, 290) followed the same line of argumentation concerning Ugaritic verse. Ley in this was followed by various others, each of whom tried to work out the metre in more detail and with varying measures of success (cf. Fensham, 1966, 10-12; Alonso-Schökel, 1971, 83, 91-92). More recent scholars who acknowledge the same principle include proponents of widely diverging views. Broadly speaking these scholars fall into two groups.

Those of the first group prefer counting only the main stresses and allow considerable freedom as to the number of unstressed syllables between the stresses, namely from 0 to 5 (Nelis, 1982, 1395), the most common being 2 unstressed syllables. The most frequent bicolon is scanned as 3 + 3, i.e. two cola of three stresses each. This pure tonic system is mostly called *akzentuierendes System*, i.e. accentuating system. Various forms of this system have been suggested. Scholars who adhered to some form of it include Budde, Sievers, Smith (1912, 11-12), Albright (1968, 8), Begrich, Hrushovski (1965; 1981, 58-60), Ridderbos (1972, 11) and Alonso-Schökel. Scansion according to this system mostly produces a so-called mixed metre, i.e. it appears that the poets were not bound to the use of the same metrical pattern for longer stretches of verse.

The second group of scholars for purposes of versification take into account the main and secondary stresses. They tend at the same time to limit the number of unaccented syllables between stresses rather strictly, namely between 0 and 2, with 1 being the most common by far. This *alternierendes System* often produces scansions of four stresses per colon, and demands a minimum of two stresses per colon. Proponents of the system include Hare (cf. Broadribb, 1972/3, 68-70), Bickell, Hölscher, Mowinckel, Horst and Böhl. As to detail there is again variation among them and scansion mostly does not produce consistent metrical patterns.

In addition some scholars would accept both these systems but for different periods in the history of Israel. Segert, for example, accepted the accentuating or pure tonic system for the period roughly from 1000 B.C. to 600 B.C., whereas he preferred the alternating system for the postexilic period (Segert, 1969, 315-316). Similar, though not identical, views on a probable change of metrical system in the course of time have been expressed by Böhl (1957/8, 136), Fensham (1966, 17-19) and Van der Westhuizen (1973, 78-79), all of whom seem to be at least partly influenced by Segert. Possibly Segert's view was anticipated by Horst (1953, 103). If such a change or changes in the versification system did occur, the question arises whether there was any other formal factor which remained and in effect bridged the gap or gaps between the various stages.

The large differences between the views of these scholars can be passed over, because it is their common acceptance of the prominence of the *stressed syllable* in Hebrew versification which is of interest here. The number of stressed syllables as counted by them range between 2 and 4 per colon. Because of this variation allowed in the number of stresses per colon, the number of stresses cannot of itself be indicative of where a caesura or colon boundary should be placed, i.e. of colon delimitation. Further it is noted that, as pointed out by Begrich (1934, 171), somehow scholars in favour of the accentuating system and those preferring the alternating system usually divided the cola in the same way. The criteria for such division are usually not spelled out.

It must be determined, then, what factor in Hebrew verse caused these scholars to divide the cola as they did.

Mowinckel, writing on "sense metre" which he regarded as the original metre, claimed:

> Die natürliche rhythmisch-metrische 'Reihe' ('Stichus') ist der abgerundete, sinnausdrückende grammatische Satz, *wie es bekanntlich noch in der hebräischen Poesie die fast ausnahmslose Regel ist* . . . (1950, 380; emphasis added).

Although one might think that Mowinckel had the bicolon in mind here, that is not the case. He was very explicit on the point that *Reihe* or *Stichus* as used in the statement just quoted meant the *colon*. Perhaps Mowinckel overstated what he had in mind. Be that as it may, it is clear that he acknowledged being influenced strongly by syntactic (and semantic) boundaries in his delimitation of cola.

Later Mowinckel wrote (1967, 169): "The separate colon is a complete thought and sentence, or a comparatively independent unit of meaning within the sentence". He continued (1967, 170):

> In later style one thought or one description may continue through several bicola . . . . But even here the unity of rhythmical and logical syntactical members is observed; each colon or bicolon constitutes a separate member in the description or the train of ideas.

To this he added (1967, 170):

> The true 'enjambement'... occurs rather seldom.... Even
> where the bicolon makes one logical unit, the rhythmical caesura
> falls between two comparatively independent units of meaning
> within the sentence...

Again there can be no mistaking the fact that syntactical boundaries,
both within and at the end of the sentence, play a prominent role in
Mowinckel's delimitation of cola.

Alonso-Schökel, in summarising his views as to the counting of
stresses per bicolon, wrote (1971, 185): "Die häufigste Formel ist
3 + 3. Sie wird durch die syntaktische Struktur des Hebräischen
begünstigt." This statement in itself may not seem very illuminating,
but it should be considered together with his conviction that there
was *no enjambement* in Hebrew verse (1971, 187). Thus it is clear that
Alonso-Schökel, although he did not state it in so many words, was
convinced that the ends of cola were syntactical boundaries.

There seem to be good grounds then to search for the factor which
determines colon delimitation on the syntactical level of the language.
It seems possible also that the same factor was responsible for the
continuity in Hebrew versification when changes in the structure of
the words presumably brought about changes in the phonological
component of the versification system.

That the relationship between colon and sentence is not a simple
constant relation, however, is evidenced by the findings of Begrich. As
point of departure Begrich (1934, 171) took the observations that the
end of the poetic verse - not to be confused with the Massoretic
verse - concurs with the end of the sentence and that likewise the
caesura concurs with a logical break in the sentence. Begrich then
found

(a)   that the sentence in the *Fünfer* or *Qina* verse form sometimes
      continued through two times 3 + 2 (1934, 171-172), and
(b)   that often the logical break in the *Fünfer* came between the
      second and the third stressed syllable, in effect reversing the
      relation of length between the clauses (1934, 178).

The second of Begrich's findings is of special significance here. What he termed the "logical break" should preferably be called a syntactical boundary. Despite the reversal of the relation of length between the clauses Begrich retained the division of cola as 3 + 2, and understood the phenomenon as enjambement. Such a treatment of the phenomenon presupposes that the numerical relation of the cola to each other had a stronger effect on the structure of the verse than the syntax had.

The same phenomenon was observed by others but interpreted differently. Alonso-Schökel (1971, 187) referred to such cases as "Verschiebungen der Zäsur" and emphatically stated that they were not comparable to enjambement. From Alonso-Schökel's (1971, 141) slightly misleading summary of Begrich it is clear that he differed from Begrich in retaining the division of cola according to the logical or syntactical breaks, i.e. where the more prominent syntactical boundary occurs after the second main stress, Alonso-Schökel divided the cola as 2 + 3.

Two facts should be clear in the light of the above discussion, namely:

1. the delimitation of cola cannot be undertaken on the basis of the number of stresses alone, and
2. syntax plays a central role in colon delimitation, but exactly how it does so has not yet been determined.

2.3 Word count

Logically and in some respects chronologically the approach of counting words precedes that of counting stresses. In order to make the proper distinction between these two approaches, however, it is discussed here after the stress counting approach. Because of the way first Budde and then Sievers took up and modified Ley's original system, scholars have tended to equate the word count approach with the accentuating system (e.g. Mowinckel, 1950, 385). Of course the two are related, but they are not the same. It was only after Mowinckel had challenged the accentuating system that a clear recognition of the difference between them was obtained.

As mentioned above Ley took the *Begriffswort* or *concept-word* as
the regulated element in Hebrew versification, counted those
meaningful words per colon and regarded each as carrying one
accent. Already in 1857 Peters had taken this view. His formulation of
the principles involved, as quoted by Segert (1953, 502-503), is
remarkably clear. Moreover, it has been claimed repeatedly that
Azariah de Rossi had had something similar in mind. Clearly Lowth
understood De Rossi to have been thinking along these lines, for
Lowth (1848, xxviii) wrote:

> Rabbi Azarias . . . makes the form of the verse depend upon the
> structure of the sentence, and the measures of the verse to be
> determined by the several parts of the proposition.

This statement by Lowth contains the essence of the extensive translated quotations from De Rossi with which Lowth (1848, xxix-xxxiv)
and Segert (1953, 500-501) provided us.

It has been generally accepted that Ley, after having discovered
and formulated the relationship between the word and the accent in
Hebrew verse, concentrated on the number of stresses, but Robinson
(1953, 133), Ernst Vogt (cf. Eissfeldt, 1964, 988-989) and more
recently Margalit (1975, 289-290) pointed out the importance of Ley's
identifying the concept-word as the regulated element in Hebrew
versification.

Like Ley, some other scholars who did not limit themselves to
Wortmetrik, also showed an awareness of word boundaries and their
importance to the versification system. So Budde (1882, 6), who
previously had been very sceptical about the existence of metre in
Hebrew verse, started his work on metrics by counting the words in
the colon. In Gray's method of assigning letters to the terms in the
parallel cola (1915, 59-60) and in much of his criticism of the metrical
theories of his day (1915, 201-240) the same awareness is reflected.

Robinson was aware that "a thought rhythm and an accent-
rhythm" would "largely coincide" (1953, 142) and that "the phonetic
element" would play a role in the form of Hebrew poetry, but he
preferred to scan in terms of "thought-units", "thought-elements or
significant words" (1936a, 32-33), also simply called "units" (1947, 25,
30). Later he referred to them as "independent terms", "sense units"
and "verse-units" (1950, 444-446) and, having translated Ley's term

Begriffswort as "significant word" (1953, 133), he also spoke of
"significant ideas" and "significant terms" (1953, 140). He pointed
out that Budde's term *selbständige* excluded "suffixes and short words
which merely modify the main terms" (1953, 133 n.3) and that by
contrast Mowinckel (1950, 385-386) referred to "logische Einheiten"
which were "sinngebend" in the sentence (Robinson, 1953, 144), i.e.
including suffixes, which accords well with Mowinckel's preference
for the alternating system. The large variety of terms used by these
authors reflects a confusion which needs to be clarified, namely
whether *word* here is to be regarded as a syntactical or a semantic
category. Returning to Robinson's own treatment of Hebrew verse, it
can be concluded that he used a kind of word count for scanning.

A strong argument in favour of regarding the word as the
regulated element at least for the earliest phase of Hebrew verse was
made out by Segert (1953). He added that the user of the language
would be so conditioned to the form of the words that he would
instinctively know where the word boundaries occurred (1958, 234-
235). He maintained this view in his later publications (1960, 1969)
and was followed to some extent by Böhl (1957/8, 135-137) and Van
der Westhuizen (1973, 79).

The writings of Bruno contain a different approach, seeing that he
concentrated on the rhythm of Old Testament literature without
distinguishing prose from verse. This also implies a denial or at least
an ignoring of the difference between rhythm and metre.
Nevertheless, Bruno's elaborate system for the counting of words (cf.
Bruno, 1953, 8-14; 1954, 233-235) is in some essentials similar to the
word-metre approach, and should, therefore, be noted in this context.

Another effort to arrive at the versification system of Hebrew verse
by counting words, apparently independently from Segert and with
only slight reference to Robinson, was launched by Kosmala (1964,
1966, 1967). He shared with Segert the conviction that sometime
around the exile there was a change in the system of Hebrew versification (1964, 427). In two respects, however, Kosmala's work
contrasts with that of Segert, namely

(a)   it lacks the broad knowledge both of versification in general and
      of studies in Hebrew versification in particular, and

(b) it has apparently not received much attention from other scholars. It was treated with scepticism by Broadribb (1972/3, 80-81). The reaction of Stek (1974, 25-28) was positive and he added a few examples which showed symmetric strophes when treated according to Kosmala's principles. On the other hand O'Connor (1980a, 49, 54, 65) accepted Kosmala's view that regularities existed on the syntactical level, but rejected nearly all details of his approach.

Gordis, in an English revision of his Hebrew article from 1944/5, claimed explicitly that De Rossi had discovered the *metre* of Hebrew verse (Gordis, 1971, 63), and proceeded to expound his own view:

> ... biblical prosody depends not on the form of the words employed, but upon the ideas they express.... The meter in Hebrew poetry is determined by the number of important words, each of which constitutes a thought unit, with each normally receiving one accent ... (Gordis, 1971, 64-65).

He followed this statement with an explanation of some subordinate principles. These concern the allocation of stress, allowing cola of two to five stresses (1971, 65-68), and, secondly, the variation - in his terms "change" - of metre, mainly forms of lengthening in order to bring about poetic closure (1971, 68-71). According to Gordis metre, in terms of stress or accent, takes precedence over the number of words where these are not in agreement with the number of stresses in the surrounding cola (1971, 65-67). Nevertheless, his system of versification is based on the number of words per colon. The lack of clarity in Gordis's explanation as to the relationship between thought, word and stress led to his view being misunderstood by Watson (1984, 104) as an approach different from the word count approach, the misunderstanding revealing again the problem of what a *Begriffswort* is.

Margalit, though primarily interested in Ugaritic versification, stressed that he regarded his "system of structural-prosodic analysis" to be valid "in essentials for OT Hebrew poetry as well" (1975, 289) for the two formed "a single *literary* tradition" (1975, 290; cf. also 298 n.15). Of all authors making use of word-metre he most explicitly claimed affiliation to Ley. Margalit, however, translated Ley's term *Begriffswort* as "word-concept" instead of "concept-word", which

again, to our mind, reflects the confusion as to whether *word* is a
syntactical or a semantic category. Determined to rid the system of its
"residual, methodologically superfluous, 'phonetical' elements" (1975,
291) he proceeded to formulate the rules of Ugaritic scansion, which
specify which words or word combinations have one unit valence or
more and under what circumstances (1975, 291-298). This he
followed with definitions of the verse and its parts (1975, 298-300),
stating *inter alia*:

> The number of *membra* in a verse is syntactically determined.
> The principal prosodic 'break' or caesura corresponds to the
> principal break in the sentence which is the verse . . . . Many
> distichic verses do in fact contain two grammatical sentences, or
> better, independent clauses (1975, 298).

He also provided a description of the structure of the strophe (1975,
300-310) and of the role of alliteration in Ugaritic versification (1975,
310-313), expanded in later studies. His is definitely a system of word
counting, and one in which syntax plays a role. His later studies
applied his system (for a convenient summary of which cf. 1980, 219-
228).

Wahl's (1976, 20-21) description of his method for the delimitation
of cola, places him squarely within the word count approach, for he
counted words and delimited the cola in terms of syntactical
boundaries and, where possible, in terms of the correspondence of
cola with one another. In his own words:

> Indeed, so regularly do we find this type of rhythm measurable by
> parallel terms that we feel justified in dividing other parts of the
> poems into similar cola, even if they lack parallelism, simply on
> the grounds that the syntax tends to group the words in units
> which admit of the same type of division (Wahl, 1976, 21).

In 2.2 it was noted that Begrich and Alonso-Schökel differed on those
cases where the most prominent syntactical boundary within the
bicolon occurs before its middle, especially in contexts making overwhelming use of the *Qina*. Amongst proponents of word counting the
same difference of opinion exists.

Gray (1915, 176-181) and Robinson (1947, 38-39; 1953, 140)
accepted that at least in some of the cases the cola should be divided

2 + 3 in accordance with the syntax and in spite of the fact that the division 3 + 2 was the norm and more common by far.

According to Gordis it occurs sporadically in Hebrew verse that "the poetic caesura will diverge from the logical caesura" and this divergence is so common in Lamentations "that it may fairly be regarded as a special characteristic of the poet" (Gordis, 1974, 120). He would in such cases divide the cola in accordance with the *Qina* metre, and not in accordance with the syntactical boundary. This had also been the view of Budde (1882, 7).

Previously Gordis (1971, 66-67) had stated that in a bicolon the order short-long, e.g. 2 + 3, is "extremely rare", but he explicitly dealt with variation of the metre by the poet "in order to increase the beauty of his poem and its interest" (1971, 69) and more specifically discussed lengthening of cola and/or verses to achieve poetic closure (1971, 70-71; cf. also Smith, 1912, 20). These aims and techniques may well provide the rationale for the existence of the 2 + 3.

Margalit found a very similar situation in Ugaritic verse:

> A (2 + 3) or a (3 + 4) will occur only, and then most rarely, as counterpunctal variations, i.e., when the rhythmic pattern is deliberately set at odds with the thought-parallelism of the verse. But this exception is at once so infrequent and well-defined that it cannot invalidate the rule that in Ugaritic poetry there are no 'umgekehrter fünfers' or 'siebeners' (sic), i.e., no (2 + 3)'s or (3 + 4)'s (Margalit, 1975, 299).

In concluding this survey of the word counting approach to Hebrew versification the following are noted:

1. In spite of the fact that the approach has been used for a long time, no unitary system has emerged supported by even a modest number of scholars.
2. Nevertheless, there seems to be some reality in Hebrew verse reflected by the repeated and varying efforts to use a word counting system.
3. The sophistication required of such a system does not seem to lie in the direction of a more minute distinction between classes of words in terms of valence or unit status.
4. Clarity will have to be obtained in any proposed versification system using the concept *word* whether a semantic category or a

syntactic category is meant, or if both are meant, how they are related.

5. Scholars using a system of word counting delimit the cola in terms of syntactical boundaries. This is clear from Lowth's summary of De Rossi quoted above, and from the writings of Gray (1915, 54-55), Robinson (1936a, 30; 1947, 22; 1953, 129, 140), Segert (1953, 484, 493), Kosmala (1964, 424, 434), Gordis (1971, 71-82; but cf. 1974, 120) and Margalit (1975, 298-299).

2.4 Syllable count

Albright believed Canaanite verse to be "partly accentual and partly syllabic (i.e. it depended partly on counting syllables)" and he pointed out that certain passages of Ugaritic verse were very exact as to the number of syllables per colon or per bicolon (1942, 117). However, as to Hebrew verse which he regarded as a derivative of Canaanite verse, he also stated:

> I agree almost entirely with Robinson's modification of the Ley-
> Sievers system, except that I emphasize certain phonetic and
> alternating principles which he does not bring into the
> discussion . . . (Albright, 1950/1, 7 n.15).

Even in his later work Albright made use of the counting of accents (e.g. 1968, 8). It is clear, then, that Albright did *not* regard the number of syllables as the essential regulated element of Hebrew versification.

It was, nevertheless, students of Albright's who advocated and practiced syllable counting as a viable approach to Hebrew versification. Most prominent is Freedman, who suggested this approach, stating:

> It is not likely that the Israelites counted syllables carefully, or
> even accents for that matter, when composing their poetry. But it
> is convenient for us to do so in tabulating the evidence
> (Freedman, 1960, 101).

Although he at times seemed to equate syllable counts with metrical structure, he later made it clear that he did distinguish between the two (cf. the discussion of Freedman's work by Longman, 1982, 232-233, 236 n.36). Other proponents included Cross and Dahood, and their students as well as Freedman's.

Logically there are two points of view possible for the syllable counter - distinguished already by Culley (1970, 16, 28) - namely either

1.   that the ancient Israelite poet - wittingly or unwittingly - made use of the counting of syllables in the construction of his verse, i.e. that syllable counting is the versification system of Hebrew verse, or
2.   that there exist regularities in Hebrew verse which can be expressed in terms of the number of syllables per colon and/or bicolon.

An exponent of the former point of view is Stuart (1976), whose book originally was a dissertation completed in 1971 (Cooper, 1976, 148). Since its publication Stuart's work has been severely but justifiably criticised by Cooper (1976, 27-32; 1979), Alonso-Schökel (1978), Culley (1978), Good (1978), O'Connor (1980a, 35-37), Pardee (1981, 117-122) and Longman (1982, 234-238, 248-252). Stuart studied early Hebrew and some Ugaritic verse, and repeatedly referred to the Hebrew versification system as "syllabic meter" (1976, 9, 16, etc.), possibly reflecting views then - i.e. about 1971 - held by his mentor, Cross, and by Freedman. The idea of syllabic metre was later explicitly rejected by Cross (see below). The most important criticisms of Stuart's work, with which we are in agreement and which concern us in this context, can be summarised as follows:

1.   Terminological obscurity.
2.   Subjective vocalisation.
3.   Drastic emendation of the Massoretic Text, often so as to obtain more syllabic regularity.
4.   Inability to obtain consistent results.

In the light of these points of criticism, as well as the strength of the alternative view, Stuart's postulate of syllabic metre is to be regarded as erroneous. Of course, "it is still quite possible that a regular number of syllables was employed, like rhyme, as a special effect for a particular saying or passage", as suggested by Parker (1974, 286). This was the view of Halle and McCarthy (1981) on the versification of Psalm 137, for which they claimed Freedman's support (but cf. Freedman, 1971, 189 = 1980, 305). Unfortunately Halle and McCarthy only stated their view and offered little proof that it was either correct or better than other treatments.

The said alternative view is that of Cross who stated it, firstly as to Ugaritic verse, as follows:

> Usually the formulaic structure gives an extreme symmetry or regularity to Ugaritic verse.
> This symmetry can be illustrated by syllable counting in a vocalised text. We should not be prepared to argue that the ancient Canaanite singer counted syllables; only that this device yields a higher index of symmetry than the more usual stress analysis (Cross, 1974, 1).

More recently he expressed the same view as to Hebrew verse:

> I have no doubt that Hebrew poetry, especially archaic poetry, reveals a level of symmetry and repetition inadequately represented by the usual stress or quantitative analyses. Syllable counting has proven a useful technique in isolating metrical structures. Yet this does not mean necessarily that the ancient poet counted syllables. Early Hebrew poetry was formulaic, I believe, its symmetry in part 'prefabricated'. Assuming the oral composition of at least the more archaic poetry, I remain doubtful that the poet engaged in 'long distance' syllable counting - my scepticism mounting as one moves from verses to strophes to complete poems - and have sought alternate modes of dealing with syllabic and structural symmetry (Cross, 1980, vii-viii).

In his recent studies Cross (1983a, 1983b) counted syllables, but only in order to establish which cola are to be regarded as long (indicated as l = *longum*) and which as short (indicated as b = *breve*), the terms in which he has for many years described the length relationships between cola (1983a, 132). Cola of six or seven syllables may be either l or b, depending on "the relative length of each in a bicolon" (1983a, 152), and this overlap strengthened his conviction "that the

ancient Canaanite and Hebrew poets were not counting syllables ..."
(1983a, 132; cf. 152). Thus, for Cross's aims, even approximate
syllable counts would be quite satisfactory in many cola.

Freedman, having experimented with accent counting and vocable
counting (1974, 195 = 1980, 219), expressed essentially the same view,
though perhaps less carefully formulated:

> There is no single solution to the problem of Hebrew meter and
> poetic structure, but there are many possible descriptions, some
> more adequate than others.... there is no single best
> system .... the principal object is to devise a measuring system
> that is symmetry-sensitive and will describe the metrical pattern
> as clearly and as simply as the data permit. That is why I have
> opted for a syllable counting system ... (Freedman, 1977, 11 =
> 1980, 7).

From the context it is clear that by "metrical pattern" Freedman
simply meant the length relationships between cola and/or bicola, for
he also wrote: "Our objective is not to find or devise a key to Hebrew
metrics, but rather to achieve an adequate description of the
phenomena" (Freedman, 1977, 11 = 1980, 7; cf. already 1971, 188-189
= 1980, 304-305). Thus, what he is interested in is only a relatively
accurate description of colon length by the modern scholar, not the
versification system used by the Hebrew poets.

It is also noted that, whereas Cross is primarily interested in
contrasts of colon length even where the difference between cola is
not great, Freedman somehow tends more to emphasise *equality* of
either colon or bicolon length. In this respect his summary of the
structure of Exodus 15 in terms of short and long cola (1974, 201 =
1980, 225) is an exception.

Another exponent of the syllable count approach is Culley, who
warned "that the numbers of syllables counted in cola and lines are
only to be considered approximate and not absolute figures" (1970,
17) and then pointed out that: "In order to count the syllables in lines
and cola it is necessary first of all to establish clearly these divisions in
the text" (1970, 18). These are both very important considerations.

In so far as cola of equal length exist in Hebrew verse the counting
of syllables could provide a means for delimitation of such cola, but
cola in Hebrew verse, especially in prophetic literature, often are not
of equal length in terms of syllables. Scholars making use of syllable

counts therefore have to rely on some other criterion for the delimitation of cola. Culley mentioned two criteria, namely *parallelism* and *clause boundary*, and again warned that since syllable counting

> is intended to be a strictly descriptive technique . . . , no count may be made where divisions into lines or cola are not evident from the text itself through the presence of parallelism or of relevant syntactic structure. This means, of course, that there may be parts of poems, or even whole poems, which cannot be analysed by means of a syllable count (Culley, 1970, 18).

On this basis it would in other cases be possible only to count the syllables in the line, i.e. mono-, bi- or tricolon, but division of cola can also be made at phrase boundaries (1970, 25-27).

Culley has made it clear that he and many other syllable counters relied on parallelism and syntactical boundaries, namely clause boundaries and phrase boundaries for the delimitation of cola. This means that syntax is of prime importance for colon delimitation, but it does not solve the problem, for neither all the boundaries between parallelistic expressions, nor the boundaries between all clauses, nor the boundaries between all phrases are colon ends. It still has to be determined which of these boundaries do constitute colon ends.

The lack of concensus amongst scholars as to which boundaries do constitute colon ends becomes most visible when the colon delimitation by Dahood and his students is compared with that of other syllable counters. Significantly, Althann (1983, 4) wrote:

> Stuart's own procedure is in line with the work of . . . Cross and . . . Freedman in relying primarily on the length of cola obtained by counting syllables to determine the metre.

Clearly Althann implied that Stuart, Cross and Freedman delimited cola primarily by counting syllables, which was seen not to be the case. Althann's statement does, however, reveal that in his own approach syllable counting is the primary factor, as is also clear from his treatment of several passages (cf. e.g. 1983, 39, 63, 73, 75, 104, 108). He confused parallel *terms* with parallel *cola*, breaking up short parallel expressions into even shorter "cola" and thus creating cases of enjambement, which we believe to be foreign to the text. In this he was following the example of Dahood (1967) who allowed "cola" of three and even two syllables in order to obtain more equal cola - measured in syllables - preceding and following these brief ones. Such a procedure has firmly and rightly been rejected by Watson (1984, 214 n.34). The value Dahood attached to syllable counts is clear from his referring to "Such careful . . . syllabic parallelism . . ." (1976, 670). Dahood and Althann, then, assumed that the Hebrew poets either wittingly or unwittingly counted syllables and that the poets based their colometry on such counting, an assumption not reconcilable with the views of Cross, Freedman and Culley. Dahood and Althann also introduced a large measure of subjectivity into their colometry by letting syllable count take precedence over the syntactical boundaries.

The counting of syllables practically means a counting of vowels, and it is precisely these that are often disputed, the vocalisation being of a much later date than the consonantal text. Anyone who considers the versification to be based upon a syllabic metre runs into serious difficulties on this point, for he is forced to reconstruct the traditional text. Because of the uncertainties concerning the vowels used by the Hebrew poets, such reconstruction easily becomes subjective, as was noted in the case of Stuart. In an effort to avoid an arbitrary reconstruction of the syllables to be counted, Althann (1983, 6) decided to count all vowels in the received text, including *shewa mobile, shewa compositum* and even the *patach furtivum*. This decision is just as arbitrary, however, because it is highly unlikely that all these vowel signs represent sounds which really occurred in Hebrew during the Old Testament period. Such a count could create symmetry where the text did not have it, or hide intentional symmetry from the scholar, i.e. if symmetry or asymmetry in terms of the number of syllables was intended. If, on the other hand, a scholar uses the number of syllables only as approximate and not as absolute figures, as Culley wisely suggested, the value of the counts is severely limited. Moreover, even in such a case the uncertainties of vocalisation are not avoided, as is clear from the different stances taken by Cross, Freedman and Culley.

It has to be stressed that there is not necessarily a *fixed relation* between the regulated element in Hebrew versification and the number of syllables. Should, for instance the number of stresses prove to be regulated in Hebrew verse, there would be no fixed relation between the number of syllables and the number of stresses. Both the appearance of symmetricality and of asymmetricality in terms of syllables can be misleading.

The objections to syllable counting as an approach to Hebrew versification can be summarised as follows:

1. A measure of uncertainty as to the number of syllables cannot be avoided, and the counts are therefore only approximate.
2. It is highly unlikely that the poets as a rule counted syllables and, if they did not, the number of syllables does not directly relate to the versification system.
3. Syllable counting can only be undertaken after cola have been delimited by other means, namely in accordance with parallelism and syntactic boundaries.

In the light of these objections syllable counting can only be used as an approximate check on the length of already delimited cola, and nothing concerning the versification system used by the poets can be deduced from such counts.

2.5 Consonant count

In order to escape the subjectivity of counting either stresses or syllables (or vowels) Loretz has advocated the counting of consonants in both Ugaritic and Hebrew verse. He was quite blunt about the fact that this approach supplies statistics only about the length and length relationships of cola in a highly abstract form, and that these statistics precede any metrical or other versification theory. He left the determining of such a theory for later. He also warned that the approach has to reckon with mistakes of writing, with glosses and with additions (Loretz, 1975, 267-269). Of course the presence of *matres lectiones* further complicates matters.

Another important aspect of his approach is the explicit and repeated statement that the counting of consonants, and any other description of the colon for that matter, can only be undertaken *after* the cola have been delimited (Loretz, 1975, 267, 269; 1979, 10). Initially he used the terms *Stichos* and *Stichometrie* - the latter indicating the delimitation of cola - but because of their ambiguity he later rejected them in favour of *Kolon* and *Kolometrie*, which are

in agreement with his use of *Bikolon* and *Trikolon* (1979, 10). After
such colometry, then, the number of consonants in each colon is
counted, which may of course lead to a redivision of cola (1975, 268),
for he was convinced that the Ugaritic texts provide proof that there
are rules as to the maximum and minimum length of cola (1979, 7,
10).

Loretz rightly stressed the importance of the correct colometry,
following the example of Pope (1966) in this regard. Yet in spite of
this Loretz did not provide clear principles for determining the
correct colometry, apparently thinking that these were well-known. In
addition to the acceptance of maximum and minimum lengths of cola,
expressed in terms of the number of consonants, the following factors
seem to play a role in Loretz's colometry:

1.   *Parallelismus membrorum* (1975, 269).
2.   Semantic unity of the colon (1975, 267 n.14).
3.   The relative absence of enjambement (1979, 478).
4.   Loretz's resistance towards the acceptance of tricola, i.e.
     emphasis on the preference for duality, following Mowinckel
     (Loretz, 1979, 7, 479, 505-506).

The role of the number of consonants per colon in the process of
colometry is, thus, severely limited by Loretz. Nevertheless, it does
play an important role in his deciding which cola and/or words are
part of the original poem and which are to be bracketed as later
additions. In this way a large measure of subjectivity is introduced,
which can damage the evidence presented by the text in order to
make it conform to the scholar's preconceived notion of the verse
structure (Ceresko, 1981, 280).

Although the numbers obtained by consonant counting can be of
value in the comparing of colon lengths and thus could provide a
check on colometry, such numbers do not relate to any meaningful
factor of versification and therefore provide no information as to the
versification system used by the poets themselves. Because of this fact
the description of consonant counting as *pre-metrical* (Watson, 1984,
105) is quite apt. If, for example, the important factor in Hebrew
verse should prove to be the number of stresses per colon, there
would be no direct, constant relation between the number of stresses

and the number of consonants. This implies that the counting of consonants may create the impression of symmetry where the poet intended asymmetry and vice versa. For that reason the value of this approach to Hebrew versification is extremely limited.

In conclusion, the emphasis which Loretz placed on the correct colometry and its primacy is welcomed, but nevertheless his approach is found wanting in the following respects:

1.   The basis of his colometry is unclear.
2.   His treatment of data that do not suit his theory is subjective.
3.   He does not deal with the versification system itself.

Whereas the first two of these defects can be remedied, the third is inherently bound to the choice of counting consonants, and therefore principially relegates the approach to a pre-metrical and unsatisfactory one.

2.6 Conclusion

In this survey of versification systems presently applied to Hebrew verse two aspects were concentrated on, namely

1.   the inability of the systems to provide a reliable and valid delimitation of cola, and
2.   the role syntax is allowed to play in these systems or in their application.

The discussion of the *parallelistic approach* to Hebrew verse has led to the conclusion that the concept is problematic, that parallelism is not always present in Hebrew verse, and that all parallelisms present are not necessarily *parallelismus membrorum*. The colon ends as established by those who follow this approach are syntactic boundaries or at the least coincide with syntactic boundaries.

Those who count *accents* dispute the method of counting and they are forced by the evidence of the verse itself to allow the number of stresses to vary. Yet their colon delimitation is similar, namely according to syntactic boundaries, but how they do so is left unexplained.

Those who count *words* are confronted with the question of what a *word* is, i.e. what kinds of words are to be counted and whether levels are to be distinguished. They delimit cola according to syntactical boundaries but do not supply the criteria for doing so.

Those who count *syllables* are prone to subjectivity of vocalisation. Their method supplies an approximate description of colon length only, not of the versification system. It can, therefore, serve only as a check on already delimited cola. Such previous delimitation is done according to syntactical boundaries but again the criteria are not spelled out.

The counting of *consonants* is not free from subjectivity, it is descriptive of colon length only and thus does not touch on the versification system. It can function as a check on previously delimited cola. The basis for such previous delimitation is unclear, but apparently syntax does play a role therein.

Another approach is noted here, which, however, was used only as a part of comparative experiments and only for descriptive purposes. It has been called a *vocable count* (Freedman, 1974, 195-200 = 1980, 219-224) and a *phoneme count* (Powell, 1982, 50, 57-58, etc.). Because it entails the counting of both consonants and vowels - taking into account also the length and stress of vowels - it has all the disadvantages of both syllable counting and consonant counting. It produces a mere quantification of colon lengths and thus cannot describe the versification system of Hebrew verse.

The conclusion is reached, then, that all the non-syntactical systems presently applied to Hebrew verse are unable to provide a valid and reliable delimitation of cola. With the partial exception of the approach through parallelism, this is so because the systems are all descriptions of some facet or facets of previously delimited cola, instead of descriptions of the colometric system itself.

The role of syntax in constituting line-breaks or colon ends is assumed throughout, but it is seldom highlighted. The fact that adherents to all the different approaches rely on it, is very meaningful. The study of Hebrew verse is desparately in need of more specific guidelines as to this role. The role of syntax in Hebrew verse is therefore to be studied, and especially the syntactical status of the line-breaks or colon boundaries has to be determined.

Chapter 3

The Syntactical Approach

3.1 General characterisation

As an outgrowth of and in part as a reaction against traditional metrics, which concentrated only on the aspect of sound, there was developed a more comprehensive view of metre which takes into account the role syntax plays in metre. This approach is fairly diversified, and the exact role assigned to syntax by different researchers in the versification systems of diverse languages varies greatly. This fact, of course, does not invalidate the syntactical approach, as it is only to be expected that widely differing languages will not function in the exact same way in versification, and that, therefore, the role of syntax in versification will vary. The common factor which makes possible our viewing these divergent descriptions given by researchers as *the syntactical approach*, is the emphasis upon syntax as one - whether the most prominent or a less prominent - component of each of these versification systems.

Syntax is often defined as part of linguistic *theory*, e.g.:

> Syntax is the part of linguistics that deals with how the words of a language are arranged into phrases and sentences and how components (like prefixes and suffixes) are combined to make words (Winograd, 1983, 35).

The word syntax, then, can be used to refer to the linguistic study and description of certain language phenomena. However, the language *phenomena* with which such description or theory deals and to which it should correspond, have a reality of their own in the language. These phenomena can be termed syntactic phenomena, or simply syntax. A paraphrase of the word syntax as "the relationship of words to one another" (Williams, 1976, 3) focuses on this meaning of the word. To express the relationship of words to one another the user of the language has at his disposal certain conventional means, which can be called syntactic means. These means the user of the language uses to combine words into identifiable conventional units. Akmajian

et al (1979, 147, 149, 150, 164) stressed that the units created by
syntactic means are structured units, having at least the following four
important aspects:

1. linear order of words
2. morphological categorisation of words into parts of speech
3. grouping of words into structural constituents of sentences
4. functional or relational role of any given phrase.

Syntactic description takes these four aspects into account.

Scholars who apply the syntactical approach share the assumption
that it should be possible, at least in principle if not in practice in any
specific case, to make use of syntactic description, i.e. description in
terms of syntactic categories or components and structures, on
further levels of language and literary study, such as stylistics,
pragmatics, rhetoric, the analysis of verse structure and the description of a versification system.

3.2 The syntactical approach to the versification of literatures other than Hebrew

It is conceivable that no other known literature will have a
versification system based on syntax, similar to those proposed by
Collins (1978a) and O'Connor (1980a) for Hebrew verse. If such
were the case, it would be no proof against the possibility of Hebrew
verse having such a syntactic base. Nevertheless, if similar systems do
function in the verse of other literatures, the case for seriously
considering these proposals for Hebrew verse would be stronger.
Therefore, descriptions which have been given of some verse systems
and in which syntax is assigned some role, will be briefly examined in
this section.

This survey does not aim at an evaluation of the various descriptions, which could, after all, only be given by specialists in each of the
literatures concerned. Neither is this an effort to represent all existing
descriptions of this type. The examples used have been picked rather
at random. Especially noteworthy is the absence of any similar
description of the verse of those languages most closely related to
Hebrew, namely the Northwest Semitic languages. No such descriptions of, for instance, Ugaritic verse is known to the present author.

Wilson's (1982) study of word order and sentence structure in *Krt* does not refer to verse structure at all. Perhaps one might, however, regard Collins' (1970/1) study of the Phoenician Kilamuwa inscription and Krahmalkov's (1975) study of Punic verse as efforts in this direction, from which, unfortunately, very little is to be gained as to the role of syntax in the versification systems concerned.

3.2.1 Russian verse

In his chapter on "Verse Structure: Sound and Meaning" Erlich (1955, 185) described how the Russian Formalists, dissatisfied with the notion of foot in the description of prosody, regarded "the verse line, seen as a distinct 'rhythmico-syntactical' or 'intonational' segment" to be "the basic unit of verse rhythm".

Moreover, Osip Brik argued that in many poems

> the rhythmical movement hinges not only on strictly prosodic factors, for example stress distribution, but on the word order as well. Syntax takes its cue here from rhythm. The tendency toward regular ordering of the verbal material finds its additional expression in the parallelism of sentence structures occuring in contiguous or otherwise correlated verse lines.
>
> Brik labeled this phenomenon 'rhythmico-syntactical parallelism' and proceeded to trace it through Russian poetry of the Pushkin era. He found in Russian iambic tetrameter, the most 'canonic' of Russian metrical patterns, a number of persistent rhythmico-syntactical 'figures'. These were such sequences as noun plus adjective plus noun . . . or personal pronoun plus adjective plus noun (Erlich, 1955, 190).

Similar "figures" do occur in many kinds of verse as exceptions, but as Brik has demonstrated,

> there are periods or schools in the history of poetry for which the approximate coextensiveness of rhythmical and syntactical units is the rule rather than the exception (Erlich, 1955, 191).
>
> Eichenbaum went Brik one better in a spirited attempt to prove that such a syntactical phenomenon as phrase melody can, in a certain type of verse, become *not merely a contributing factor, but the 'dominant' element - the formative principle*. (Erlich, 1955, 191; emphasis added).

Although Eichenbaum's thesis was contested by Zhirmunsky (Erlich, 1955, 192), it should be noted here that, as long ago as 1922, such a thesis was advanced.

3.2.2   The earliest Hungarian verse

In their summary of "Directions in Hungarian Metric Research" Kecskés and Kerek (1980, 321) pointed out that

> Prehistoric Hungarian verse (much like versification in other Finno-Ugric languages) did not utilize either syllable counting or syllable length as organizing principles. Originally, every line in a verse coincided with a major syntactic unit (usually a sentence), and poetic effects were created by the partial or complete repetition, logical parallelism, contrast, or expansion of these sentences.

This early Hungarian verse was studied by Vargyas in 1952.

> Vargyas's examples and analyses convincingly demonstrate that the development of the traditional Hungarian verse rhythm closely parallels the syntactic and semantic segmentation of normal speech into *phonological phrases* (henceforth 'phonophrases'). According to Vargyas, such phrases are the primary formative factor of Hungarian verse; it is, above all, the segmentation of the verse text into phonophrases that determines the number of beats in a line. A phonophrase ... either fully constitutes a beat or consists of more than one beat, but a single beat must take all its syllables from a single phrase (Kecskés and Kerek, 1980, 329-330).
>
> Vargyas further supplements his *basically syntactic interpretation* (emphasis added) with an acoustic-auditory observation .... he claims that regardless of the number of syllables in the line, the perceived duration of successive beats shows a *levelling* tendency, so that all beats are perceived as if they had the same objective length (Kecskés and Kerek, 1980, 330-331).

3.2.3   American Indian verse narrative

A number of scholars have in recent years taken the view that some narratives of various American Indian peoples are to be understood as consisting of lines of verse rather than as prose.

> A step toward demonstrating the existence of such lines in American Indian narrative was taken by Tedlock . . . in his translations . . . . although Tedlock does not explicitly point out many linguistic features which would identify Zuni narratives as poetry, his organization into lines on the basis of pause strongly points to a poetic structure in the Zuni originals (Bright, 1981, 275-276).

Hymes, however, realised that pause cannot on its own be proof of the existence of verse lines and wrote:

> . . . even if pause is basic to poetry, there remains the problem of differentiating pause that is motivated, that heightens the organization of lines, from pause that is inherent in the spoken medium . . . . Exciting as is the possibility of initial demarcation through pause, it is only a step toward poetics (Hymes, 1977, 453).

Hymes then pointed out that Tedlock was aware of other factors besides pause which might well play a role in the poetic structure, for instance stress, marked chanting of certain lines, and pitch. To this he added:

> Perhaps it is not accidental that the passages cited to illustrate such points also show parallelism of structure, enclosing an apposition, . . . full clauses . . . and also threefold repetition . . . . Not only is pause not the only phonic marker of lines; one begins to suspect that lines have a grammatical aspect as well . . . . Perhaps pause does not so much define lines, as provide a counterpoint to them . . . (Hymes, 1977, 453-454).

It is quite apparent that Hymes did not regard the latter possibility as likely, for he relied to a very large extent on syntactic arguments for his delimitation of lines, especially on recurrent initial particles and the presence of verbs (cf. Hymes, 1977, 438-440; 1980, 37-38). Indeed, the verse narratives studied by Hymes, not having metre (in the traditional, i.e. phonological sense) or rhyme, could hardly have such counterpoint; on the contrary, these narratives have "a characterizing grammatico-semantic repetition within a frame as its base" (Hymes, 1976, 154).

Bright's summary (1981, 276) of Hymes's approach is significant:

In seeking a basis for the analysis of measured verse, Hymes has
put great emphasis on the use of sentence-initial particles . . . .
With this concept of verse as basis, Hymes finds it possible to
recognize other structurally defined units, both smaller - such as
*the line, defined typically in terms of its unity as a grammatical
predication* - and larger, such as the scene and act . . . (emphasis
added).

Following Hymes a number of researchers studied oral narratives of
various American Indian peoples and in some of these found similar
systems functioning (cf. Hymes, 1980, 34-35; Bright, 1981, 280 n.13).
Bright combined the methods of Tedlock and Hymes and found that
"the two approaches coincide 90 percent of the time in their identifi-
cation of basic units", which result gave him "confidence that
occasional ambiguities of one approach can be resolved by reference
to the other . . ." (Bright, 1981, 276, 280 n.11).

To be fair, it has to be added here that some reservations as to the
applicability of a verse - prose distinction to American Indian oral
literature have recently been expressed by Tedlock (1977) and
McLendon (1981). A careful response to this problem was that of
Bright (1981, 277-278), who mentioned the possibility that perhaps all
literature was in verse form and that prose was used only for non-
literary discourse.

3.2.4   Bantu praise verse

O'Connor (1980, 157-158), following Opland, pointed out that certain
Xhosa praise poems, called *izibongo*, are composed using techniques
similar to those found in Hebrew verse, and using what O'Connor
called "a constrictional system", i.e. with a syntactical base similar to
that which he formulated for Hebrew verse. It seems, however, that
the comparison can be made more explicit.

Writing on Southern Bantu praise poems Finnegan commented on
their versification system:

This is a difficult topic, but it seems that there is some kind of
dynamic stress which, in addition to other stylistic features
mentioned below, is one of the main characteristics which
distinguish this art form as 'poetry'. The division into lines is in
most cases indicated fairly clearly by the reciter's delivery, so that
certain groups of words are pronounced together in the same

breath, followed by a pause, and fall together in terms of sense, sometimes consisting of a formalized 'praise verse' . . . . Within each of these lines there are normally three or four groups of syllables (or 'nodes' as Lestrade terms them), each group marked by one main stress but containing any number of other syllables. This 'node' sometimes consists of just one word (or is dynamically treated as one word) . . . . A stanza - and, ultimately, a whole poem - is thus made up of succession of these lines, each consisting of three or four 'nodes' following each other indiscriminately. There seems to be no attempt at regular quantitative metre, for the stanzas are made up of irregular numbers of lines each with varying numbers of syllables, but the variety in syllable numbers . . . is bound together not only by the overall pattern of this strong stress rhythm, but by repetition, parallelism, and other devices . . . (Finnegan, 1970, 129-130).

As devices of the poetic style Finnegan (1970, 131-132) then mentioned alliteration and assonance, syntactic constructions peculiar to the poems, parallelism and repetition in various forms, binomination, chiasmus, deliberate change of word order in the second of three parallel lines, and linking by repeating a phrase from the end of a line in the first half of the next line.

In the light of the above description Opland's remarks on Xhosa poetry are more clearly relevant to the present problem. Opland (1976, 121) distinguished four types of poetry among the Xhosa, namely:

(a)   that of the ordinary tribe member,
(b)   that of the memoriser,
(c)   the praise poem, and
(d)   written poetry by literate Xhosa poets.

Of interest here is his descriptions of the praise poems or *izibongo*, which he firstly contrasted with the spontaneous poetry of an ordinary tribe member. In the latter he found that

the words are rushed, as many words as possible being squeezed into a breath group: there is generally not the rhythmical cadence of the typical *izibongo* of an *imbongi*, or the relation one finds in the latter's poems between sense, breath and intonation (Opland, 1975, 187).

On the other hand, when Xhosa poets compose written poetry this also clearly differs from the praise poems.

> The lines no longer have the variable length of the oral *izibongo*, and there is frequent enjambment. This too is the product of literacy: the line is now thought of as a fixed metrical unit . . . rather than as a unit of sense (Opland, 1975, 204).

In the praise poems

> the lines do not display either syllabic or quantitative meter . . . though there is some reason to believe that one may be able to determine certain recurrent intonational patterns that function as meter (Opland, 1975, 194).

Opland continued his description (1975, 196):

> One may seek the meter of Xhosa poetry in the technique of parallel repetitions, or one may seek it in the intonation of the lines . . . The latter would seem to me to be the more profitable approach. Rycroft is certainly correct in drawing attention to recurrent patterns that act as tonal rather than verbal formulas . . . . The *imbongi*'s lines display control of tone, breath and sense . . . . A breath group is thus also a sense group, and it has a distinctive pattern of intonation.

The fact that Opland (1976, 124) at a conference in 1974 was unable to describe the metre of Xhosa praise poems perhaps indicates that his decision quoted above to seek the metre in the *intonation* of the lines rather than in the *recurrent patterns* was a mistake. Even later he wrote: "The meter of Xhosa *izibongo* awaits definition" (Opland, 1983, 159). Having surveyed various efforts to describe the versification system of Southern African praise verse Rycroft recommended that the search be given up in favour of a broad perspective of the oral performance as it is accompanied by bodily movements, gestures or hand-clapping. He believed that these actions provided "a kind of *extrinsic* metre", against which the oral delivery is timed and regulated (Rycroft, 1980, 298). It seems likely that the versification system which Opland was seeking and which Rycroft despaired to find, will be similar to that described by O'Connor (1980a).

3.2.5   Babylonian verse

In his recent dissertation on the Babylonian poem *ludlul bel nemeqi*
Van Rensburg gave a metrical, syntactic and semantic typology of
verse lines. His approach was inspired by the work of Collins (1978a)
on Hebrew poetry and aimed at the integration of grammar and
stylistics within verse lines. Syntax was given a central place in his
argumentation (Van Rensburg, 1983, 1-2).

Van Rensburg's additions and modifications to Collins' approach
are no radical alterations thereof. In Van Rensburg's approach,
however, verse line division played a more important role than in
Collins'. The characteristic of Babylonian verse that makes possible
the application to it of such a modification of Collins' approach, is
specifically of interest here. Von Soden (1952, 242) formulated this
characteristic: "Die rhythmische Gliederung entspricht genau der
syntaktischen bzw. der Sinngliederung." This statement of Von Soden
was also quoted with approval by Böhl (1957/8, 141 n.43) as a reliable
point of departure in the metrical study of Babylonian verse (cf. also
Von Soden, 1982, 177).

This means that the relationship between verse line and sentence,
clause or phrase in Babylonian verse is similar to, though not necessarily identical with, that in Hebrew verse.

3.2.6   Egyptian verse

Starting from Khety's *Hymn to the Inundation* Foster expounded his
theory of Egyptian verse in three publications (1975; 1977; 1980).
There are amazing similarities between O'Connor's description of the
Hebrew verse system and Foster's views on Egyptian verse. For that
reason it is necessary to present Foster's description in some detail,
the more so as these researchers apparently reached their conclusions
independently of each other.

In the *Hymn to the Inundation*, commonly recognised as a poem,
Foster observed that red dots called verse points were used "in
identical positions from copy to copy . . . and, ultimately of the most
importance, *the verse points coincide absolutely with grammatical
clauses*" (his emphasis).

Foster (1975, 7) continued:

> Furthermore ... we infer that the ancient Egyptian line of verse
> was not metered but rather was a matter of stresses and
> cadences. Cadences can be defined as rhythmical units of
> phrasing, varying in length, much more loosely and irregularly
> structured than meter, varying also in number of stresses and
> syllables per unit and separated by the instinctive pauses of the
> speaking voice ('mouthfuls of verse').... one ... finds that
> individual lines employing essentially identical grammatical
> patterns can be longer or shorter, primarily through the presence
> or absence of a complement ...

Foster (1975, 7-8) then reached the conclusion that "in a rhythmic
scheme based on cadences ... *the poetic line of verse coincides with
the grammatical clause.*" He pointed out that in literary studies this
phenomenon was termed the "end-stopped line" and suggested that
rhythmically Walt Whitman's verse and ancient Egyptian verse
employed the same scheme.

He was convinced that his reconstruction of the *Hymn to the
Inundation* proved his hypothesis, namely that the red dots mark the
end of the single line of verse, to be sound. He added a point with
wider implications (1975, 8): "... by rhythmic criteria alone,
cadenced verse cannot be distinguished from literary prose." He
pointed out that the latter was what Fecht had tried to do and that it
had resulted in Fecht's assertion that all Egyptians wrote in verse.
(One notices a similarity between Fecht's view and the views of
Sievers and Bruno on Hebrew literature.)

The use of the term "parallelism" or "parallelism of members" in
Egyptology Foster (1975, 9) found somewhat misleading and he
wanted it replaced by the term "thought couplet". This he described
as

> something both stricter and more varied than mere parallelism of
> members .... Parallelism is merely one of its devices.
>
> The ancient Egyptian thought couplet, then, is a pair of verse
> lines which form an independent unit of thought, syntax and
> rhetoric. Rhythmically, the lines are composed of cadences
> (rather than the feet of a strict meter) of irregular length; and
> there is a pause at the end of each (the end-stopped line), a
> pause especially prominent at the end of each second line. These

lines can be built into larger units, but always as multiples of two. There are no run-on lines, where the grammatical, or rhetorical, or thought content continues without break into the next couplet (Foster, 1975, 9).

He then described the *individual line* of Egyptian verse *in terms of syntax*, stating (1975, 11) that it

can consist of either an independent or a dependent clause; it can even be a complete short sentence. Each such clause must have a verb or verbal notion and one of three types of clause must occur . . .

He called the single clause an "element" and stated (1975, 12): "There are both one element and two element lines of verse . . . . and I suspect there is no such thing as a three element verse line." Foster (1975: 15-17) realised that

if we can come to rely on certain rules for the maximum number of grammatical elements per line, or if we can develop rules strictly limiting the kind or number of phrases that can occur in a line

it would be of great value in textual criticism and in syntactical studies. It is important to note the fact that Foster regarded it as possible to describe the *single verse line in syntactical terms on various levels*, i.e. in a way very similar to O'Connor's description of Hebrew verse. Of course, with the individual lines already clearly marked in the text, as Foster believed, he was not so much interested in the description as such, but rather in the traditional problem areas to which the description might be fruitfully applied.

3.2.7   Arabic verse

O'Connor (1980a, 154-156) claimed that the Arabic *saj'*, usually understood as rhymed prose (cf. for instance Krenkow, 1934, 43-44), should be understood as verse composed according to a prosodical system of the same type as the constrictional system which he discovered in Hebrew verse. At least one scholar of Hebrew literature had previously recognised the poetical nature of *saj'* and the similarity of its structure to that of Hebrew verse, namely G.B. Gray (1915, 44-

45). O'Connor's claim is, of course, more specific and should be evaluated by specialists in the field of Arabic literature.

In the meantime the way in which one such specialist has recently described the structure of early Meccan suras can be compared. Neuwirth (1981, 118) pointed out, like Gray and O'Connor that these early suras originated from the *saj'* and that they are not prose, i.e. they should be regarded as verse. She also repeatedly stressed that syntax played a decisive role in the delimitation of lines (1981, 6, 18-20, 119-122), even listing five syntactic units ("syntaktische Einheiten") which function as poetic lines, namely (1981, 121-122):

(a)   all main clauses (having more than two words)
(b)   all syndetic relative clauses (having more than two words)
(c)   the protasis of a conditional sentence (having more than two words)
(d)   other subordinate clauses, if they have a change of subject vis-à-vis the clause on which they depend
(e)   single syntagmas in sentences of more than average length, if they have enough bulk (i.e. length) and semantic weight.

It is of import that Neuwirth, like O'Connor, realised the necessity of taking into account *different levels*, not only clauses and phrases (= syntagmas), but also the number of words. Whereas O'Connor refused to take semantics into account and has been criticised on that account by Kugel (1981, 321-322) and Blommerde (1982, 163, 166), Neuwirth did reckon with it, but clearly as a lesser factor (1981, 19-20; cf. also d and e above).

The descriptions proposed by O'Connor and Neuwirth are far from identical - that of O'Connor being much more formalised - but the similarities in their approaches imply a large similarity between the versification systems which they attempted to describe.

3.2.8   Conclusion

From the above survey it has become clear that a number of scholars are convinced that syntax does play a role in the versification systems with which they are acquainted through research. In each case the versification system is (or was when it still functioned) part of an oral tradition, or was based upon an oral tradition of verse-making with which it interacted, as was also most probably the case with the phase of biblical Hebrew verse with which this study is concerned (cf. Cross, 1983a, 129, 133, 137). It is noteworthy that in some of the cases the languages and literatures concerned are related to those of Hebrew. In our opinion the proposal of versification systems based on syntax for literatures other than Hebrew do warrant the serious consideration of similar systems proposed for Hebrew verse. The use of various syntactical levels in the description of the systems suggested for Babylonian, Egyptian and Arabic verse probably indicates that such levels will have to be taken into account in the description of the Hebrew versification system.

3.3   The syntactical approach to the versification system of Hebrew verse

In the past decade and a half several studies were undertaken and published in which syntactical description was used as a more or less important part of the versification system of Hebrew verse. Some of these were done independently of one another and roughly simultaneously (cf. O'Connor, 1980b, 91), with the result that the precise order of their completion or publication is not necessarily important for our purposes. In each of these studies the syntax is assigned a different role in the versification system. The purpose of this section will be to make a comparative evaluation of these studies.

3.3.1   Precursors

Even though the syntactical approach to Hebrew versification is a fairly recent development it has roots going back very far into the history of the study of Hebrew verse. Basic to the syntactical approach is the assumption that words - in some definition of that term - and sentences are the elements or units of versification. Because of this, the syntactical approach is closely related to the word count approach. In a sense, then, De Rossi, Schoettgen, Lowth, Peters, Ley, Gray, Robinson, Gordis, Segert, Kosmala and Holladay can all be regarded as precursors of the syntactical approach. This applies also to Wahl from whose description of his method (1976, 20-21) has already been quoted in 1.5 and 2.3.

LaSor's (1979) attempt to deduce the colometry of Hebrew verse from the Massoretic accent signs cannot in itself be regarded as an example of the syntactical approach. However, the measure of success obtained by his method is due to the fact that the Massoretic accent signs were placed at prominent syntactic boundaries, as he himself acknowledged (1979, 328). Thus, indirectly, his system is based on the syntax of the Hebrew verse, albeit the syntax as understood by the Massoretes long after the origin of the text, and as indicated by their accent signs, which were not intended to indicate verse structure as such.

3.3.2   Kurylowicz (1972; 1975)

The versification system which Kurylowicz devised for Hebrew verse is the first of the recent theories in which syntax is a constitutive factor. Longman (1982, 231 n.5) labelled Kurylowicz's method "syntactical-accentual", because he felt that it accurately described "the main points of the method."

Kurylowicz did distinguish between rhythm and metre, but he did not regard metre as abstract. According to his theory metre was indicated in the text by the Massoretic distinction between *accentus domini* and *accentus servi*. He regarded the non-spirantisation of word-initial stops (*begadkefat* letters) following an open syllable as an additional indication that the word ending on the open syllable is the last of a metrical group (accented word-complex), carrying one metrically relevant stress. The *accentus servi* indicated, according to Kurylowicz, accents which do occur in the speech rhythm but which were suppressed in the metre (1972, 167, 175). As to the reliability of these two criteria he stated (1972, 167-168):

> ... the tradition concerning the distribution of *primary* and *secondary* accents and external sandhi (lenition of *initial* occlusives) may be considered a reliable data as long as no internal contradictions are shown up.

Kurylowicz initially limited his research to the Psalter, following Segert's (1969) conjecture that between 1000 and 600 B.C. Hebrew verse had an "akzentuierende Metrik", and observing "that the bulk of the Psalms may be safely attributed" to that period (1972, 176 n.2). Nevertheless he seemed to conclude that most or all of Old Testament verse functioned according to his system (1972, 176-177; 1975, 219-220, 223-224). Admittedly the Massoretes used a different set of accent signs for Psalms, Job and Proverbs than for the other books, but the division of the signs in *domini* and *servi* holds true.

An important aspect of Kurylowicz's system is his discounting of *parallelismus membrorum* as an indicator of colon length. He wrote (1972, 176): "Parallelism of members etc. are adornments proper to poetic style, but must be left out of consideration in the analysis of metre." He replaced the concept of parallelism with a rigid principle, namely the bipartite structure of each verse, saying (1975, 223): "Die einzige relevante metrische Konstante ist die Zweiteiligkeit des ganzen Verses." This of course excluded the possibility of both monocola and tricola, and resulted in his finding what has often been called a "mixed metre", as can be seen from his treatment of Psalm 43 (1975, 220), which he scanned as 3 + 1, 3 + 2, 2 + 2, 4 + 2, 3 + 4. Indeed, he seemed impressed by the structural independence of each verse from its neighbours, and did not attempt to explain how such a "mixed metre" was possible.

The system which Kurylowicz devised for the metrical analysis of Hebrew verse is important to the present study for the following reasons:

1. Kurylowicz claimed that Hebrew metre had a syntactic base. Firstly, he wrote (1975, 224):

> Wenn wir also den heb. Vers metrisch definieren wollen, müssen wir nicht von Takten, wie etwa fürs Germanische, sondern von Sätzen ausgehen. Die ideale Grundform des heb. Verses, wie er in den Psalmen erscheint, besteht aus zwei Halbversen, deren jeder ein Satz (Nominal- oder Verbalsatz) enthält. Als equivalente Formen sind anzusehen: a) Halbverse, in denen zwei Sätze durch 'metrische Kontraktion' zusammengezogen sind; b) anderseits Halbverse, die bloss syntaktische Gruppen enthalten, indem sie sich an das verbale Prädikat des vorausgehenden (Halb)verses anlehnen.

Secondly, Kurylowicz (1975, 216-219) claimed that the occurrence or non-occurrence of spirantisation and the metrical suppression of specific stresses originally were *syntactically determined*, though these processes were later generalised in verse to include also cases of neighbouring words which do not belong together syntactically.

2.   Kurylowicz's system served as point of departure for the metrical part of Cooper's (1976) study of Hebrew verse, in which syntax plays a fairly prominent role. A proper evaluation of Cooper's method is possible only against the background of Kurylowicz's.

In conclusion the reasons why Kurylowicz's system cannot be accepted as correct, can be briefly summarised as follows:

(1)   He failed to recognise the abstract nature of metre.
(2)   He gave no explanation as to the functioning of the very irregular "mixed metre" which he found.
(3)   He relied too heavily on signs added to the Hebrew text much later than its origin.
(4)   He refused to take *parallelismus membrorum* into account as an indicator (amongst others) of colon length.
(5)   His insistence that all verses must be bipartite is at variance with the facts.

3.3.3   Cooper (1976)

Cooper's theory (1976, 32-35) of what he called "meter" was taken over from Kurylowicz (1972, 1975) and was an effort to regularise cola to fewer accents, mostly two, using the non-spirantisation of initial stops (*begadkefat* letters) as a guide. Thus, in spite of the fact that Cooper (1976, 34) approvingly quoted Hrushovski (1960, 178-179) on the distinction between rhythm and metre and on the abstractness of the latter, he was expecting to find and trying to create a rhythmical regularity *in* Hebrew verse, which he then called "meter".

The role of syntax in this theory was simply that certain syntactical combinations, for instance "Subject + Verb and Verb + Subject; Verb + Direct Object and Direct Object + Verb" (1976, 33), could when necessary take one accent instead of the usual two.

It might seem impossible to prove Cooper wrong, simply because his approach, which can hardly be regarded as a system, was flexible in the extreme. Once one examines his approach closely, however, its weaknesses can be identified:

1. Cooper took over the principle of the reduction of stresses from Kurylowicz, who studied parts of the Psalter as being from the period between 1000 and 600 B.C., when an accentuating metre probably was in use. Cooper not only ignored the chronological limits - which Kurylowicz himself apparently relinquished, cf. the discussion above - but also, without explaining how this was possible, moved beyond the limits of the three books which the Massoretes treated as poetic when they added the two systems of accent signs.

2. Kurylowicz relied on the presence or absence of the *dagesh lene* and on the Massoretic accent signs. Cooper (1976, 49 n.59) significantly stated: ". . . I do not rely on MT as heavily as does Kurylowicz for the isolation of metrical units." This meant that Cooper could ignore either the *dagesh* or the distinction between the two broad categories of accent signs or both at will. Amongst the 20 examples which Cooper discussed (1976, 103-108) to illustrate and test his method, his treatment was in disagreement with the presence or absence of the *dagesh* in at least the following three cases:

No.4	Is 1:10	תורת
No.9	Ps 84:9	תפלתי
No.15	Ps 17:1	תפלתי

As to the accent signs, his treatment was in disagreement with the distinction between *domini* and *servi* as follows:

No.4	Is 1:10	האזינו
No.6	Ps 39:13	ושועתי
No.9	Ps 84:9	צבאות
No.15	Ps 17:1	הקשיבה
No.16	Ps 143:1	באמנתך
No.17	Ps 5:3	אליך and הקשיבה
No.19	Is 32:9	שאננות

To this can be added that:

(a)   in No.16 (Ps 143:1) Cooper's regarding V + O as carrying
      only one (metrically relevant) accent would not at all be as
      arbitrary as he thought (1976, 143 n.21), since that is
      exactly what the Massoretic accent signs would indicate if
      interpreted in terms of Kurylowicz's system.
(b)   for No.18 (Num 23:18) Cooper offered no solution,
      whereas according to Kurylowicz's system the Massoretic
      accent signs would indicate 2 + 2.
(c)   in No.20 (Is 28:23) Cooper's second "possible division",
      i.e. his second accent allotment, is precluded in terms of
      Kurylowicz's interpretation of the Massoretic accent signs.

Even if those of the above examples not taken from the Psalter
are excluded, on the grounds that the Massoretes did not read
them as verse, the examples from the Psalter clearly prove that
Cooper did not take into account Kurylowicz's use of the
Massoretic division of the accent signs into *domini* and *servi*.
This, in conjunction with his ignoring of Massoretic indications
of spirantisation, resulted in practice in a complete break with
Kurylowicz's system and a gratuitous application of Kurylowicz's
principles. When one compares Kurylowicz's counts of metrically relevant accents with that of Cooper, the vast difference
between them becomes apparent (cf. Kurylowicz, 1975, 220 on
Psalm 43 and Cooper, 1976, 103-108).

3.   Probably the most fundamental criticism one can raise against
      Cooper's approach is the complete lack of a principle for the
      delimitation of cola. Whereas Kurylowicz claimed that every
      verse must be bipartite, Cooper accepted that there were
      monocola and tricola in Hebrew verse (1976, 7-9). This is
      correct but not compatible with Kurylowicz's system.
         It might seem that Cooper regarded parallelism as the
      decisive factor for colon delimitation, for he stated (1976, 77):
      "Parallelism is the one *universally acknowledged prosodic feature*
      of the Hebrew poetic line . . ." (emphasis added), seemingly
      unaware that he was thereby reversing a fundamental principle

in Kurylowicz's system, and that this radically affected his own application of that system.

That parallelism was not the principle of colon delimitation in Cooper's approach, indeed the complete lack of such a principle, is best illustrated by his arbitrary redivision of some of his examples (1976, 103-108), for example:

No.6	Ps 39:13	2 + 1	redivided as	3 (= 1 + 1 + 1)
No.9	Ps 84:9	2 + 1	redivided as	3 (= 1 + 1 + 1)
No.17	Ps 5:2-4	2 + 1, 2 + 1, 3 + 3	redivided as	
		3 + 3 + 3 + 3		

Although the emphasis Cooper placed upon syntax is to be welcomed, one has to conclude that his approach to the problems of metre and colon delimitation was so arbitrary as to be completely unacceptable. This conclusion is essentially the same as that reached by Longman (1982, 252-253) and Garr (1983, 57-58 n.25), both of whom paid less attention to the detail of the differences between Kurylowicz and Cooper than has been done above.

3.3.4   Collins (1978)

In his Manchester dissertation of 1974 Collins proposed that a valid description of the Hebrew poet's art could be given in terms of the syntax and word order of the verse-line (by which he usually meant the bicolon or tricolon), rather than in terms of either parallelism - usually tending to be semantic parallelism - or metre (1978a, 5-10), the latter being understood in its usual, i.e. phonological sense.

Making use of a simplified form of Transformational Generative Grammar, he distinguished only four types of constituents, namely:

NP1 = subject
NP2 = direct object
V = verb
M = modifier

He theorised that there were four possible *general line-types*, which could be differentiated into a large number of *specific line-types*, which in turn could be divided into *individual line-forms* according to the order of the constituents in the verse-line (1978a, 22-24). "These Line-Forms are still abstract notions, in the sense that they refer to theoretically possible arrangements of a given set of constituents, and they may not in fact occur" (1978b, 235).

With the aid of this classification system Collins analysed the poetic portions of the prophetic books. He explicitly drew attention to the fact that he was interested primarily in the stylistic study of the prophets (1978a, 22), i.e. he was not studying syntax for its own sake. This aim severely limited the attention that he could pay to the finer points of syntax, *inter alia* restricting his description of the verse-line to the level of *constituents*.

Of the various criticisms that have been raised against the work of Collins the following concern the *method* that he applied, but are not directly concerned with the system which he devised to describe verse-lines:

1. He left out of consideration units of syntax (and meaning) larger than the bi- or tricolon (Smend, 1981, 192; Van Rensburg, 1983, 82, 85).
2. He did not take into account previous research as to either exegesis or Hebrew syntax (Watson, 1980, 582; Smend, 1981, 193).
3. He ignored known poetic techniques (Watson, 1980, 582).
4. His treatment of the passive was superficial (Watson, 1980, 582).
5. He was inconsistent in his treatment of apposition (Watson, 1980, 582).
6. To be of value his results have to be compared with results obtained by similar methods from non-poetic texts and non-prophetic poetic texts (Watson, 1980, 582).
7. He ignored the *maqqeph* (Sawyer, 1981, 124).
8. He included some prose in his corpus, according to one reviewer (O'Connor, 1980b, 92).
9. He did not supply a list or statistics of either the verse-lines containing nominal sentences or the verse-lines which he had to leave out of consideration due to textual uncertainties (Van Rensburg, 1983, 84-85).

The criticisms regarding Collins' *system* of verse-line description are as follows:

1. He oversimplified the relation between verse-line and sentence (Smend, 1981, 192).
2. His syntactical categories are not specific enough (Richter, 1980, 222 n.852; March, 1980, 301; O'Connor, 1980b, 92; Smend, 1981, 193; Talstra, 1984, 454-455). This criticism relates both to sentence types and constituent types. A suggested more complete system of line description would distinguish higher and lower constituents, as well as simple and complex constituents, would indicate the grammatical content of constituents, and would also distinguish lines with gapped constituents, i.e. elliptical lines in which a constituent is implied (Van Rensburg, 1983, 81, 82-83, 86).
3. He did not discuss the status of particles (O'Connor, 1980b, 92; Sawyer, 1981, 124; Talstra, 1984, 455).
4. Some of his line-types were incorrectly differentiated or overlap and it would be useful to distinguish more line-types in order to accommodate some of those which he regarded as variations on his line-types (Van Rensburg, 1983, 84-85; Talstra, 1984, 454).
5. His line delimitation was unsatisfactory (Watson, 1980, 583), *inter alia* because of his "insistence on the bi- and tricolonic character of Hebrew verse and the resultant recognition of one word cola . . ." (O'Connor, 1980b, 92).

A brief discussion of the latter group of five criticisms is necessary here. The criticisms relate also to syntax as such, but in this context they are discussed only in so far as they affect, or are likely to affect, line delimitation and the development of a valid and adequate description of the line in syntactical terms. In order to refer accurately to the cola of Hebrew verse involved use will here already be made of the letters applied below in **4.2.1**; cf. also **4.1** for an explanation of the letter system.

As to the relation between *verse-line and sentence* (criticism 1 above) it will be seen that Collins' description (1978a, 34) of the verse-lines as "self-contained entities" is unspecific and misleading. Not all bicola have the same syntactic status. Many bicola are indeed

complete sentences, which fact Collins took as his point of departure,
adding that some verse-lines consist of two sentences (1878a, 36).
Later he noted that verbs may be doubled or even tripled in the
halves of the verse-line and that some verse-lines consist of three
basic sentences (1978a, 220-224).

However, there are bicola which are not sentences, but clauses, e.g.

    Jer 2:2cd   an infinitival object clause
    Jer 2:6cd   a participial relative clause
    Jer 2:27ab a participial relative clause

There are also bicola which are neither sentences nor clauses, but
phrases, e.g.

    Jer 2:6ef   prepositional phrases
    Jer 2:26cd nominal phrases in apposition to the subject in a
                preceding colon
    Jer 4:26cd prepositional phrases

Smend (1981, 192) pointed out a bicolon in Mic 4:8ab consisting of
vocatives, which was incorrectly treated by Collins (1978a, 216) as a
nominal sentence. We have not found an equivalent bicolon in
Jeremiah, where similar double vocatives, e.g. Jer 4:4c, being shorter,
were regarded as a single colon.

On the other extreme again there are complete sentences embedded either in a bicolon forming the second colon, e.g. Jer 2:27ef, or in
a single colon, e.g. Jer 2:27ab (two examples).

Thus the relation between verse-line and sentence is much more
complicated than Collins would lead us to believe. This is a matter
which should receive more attention in further study, firstly for the
description and delimitation of the colon itself, and secondly for the
description of the relationships between cola.

We can heartily agree to the criticism that Collins' *syntactical
categories*, both as to sentence types and constituent types, are not
specific enough (criticism 2). This is at least partly due to the fact that
his system describes the verse-line at only one syntactical level. As to
sentence types he made no distinctions at all. The distinguishing of
sentences as statements or questions is hardly likely to affect line

delimitation, but differentiation between independent clauses and dependent clauses might well do so, and is very likely to play a role in the combination of cola. The four constituent types which Collins distinguished will now be examined in turn.

The *constituent NP1* in Collins' system is not specific enough as to its syntactical status because it includes not only subjects, but also vocatives, e.g. Jer 3:12a and Jer 3:22a (1978a, 178), which have a different syntactic status (O'Connor, 1980b, 92; cf. also O'Connor, 1980a, 79-80 and Richter, 1980, 158-159) and which might, therefore, play a different role in the syntactical regulation of lines of verse. Furthermore, some of the subjects treated by Collins as NP1 are in fact participles which function on two syntactical levels at the same time, being subjects on the higher of the two levels, but predicates of an embedded clause on the lower. For example: In the case of the participles in Jer 2:3c and 2:24d, treated as NP1 by Collins (1978a, 178), these two levels must be distinguished, as indicated by the presence of the direct object, in both these cases a suffix to the participle. (Cf. the discussion of Collins' constituent V below.)

The constituent NP1 is also very unspecific as to its length, referring without differentiation to

> one word, e.g. in Jer 3:19ab, 5:9bc (1978a, 73, 64)
> two words, e.g. in Jer 6:1ab, 6:3a (1978a, 62, 63)
> three words, e.g. in Jer 4:8c, 6:21de (1978a, 62, 58)
> four words, e.g. in Jer 2:34ab, 5:11ab (1978a, 63).

In Collins' system the *constituent NP2* is even more unspecific as to length and syntactical status than NP1, seeing that it refers without differentiation to

> a noun, e.g. in Jer 2:11cd (1978a, 78)
> a demonstrative, e.g. in Jer 4:18ab (1978a, 78)
> the *nota accusativi* with suffix, e.g. in Jer 2:6cd (1978a, 153)
> a two word phrase, e.g. in Jer 3:19cd, 6:14ab (1978a, 155, 83)
> a nominal sentence, e.g. in Jer 2:27ab (1978a, 154)
> verbal sentences of various lengths and a variety of constituents,
>   e.g. in Jer 2:27ab (1978a, 154), Jer 2:35ab (1978a, 149) (two
>   quite dissimilar examples), Jer 2:27ef (1978a, 86).

When Collins treated direct speech as the object of verbs meaning "say" or "speak", i.e. as NP2, in this way, the category became quite meaningless for the determination of line length. So for instance in Jer 3:19ab the second colon cannot on its own be called an NP2, as Collins would have it (1978a, 73), seeing that that NP2 actually extends from 19b right through to the end of verse 20, a total of seven or eight cola.

The *constituent V* in Collins' system is not specific enough as to either length or syntactical status. As to length Collins' line description does change in cases of doubled V, which he regarded as a "standard technique of variation", indeed as the "commonest technique for varying the lines" (1978a, 219-223). However, his line description did not change when an infinitive absolute was added to the verb, although he did regard this as an expansion of the V (1978a, 58). Examples are in Jer 51:56ef and 51:58bc, to which he added Jer 6:13ab, apparently having misread the cognate object for an infinitive absolute (1978a, 58). Another example which he treated is in Jer 6:29ab (1978a, 183). The example in Jer 3:1e he apparently missed. Such expansion of the verb affects line length on a syntactical level and must, therefore, be taken into account in a syntactical description of the line.

More important, however, is Collins' failure to distinguish finite verbs, i.e. perfects, imperfects and imperatives, from participles and infinitives as to their syntactical status. The latter two groups both have a nominal-verbal dual nature, with the result that they can function as verbs in an embedded clause, whilst at the same time functioning as substantives in a higher clause. So for instance Collins (1978a, 153) treated the participle in Jer 2:6cd as a V, whereas on a higher level it, as well as the participle in 2:6b, functions as a noun in apposition to the noun יהוה in 2:6a. The participle in Jer 2:27ab is a similar case, treated by Collins (1978a, 154) as a verb. By contrast the participles in Jer 2:3cd and 2:24de are treated as NP1 (1978a, 178), in spite of their having object suffixes, which clearly indicate their verbal nature on a lower syntactical level (as was pointed out above in discussing Collins' constituent NP1). The infinitive construct in Jer 2:2cd Collins (1978a, 140) treated as a V, which is correct, but on a higher syntactical level that infinitive is an object of the verb זכרתי in

2:2a. Similarly Collins treated the infinitive construct in Jer 4:7de as a V (1978a, 185), whereas on a higher level it can be regarded as a prepositional phrase, i.e. as an M, to the verb יצא in 4:7c. These are the only cases of the infinitive construct from Jeremiah chapters 2 - 6 which Collins gave account of, and both are located at the beginning of the verse-line as he delimited it. In Jeremiah chapters 2 - 6 a further 20 cases of the inf. cs. occur, viz. in 2:7b, 2:13d, 2:17b, 2:18b, 2:18d, 2:19d, 2:33b, 2:35d, 2:36b, 3:3d, 4:10d, 4:11e (two cases), 4:22ef (two cases), 5:3c, 5:3e, 6:10d, 6:11b, 6:14b. It remains uncertain whether Collins' line description of Jer 6:14b (1978a, 83) included the infinitive construct as part of the line, and thus of the M, though such inclusion seems unlikely. From these facts it seems as if Collins was aware that the status of the infinitive construct was problematical in terms of his constituents and that he therefore often avoided examples of it.

The *constituent M* in Collins' system also is unspecific as to both length and syntactical status. As to syntactical status alone, Collins did not distinguish between prepositional phrases which are indeed modifiers and those which are direct objects. A clear case is to be found in Jer 2:37cd (1978a, 134) to which Collins added a note (1978a, 292) in which he wrote: "Perhaps במבטחיך should be construed as NP2, in spite of the preposition in the surface structure. This would give line-form IV D/B:ii)1." Uncertainty of this sort, regarding a well-known grammatical phenomenon and influencing as it does the allocation of a verse-line to a specific line-form, is completely unacceptable. Other examples of prepositional phrases which are direct objects Collins also treated as M, namely in Jer 6:30ab (1978a, 186), Jer 8:9cd (1978a, 217) and Jer 13:25cd (1978a, 173). From the apparent absence of examples of שמע ב from the book of Jeremiah in Collins' book it would seem that he tried to avoid these problematic cases.

As to length it should be pointed out that, whereas Collins treated the doubling of verbs as a "standard technique of variation" for which provision was later made in line description (1978a, 219-223), his constituent M can *inter alia* be either one or two prepositional phrases, as is clear from his treatment of Jer 3:2ef and 4:2ab (1978a, 83, 153). Apparently the only reason for not treating such successive prepositional phrases as more than one M lay in the fact that Collins

did not posit a caesura between them, i.e. when two successive prepositional phrases occur in the same colon they were regarded as one
M. Given the uncertainty as to the length of cola, this implies that
their delimitation depended on semantics alone, the constituent M
having lost any reference to length and therefore being of no use for
the delimitation of either verse-lines (i.e. bi- or tricola) or cola. To
Collins such "doubled prepositional phrases in the M" was merely an
"interesting feature", the import of which for line description he did
not realise in spite of the fair number of occurrences which he noted
(1978a, 140), including Jer 2:2cd, 6:11cd and 17:10cd.

That the constituent M as used by Collins is unspecific as to both
length and syntactical status will further be clear from his application
of it without differentiation to:

noun + adjective, e.g. Jer 3:1fg (1978a, 131), and
preposition + noun + noun + noun, e.g. Jer 2:6cd (1978a, 153).

Additional illustration is provided by Jer 2:6fg, which Collins did not
treat but to which his treatment could be applied and where M would
then be a prepositional phrase containing two embedded clauses.

It must be concluded that all four of Collins' constituents, which
are the syntactical categories in terms of which he described the
verse-line, are not specific enough for such description, if used in the
way he did.

It is understandable that in a ground-breaking study like that of
Collins the difficult question of the *status of particles* (criticism 3) was
left out of consideration. At the same time it has to be granted that
for a syntactical description of the Hebrew verse-line to be valid and
adequate, the status of particles will have to be determined. There are
two aspects of the relation of the particle to lines of verse which have
to be distinguished here, namely:

1.   The contribution which the presence or absence of a particle
     can make to our delimitation of the lines (cola). This is due to
     the fact that some particles appear mostly in the clause initial
     position and therefore often appear as the first word of a colon.

2.   The contribution of particles to line length, i.e. the syntactical
      status of particles in a line description formulated in syntactical
      terms.

To the first of these aspects Collins gave no explicit attention,
although it may subconsciously have played a role in his line
delimitations. The second aspect he did not ignore, as he clearly
stated that "a line may have an introductory particle . . . which does
not affect its structure and hence does not change its classification"
(1978a, 28; cf. also 49 n.54). Collins did apply this policy to the short
particles, e.g.

ה   in Jer 2:32a (1978a, 144)
גם   in Jer 2:34a (1978a, 63)
כי   in Jer 2:37c (1978a, 134)
אך   in Jer 3:13a (1978a, 173)

and to some longer particles, e.g.

לכן   in Jer 2:9a (1978a, 108)
מדוע   in Jer 2:31c (1978a, 145)
למען   in Jer 4:14b (1978a, 182)

as well as to some combinations of particles, e.g.

כי לא   in Jer 5:4c (1978a, 234)
כי־גם   in Jer 23:11a (1978a, 178)
על־כן   in Jer 5:6a (1978a, 113)
עתה גם   in Jer 4:12b (1978a, 78).

There are some particles and combinations of particles, however,
which Collins treated as modifiers, taking them into account at the
constituent level on which he described the verse-line, e.g.

איך   in Jer 2:23a (1978a, 156)
למה   in Jer 2:29a (1978a, 239)
כי־כה   in Jer 4:3 (1978a, 68)

עַד־מָתִי in Jer 4:14c (1978a, 69)
לָכֵן כֹּה in Jer 23:15 (1978a, 68).

Collins gave no indication of what his criterion for this differentiation
was and one can only guess that it was of a semantic nature. Be that
as it may, we can see no reason for treating מַדּוּעַ and לָמָּה in two
different ways. That Collins was uncertain how to treat these particles
is clear from his note to מַדּוּעַ in Jer 2:31c asking: "introductory
anacrusis?" (1978a, 291), which indicates that he thought it possible
to assign constituent status to מַדּוּעַ. Had he done so, the line would
have had to be assigned to another line-type, unless the word מַדּוּעַ
was regarded as extrinsic to the line. Even more unacceptable is the
fact that he treated אֵיךְ as a constituent in Jer 2:23a, but וְאֵיךְ in Jer
12:5cd was not given the same status (1978a, 156, 136; cf. also 293).
    The combinations of particles וְעַתָּה מַה in Jer 2:18a and כִּי אִם
in Jer 2:22a were not treated by Collins and it would be very
interesting to know how he would treat them.
    From this discussion it has become clear that for a description of
the line of verse in syntactical terms to be adequate the role of the
particles must be established precisely. It must be concluded,
therefore, that Collins' treatment of the particles is unsatisfactory.
    Collins' *line-types* were indeed *incorrectly differentiated* (criticism
4). Without going into too much detail here, the following factors can
be pointed out which invalidate his differentiation of line-types:

1.   Line-type II is a subtype of Line-type IV, characterised by
      syntactic identity between the two basic sentences (Van
      Rensburg, 1983, 84), and should be treated under line-type IV.
2.   Line-type III in its turn is a subtype of line-type II, differentiated
      from it by Collins so as to reflect the phenomenon of
      incomplete parallelism. This differentiation was based on the
      number of constituents in the second colon being one less than
      in the first, and a semantic criterion, namely that the corre-
      sponding constituents be in apposition (Van Rensburg, 1983, 83-
      84). It would, therefore, be correct to treat examples of Collins'
      line-type III under line-type IV, or alternatively as variations of
      line-type I.

In order to obtain more accuracy of line description more line-types and sub-types should be distinguished so as to provide adequate descriptions of those lines only briefly illustrated by Collins under the heading "Extension of the System", referring to nominal sentences, the verb היה, and standard techniques of variation (1978a, 215-226), but also to accommodate other expansions (1978a, 58) and variations (1978a, 67).

Collins' line-types were stated in terms of categories which were shown above to be unspecific. When these syntactic categories (constituents) are combined in the form of line-types, the vagueness is multiplied.

Collins' line-types do not reflect the effect of the presence or absence of particles on line length, which was shown above to be essential to an adequate line description in syntactical terms.

Collins' *line delimitation* indeed was *unsatisfactory* (criticism 5), in the first place because he did not attempt to describe how he arrived at such line delimitation. This applies equally to his determination of the ends of bi- and tricola and to his placement of line-breaks within them. Apparently he made use of a system of counting main stresses (cf. 1978a, 56-57), "allowing one heavy stress for each main constituent ... although variations are possible if one constituent is exceptionally lengthened" (1978a, 252). To what extent such lengthening can take place without more than one stress becoming obligatory, he never stated. Moreover, a counting of main stresses is in itself insufficient for the delimitation of lines, it being widely accepted that the number of main stresses per colon is not constant. Collins was led by syntactic boundaries of varying status, and his reference to a "lesser syntactic pause" is revealing and very important, but he related this to "interpretation and performance" (1978a, 56-57), which cannot be used to determine the prosodical structure of verse; cf. 1.4.

O'Connor's criticism of Collins concerning his "insistence on the bi- and tricolonic character of Hebrew verse and the resultant recognition of one word cola ..." (1980b, 92) is an overstatement in view of Collins' wavering attitude on the role of lesser syntactic pauses just mentioned. Collins did in fact state that he accepted the existence of the *Kurzvers*, but he refrained from investigating it, only stating his impression: "In general, they come under Line-Type I, but further

investigation is needed to determine how frequent they are and in
what environments they occur" (1978a, 279 n.23). There is, however,
some truth in O'Connor's criticism, namely in so far as Collins took
the bicolon as the point of departure for his study, even as to line-type
I (1978a, 56), but here again it is vagueness and uncertainty rather
than insistence which characterise Collins' statements and detract
from their value.

When one speaks of the delimitation of the verse-line there are
three separate aspects involved, namely the beginning of the verse-
line, the breaks or caesurae in the verse-line, and the end of the
verse-line. What has thus far been said about Collins' line delimitation concerned the latter two aspects. Each of the three aspects will
now be taken in turn, and illustrative examples examined to show the
deficiency of Collins' handling of them:

(a) The *beginning* of the verse-line is problematic in cases where
     anacrusis is suspected. When that is the case the word (or
     words) concerned may be treated in one of two ways. Firstly, it
     may be kept as part of the line in spite of its being regarded as
     not conforming strictly to the versification system, or secondly, it
     may be regarded as being extrinsic to the line, in which case it
     would in printed form be placed on a line of its own. Collins'
     treatment of מרוע in Jer 2:31c and his note to it (1978a, 145,
     291) prove his uncertainty on this matter.

(b) As to the breaks or caesurae in the verse-line - assuming that
     one takes the bi- and tricolon as the basis of Hebrew verse as
     Collins did - there is much uncertainty. Collins placed a break
     in Jer 2:13a, separating the direct object from the verb and the
     subject (1978a, 74). Having treated Jer 2:27cd as a bicolon as in
     BHS, Collins mentioned the possibility, without argumentation
     either way, that it might instead be divided before ערף (1978a,
     155, 291). Indeed, in Collins' approach there would be no
     objection to treating both Jer 2:13a and 2:27cd as single cola,
     excepting of course the accustomed preference for bipartite
     verse-lines.

(c) What determines the *end* of a verse-line for Collins remains
     unclear. In some cases it is the end of a sentence, but not
     always. From his mentioning Jer 6:14ab as an example of line-

form IID: ii)1 (1978a, 83) it is not known whether he included the word לאמר in this bicolon or excluded it, his constituent M often containing more than one prepositional phrase. Even if he had written the example in full it would still be unknown on what grounds he had included or excluded the word.

It must be concluded that Collins did not really attempt a motivated colon delimitation. This is due to the following two closely related assumptions on which he based his approach:

1. He assumed that the bicolon is the basis of Hebrew verse, and that, therefore, the tricolon and the monocolon are derived from it. This approach gives too little attention to the colon boundary (pause or line-break), as was seen.
2. He assumed that he knew exactly what the term "self-contained entities" meant when applied to verse-lines. This assumption led him to an oversimplification of the relationship between verse-line and sentence.

This conclusion implies that it will be necessary to reconsider whether the single colon might be a more reliable basis for the description of Hebrew verse in terms of syntactical categories, and also to take into account syntactic structures larger than the bi- or tricolon.

One further matter should be briefly discussed here, namely the relationship between the syntactical description of the verse-line and metre. On the one hand Collins was reticent to take a firm stand on the matter, saying: "There is nothing to be gained from futile hen and egg arguments as to which comes first." However, he realised the possibility that

> the line-types and line-forms can be looked on as a system of measurement, determining what is a well formed verse-line and thus performing the same function as the more familiar systems of metre (1978a, 251).

Indeed, in a later formulation on the same topic he seemed to have made his choice:

> In the poetry of the prophets, syntax and constituent order take on the role of a formal principle of measurement. They are

'metrical' in the sense that they determine what constitutes a well
formed line according to a limited number of basic patterns and
variations. Rhythmic stress patterns and the number or length of
syllables are significant, but they are dependent on and
controlled by the syntactic pattern which is the fundamental
framework (1978b, 244).

It is clear that the relationship between the syntactical patterns and
metre needs further investigation.

3.3.5   O'Connor (1980)

In his approach O'Connor was able, to some extent, to build on
previous work that took the *word* as the regulated element in Hebrew
versification. Research in metrics from outside the field of Semitics,
however, contributed largely to O'Connor's approach. He acknowledged his indebtedness to Austerlitz, who had studied Ob-Ugric
poetry in this way. Austerlitz was following the example of Lotz, who
supervised his research, and of Jakobson (Austerlitz, 1958, 127). One
might note in passing that this earlier work of Jakobson and Lotz
belonged to the second of three important stages in East European
general metric research during this century (Gasparov, 1980, 17-18).
In a sense, then, the method applied by Austerlitz and O'Connor is
outdated, which of course does not mean that it is useless. It should
be kept in mind that at the least O'Connor had more advanced
linguistic knowledge at his disposal than previous researchers had,
and that similar research is still being done elsewhere.

The influence of syntax on the stress pattern of the verse line in
English was fairly recently examined by Kiparsky (1975), and the role
of syntax in general metrical theory was described by Lotz (1972) and
Lotman (1980). To certain varying extents the views of *inter alia*
Kosmala, Kurylowicz, Cooper and Collins on Hebrew verse and that
of Margalit on Ugaritic verse also took syntax into account; cf. 2.3,
3.3.2, 3.3.3, 3.3.4.

3.3.5.1   O'Connor's approach

O'Connor took as point of departure the concept of *metre* and, being
convinced that Hebrew verse had no metre in the usual phonological
sense of the term (1980a, 65, 138), he pointed out that even in some
such phonological metres there are regulated elements of a

syntactical nature (1980a, 60-64). He then proceeded to develop a versification system for Hebrew verse, keeping in mind that metre in verse comprises regulation of more than just the phonological elements. In O'Connor's new versification system the regulation of syntactical elements plays the main role, the regulation of phonological elements being regarded as concomitant (1980a, 148-149). For this reason he decided not to call his versification system a metre, fearing that such an extension of the use of the term would cause confusion (1980a, 67). The whole system he called a *constriction* and to its components he referred as *constraints*.

In spite of this new nomenclature O'Connor was well aware that what he had actually done was to extend the concept of metre in a perfectly acceptable way for he wrote (1980a, 67): "The system we describe will be of the same sort as a meter . . ." and he then referred to Lotz's definition of metre, namely (Lotz, 1972, 2): ". . . the numerical regulation of certain properties of the linguistic form" of verse, which definition would allow the application of the term metre to versification systems in which the numerically regulated elements are syntactic, as duly pointed out by O'Connor himself (1980a, 67). This would also be the case in terms of Hartman's definition: "A meter is a prosody whose mode of organization is numerical" (Hartman, 1980, 17, cf. 14). Thus there is in principle no reason not to call O'Connor's constrictional system a metre, and indeed it functions as a metrical system.

As a convenient summary of the system which O'Connor found in the Hebrew colon his "restatement of the constriction" (1980a, 86-87) can be quoted, keeping in mind that he used the term *line* where we use *colon*:

> *Definitions.* A clause predicator is a finite verb; an infinitive which is not used absolutely or which governs only an agent; a participle which is not used absolutely or which governs only an agent, object or possessor; or a 0 predicator of a verbless clause (the major predicators); or a vocative or a focus-marker (the minor predicators). A constituent is a verb, or an argument of a predicator which appears on the surface, unless it includes a prepositional phrase, in which case it is split. A unit is a verb or an individual nomen.
>
> *Constraints.* 1. *On clause predicators.* No line contains more than three. 2. *On constituents.* No line contains fewer than one or

more than four. 3. *On units*. No line contains fewer than two or
more than five. 4. *On the units of constituents*. No constituent
contains more than four units. Constituents of four units occur
only in lines with no clause predicator. Constituents of three
units occur either alone in lines with no clause predicator; or as
one of two constituents in 1-clause lines. 5. *On the constituents of
clauses*. No line of three clause predicators contains any
dependent nominal phrases. In lines with two clause predicators,
only one had dependent nominal phrases. 6. *On the integrity of
lines*. If a line contains one or more clause predicators, it contains
only nominal phrases dependent on them.

The dominant line form. Most lines of Hebrew verse contain
one clause and either two or three constituents of two or three
units. A lineation which yields lines of these constellations is
preferred to other lineations.

From this long quotation its should immediately be noted that the
definitions concern three *levels* of syntax on which according to
O'Connor three separate line level, i.e. colon level, constraints
operate, namely constraints numbers 1, 2 and 3. The same information O'Connor (1980a, 75, 138) also presented in the form of a
matrix, which form makes the levels more visible, as follows:

clause predicators	0	1	2	3
constituents	1	2	3	4
units	2	3	4	5

For the present study the work of O'Connor is of special interest,
seeing that he substituted a system of syntactical constraints for metre
(1980a, 146-150). Moreover, if his findings have any validity - and
surely they must have some, even if they have to be adapted and
refined in some ways - then these rules are basic not only to the
delimitation of cola of Hebrew verse, but also to the syntactic structure of the cola and to the syntactic relations between the cola.

Therefore, although a detailed evaluation of O'Connor's method,
system and results can only emerge from a study such as that to be
undertaken in a following chapter, it is well to take into account
beforehand some points of criticism which others have already raised,
and which will help us in our preliminary evaluation.

The criticisms raised against O'Connor's study fall into three groups, namely:

(1) criticisms regarding his method but not affecting his system for the delimitation and description of cola,
(2) criticisms regarding his choice of the single line or colon as basic unit, and
(3) criticisms regarding his system for the delimitation and description of cola.

We will treat these three groups in the order as just listed. It will not be necessary in this context to discuss the first group, as our prime concern here is with the delimitation and description of cola.

The following criticisms do not directly affect O'Connor's system of colon description, but relate to his *method*:

1. O'Connor not only used obscure terms (Watson, 1983, 131), but he also applied certain terms to areas of study to which they do not belong (Good, 1982, 112). This leads to misunderstanding and terminological confusion, and in doing so adds to the difficulty of his book for the reader, which probably contributed to the fact that a number of reviewers (Eaton, 1980/81; Fensham, 1981; Berlin, 1982; Denis, 1982; Hagstrom, 1982; Schmitt, 1982; Galbraith, 1983; Greenstein, 1983) refrained from entering into discussion with O'Connor.
2. O'Connor ignored much existing research on Hebrew verse and syntax with the result that his study, although well-informed on linguistic and literary theory, suffered from an unsatisfactory knowledge of Hebrew (Watson, 1983, 132-134).
3. O'Connor limited his study to poems of specific lengths, the very short and very long poems being excluded. This skewed his conclusions (Watson, 1983, 132), especially as to gross structure.
4. O'Connor ignored known poetic techniques as to the relations between cola and as to gross structure (Blommerde, 1982, 167; Watson, 1983, 133).
5. O'Connor was inconsistent in generally excluding semantics from consideration but relying on it for his trope of coloration (Geller, 1982a, 71-72).

6.   One reviewer was "totally unconvinced of the trope of 'construct
     combination'" (Good, 1982, 112), while another expressed
     doubt as to "the trope of coloration, especially as far as
     combination is concerned" (Blommerde, 1982, 162; cf. also
     Kugel, 1981, 321 n.5).

3.3.5.2   Criticisms of the colon as basic unit

The criticisms that have been raised regarding O'Connor's choice of
the single line or colon as the *basic unit* to be described in Hebrew
verse are the following:

1.   The bicolon and tricolon are "absent" in O'Connor's descrip-
     tion, in the sense that he regarded them as a "secondary reality
     that resists characterization" (Blommerde, 1982, 163).
2.   The single line or colon "has no perceptual reality at all in
     Biblical verse of the sort required of a basic unit" (Geller,
     1982a, 71).
3.   Grammatical parallelism and in particular "ellipsis of
     grammatical elements" or gapping make no sense "except in the
     perceptual environment of binarism", from which it is clear that
     the couplet or bicolon is the dominant or basic element in
     Hebrew verse (Geller, 1982a, 72).
4.   "A study of syntax must concern itself with the sequence A + B
     as a whole", i.e. the two or more members of the parallelism,
     not with only A or only B (Kugel, 1981, 320).

O'Connor's view that the bi- and tricolon are of a *secondary nature*
and not the basic structural elements in Hebrew verse (criticism 1) is
at odds with overwhelming scholarly opinion. The bi- and tricolon
probably are the basis for gross structure in Hebrew verse (Van der
Lugt, 1980, 176; Blommerde, 1982, 163, 166, 169). Nevertheless, when
it comes to either syntactical or metrical description of Hebrew verse,
it seems preferable to describe the bi- and tricolon in terms of
combinations of single lines, rather than describing single lines as
parts of bi- or tricola. A description taking the bi- and tricolon as its
starting point not only has to take cognisance of the difference
between the bicolon and the tricolon, but also of the existence of

monocola. If, however, an adequate description of the colon can be found, which was O'Connor's first aim, the description of larger units becomes a comparatively small problem. Furthermore, as Blommerde (1982, 163) admitted, the "absence" of the bi- and tricolon in O'Connor's description was no denial of their existence. On the contrary, his findings indicate that the bi- and tricolon occur very frequently, but then as preferred target structures or results of the combination of cola or single lines.

Geller's objection - apparently shared by Kugel (1981, 320) - that the single line has *no perceptual reality* (criticism 2) cannot be accepted as valid, because of the importance of the line-break, which was duly pointed out by Geller himself (1982a, 70). The line-break or colon boundary is the factor giving the single line its perceptual reality as a unit in versification; cf. 1.5 above and Hartman (1980, 60). Geller later (1982a, 72) referred to the single line as "a structure of limited perceptual significance", revealing by this contradiction his own uncertainty on the matter. One should also be careful not to confuse the perception of verse with verse structure.

It is true that *parallelism* and *gapping* can only function as they do in the context of more than one colon (criticism 3), but this fact is no proof that the bicolon, created by parallelism and other devices, is the basic element in Hebrew verse structure as Geller would have it. Again he contradicts himself, for he writes: "Of course, if a strict meter could be established for Biblical verse, the single line would succeed to the throne" (Geller, 1982a, 71). It does not matter what kind of metre or prosodical system Hebrew verse can be established to have, its basic unit would remain the same, namely the single line; and if a combination of lines such as the bicolon or tricolon were the basic unit, that, too, would remain intact irrespective of the discovery of a strict metre or any other versification system.

A study of *syntax* should indeed "concern itself with the sequence A + B as a whole" (criticism 4), especially in cases where either A or B on its own would be syntactically incomplete. This point of criticism raised by Kugel would be applicable to a study such as that of Garr (1983) because, although he distinguished the A cola from the B cola and then studied the constituent order of each separately, he failed to study the syntax of A + B together. O'Connor, however, did not study syntax for the sake of syntax, but rather to enable him to describe the colon. This point of criticism thus is not quite applicable to his work. Neither can one deduce the structural status in versification of either the colon or the bi- and tricolon from the fact that single cola often are syntactically incomplete.

The discussion of this group of criticisms must be concluded by stating that not one of them can be regarded as a valid and adequate proof that O'Connor was wrong in taking the single colon as the basic structural unit to be described. The points made by the various critics were seen rather to relate to other matters, namely the combining of cola, the perception of verse, and the study of syntax. The preference expressed for the bi- and tricolon as the basic structural unit in Hebrew verse is understandable in the light of their role in the creation of larger units of verse, i.e. in gross structure. It seems, however, that at least three levels of structure in Hebrew verse must be reckoned with, not only fine and gross structure, but also the structure of the single line or colon. It is at this lowest structural level that O'Connor made his best contribution, as duly acknowledged by Blommerde (1982, 169).

3.3.5.3   Criticisms of O'Connor's system
The criticisms that have been raised regarding O'Connor's *system* for the delimitation and description of cola, of which some are obviously contradictory, are as follows:

1.   O'Connor made use of a kind of descriptive linguistics which could not describe that which is specific to poetry, because it excluded aesthetics and perception (Geller, 1982a, 67-68).

2.   O'Connor based his approach on generative grammar, which according to Van Rensburg (1983, 86) is purely semantically orientated and therefore is unacceptable for syntactical description.

3.   O'Connor's distinguishing of various levels in verse obscured the "underlying functional similarity" of the varied and complicated uses of parallelism (Kugel, 1981, 322).

4.   In his colon descriptions O'Connor was interested in the number and not the nature of the constituents (Van Rensburg, 1983, 87).

5. O'Connor took too little account of contents, i.e. semantics (Kugel, 1981, 321; Blommerde, 1982, 163, 166, 169).
6. O'Connor left out of consideration certain formal elements (Blommerde, 1982, 163, 165, 169).
7. O'Connor's views on gapping and apposition, and on the relation between the two, are unclear (Kugel, 1981, 322).
8. O'Connor, "in seeking to use observations of syntax to derive a set of quasi-metrical prescriptions, ... skews somewhat the focus of his inquiry" (Kugel, 1981, 316).
9. O'Connor's numbers, i.e. the matrix of the constriction, "argue eloquently against the use he wishes to make of them", because the cola which they describe are too unequal (Kugel, 1981, 316-317).
10. O'Connor's constriction fails to describe any difference between poetry (i.e. verse) and prose, seeing that

   (a) it would exclude some passages which are commonly regarded as poetry, and
   (b) include some passages which are commonly regarded as prose (Kugel, 1981, 319).

11. O'Connor's matrix has no descriptive validity because his lines (cola) are arbitrary and "lineation in this system is entirely *ad hoc*" (Kugel, 1981, 317, 319).
12. Some of O'Connor's lineations, i.e. colon delimitations, are unacceptable and, of more general import, "the problem of what constitutes a line remains and the syntactic restraints adduced by O'Connor are valuable aids but no more" (Watson, 1983, 132-133).
13. "... the nagging doubt remains, whether reversing this process would produce a line of Hebrew poetry", i.e. whether one could work backwards from O'Connor's constriction to create cola of Hebrew verse (Ap-Thomas, 1982, 225).
14. O'Connor preferred the system of syntactical constriction to that of (phonological) metre because of the former's ease of description (Geller, 1982a, 69).
15. O'Connor's constriction is "a kind of simple meter" (Geller, 1982a, 70).

A brief discussion of the latter group of criticisms, i.e. those concerning O'Connor's system for the delimitation and description of cola, will be in place here.

Geller's criticism that O'Connor made use of a kind of *descriptive linguistics* which could not describe that which is specific to poetry because it excluded aesthetics and perception (criticism 1) is based on some misconceptions. Firstly, O'Connor was not concerned with poetry as poetry, but with poetry as verse; cf. the distinction between these two terms made in **1.1**. Secondly, O'Connor did not try to describe the essence of poetry, but the structure of verse, i.e. he did not want to say what made poetry poetical, but rather how cola were formed and combined in verse. Thirdly, in a versification system aesthetics play no role at all, and the role of perception in versification is limited to phenomena which can be described linguistically; cf. the discussion in **1.4**. Thus there is no reason to object to the kind of descriptive linguistics of which O'Connor made use, provided it is used for the description of verse structure.

Van Rensburg's criticism of O'Connor for making use of *generative grammar* (criticism 2) is incomprehensible, seeing that Van Rensburg based his own work on the approach of Collins who also made use of generative grammar, as he clearly stated (Collins, 1978a, 31-44). Furthermore, it is simply not true that generative grammar is purely semantically orientated. It is indeed suitable for syntactical description.

It seems to be true that the distinguishing of various *levels and categories* would obscure some functional similarity between the variety of uses of parallelism (criticism 3), but when one wants to describe the structure of verse, which is what O'Connor tried to do, precision is called for, not the recognition of functional similarity. This criticism by Kugel is the unfortunate result of his rejecting, "as a matter of principle, any attempt at detailed study" (Geller, 1982a, 65). Kugel himself had admired the clarity of O'Connor's use of categories and levels one page earlier (1981, 321). The use of levels and categories in the description of verse is commonly accepted practice. Recent examples of the stringent application of levels and categories to Hebrew verse with quite different aims would be the studies of Berlin (1979, 1985). The importance of O'Connor's awareness and use of levels was duly pointed out by Watson (1983, 134) and in our discussion of Collins' system above it has become clear that the use of levels is essential in the syntactical description of cola of Hebrew verse; cf. also our introduction to O'Connor's system in 3.3.5.1.

That O'Connor was interested in the *number* rather than the *nature of constituents* (criticism 4) is correct. His main aim was to give a valid description of the colon in syntactical terms, not to study syntax in itself. For that aim all the details as to the nature of the constituents do not seem to be neccessary. A partial indication of the nature of the constituents is given, nevertheless, by the various levels of his description.

That *content* or *semantics* should be taken into account (criticism 5) seems to be correct. There can be difference of opinion as to the exact role content should be allowed to play in structural description, but in Hebrew verse, where formal units and units of meaning usually coincide, content must be taken into account as a guide to structure. This, however, does not influence the syntactical description of the colon itself, because semantics does not play a role in the structure of the colon, except superficially in the case of parallelism within the single colon. Semantics does play a significant role in the combinining of cola and upwards towards gross structure. Nevertheless, Blommerde (1982, 163, 166, 169) may be expecting too much by asking that content should be assigned more than a secondary role and be given "heavy attention". Surely Blommerde, who himself is keenly aware of the role of formal elements in structure, did not mean to assign them a role secondary to that of content.

That there are *formal elements* left out of consideration by O'Connor (criticism 6) cannot be denied. However, all the formal elements mentioned by Blommerde (1982, 163-166) - cola of certain lengths, change of number, repetition, inclusion, chiasmus - serve the combining of cola into pairs or larger groups, not the structure of the colon itself. Indirectly they might contribute to colon delimitation in any specific case, but that does not make them part of the structure of the colon. Exactly which formal elements, if any, do play a role in the structure of the colon will have to be determined by further study. Possibly certain particles, which Blommerde mentions only in connection with gross structure, might be amongst the formal elements playing a structural role in the colon. This criticism, then, can be applicable only to the delimitation of cola by O'Connor, not to his system of colon description.

It may indeed be possible to improve on O'Connor's views on *gapping* and *apposition* and the relation between the two (criticism 7). Although one will have to acknowledge that these matters are not so directly related to the functioning of syntax in the versification system, they will have to be addressed in further syntactical study. Again this is a factor relating to colon delimitation, but not to colon description.

The criticism that trying to derive a set of so-called *quasi-metrical prescriptions* from observations on syntax "skews somewhat the focus" of O'Connor's enquiry (criticism 8) is valid in so far as O'Connor never completed his description of the versification system, specifically the phonological patterning, but the fact that he tried to discover and describe formally the syntactic patterns *in* the versification system surely cannot be criticised. The case is somewhat similar to that of Wimsatt (1971); cf. especially the following comments on his paper:

> ... that it was essentially a linguist's theory rather than a metricist's theory, that it was more concerned with accounting for meter by linguistic theory than by finding out what meter is (1971, 218) and
> Like Halle and Keyser, Wimsatt was simply trying to describe what was there (1971, 220).

The *inequality* of the cola which O'Connor's constriction describes (criticism 9) is no argument against the validity of the numbers of the constriction. Reference can here be made to our discussion in **1.4** concerning the nature of metre and especially so-called free (more accurately pure tonic) metre, in which not even the number of stressed syllables per line or colon is fixed. The inequality of cola is no argument against the classification of literature as verse, nor against the possible metricality of that verse (cf. Hartman, 1980, 18-21).

The criticism that O'Connor's constriction fails to describe any *difference between prose and verse* (criticism 10) will have to be taken up further on in the present study, at least as far as the asserted exclusion of verse is concerned, seeing that it might be possible to adjust or refine O'Connor's constriction. The argument as to the inclusion of prose can be repudiated. In spoken and written prose there do occur sentences which comply with the metrical requirements for verse (Cunningham, 1976, 266-267, quoted with approval by Bjorklund, 1978, 18). There is no reason why this should not also happen in the case of biblical Hebrew. One must remember that verse makes use of the resources of the natural and the literary language, being in some cases more closely related to the latter (Mukarovsky, 1977, 7-9). In Hebrew verse the language seems to be more closely related to the natural language of speech, than to the language of literary prose, at least as far as the verb functions and verb positions are concerned (Gross, 1982, 70).

The criticism that O'Connor's matrix has no descriptive validity because his cola are *arbitrary* (criticism 11), is directly related to the previous three already discussed briefly. The problem of colon delimitation is a central problem in the study of the versification system, and a very important factor in the study of Hebrew verse syntax. It will be treated in detail in the present research. It would suffice to say here that from Kugel's statement: "... lineation in this system is entirely *ad hoc* ...", at least the word "entirely" should rather be deleted. Kugel's earlier statement (1981, 317) that O'Connor's concept of the colon is a "potentially arbitrary entity" is more careful and perhaps closer to the truth. The criticism of arbitrariness was also raised by O'Connor (1977, 15, 16, 18) against the cola which Collins (1970/1) found to exist in the Kilamuwa inscription. One would expect O'Connor, then, to be more careful to avoid arbitrary delimitation, and his delimitation of Hebrew verse in fact seems to be less arbitrary than that of Collins.

That some of O'Connor's *lineations* (i.e. colon delimitations) were regarded as unacceptable (criticism 12) is nothing unusual in our field of study, seeing that scholars tend to differ to some extent in their delimitation of cola in Hebrew verse for reasons already mentioned; cf. **1.5**. However, the view that O'Connor has supplied us with valuable *aids but no more* and that therefore the problem of what constitutes a colon remains, casts very serious doubt upon the validity of O'Connor's approach. This means that his approach will have to be tested extensively, and possibly that the status of his constraints will have to be examined.

The uncertainty whether one could *reverse the process* and work backwards from O'Connor's constriction to create cola of Hebrew verse (criticism 13) is directly related to the problem of what constitutes a colon. Ultimately the question is what system the Hebrew poet used when creating his verse. To state it another way: One can ask whether O'Connor's constriction is just a description of Hebrew verse, or whether it is *the system* of Hebrew verse. It would seem at this stage, however, that O'Connor has discovered at least part of that system, a part of which the importance had not been made explicit before.

That O'Connor preferred the constrictional system to that of phonological metre because of the former's *ease of description* (criticism 14) is a misrepresentation of the facts. In the first place, it seems unlikely that O'Connor would have come up with such a diversion from standard metrical practices as far as Hebrew verse is concerned if it had been only for ease of description. It must after all not have been so very easy to devise such a description. Secondly, the fact that others - Kurylowicz, Cooper and especially Collins - simultaneously applied similar approaches and, in the case of Collins, achieved a fair measure of success, indicates that this approach corresponds to some reality in the verse. Thirdly, the very statement of O'Connor's which Geller (1982a, 69) quoted goes to show that O'Connor took more into account than just ease of description:

> The ease of syntactic treatment combined with the *obtusity of phonological treatments* suggests that Hebrew verse *uses* a constriction, a poetic system with primary syntactic features and *concomitant* phonological features (O'Connor, 1980a, 148; emphases added; cf. also 149).

Geller's view that O'Connor's constriction is a kind of *simple metre* (criticism 15) makes a very important contribution to our evaluation of O'Connor's system, pointing out as it does some uncertainty on O'Connor's part as to the theoretical status of the system which he devised. At times O'Connor flatly stated that Hebrew verse had no metre (1980a, 65, 138), and announced that he had decided not to call the constrictional system a metre (1980a, 67), but then again he stated that it was of the same sort as a metre (1980a, 67) and indicated an awareness that the constriction is related to metre (1980a, 147-149,

159-161). This ambiguity is the result of the fact that he developed his constrictional system from the concept of metre by extending that concept and then illogically excluding the constriction from metre, hoping in this way to prevent terminological confusion. In our view O'Connor's constriction is metrical, i.e. is metre or part of metre in an unconventional extended sense of the term; cf. our discussion in 1.4. This means that we can agree with Geller that the constriction is a kind of metre, though not on the grounds of its phonological effect as he would have it; rather it is metrical by virtue of its being a "numerical regulation of certain properties of the linguistic form", to quote Lotz (1972, 2) again.

3.3.5.4 Further criticisms
To the foregoing discussion of scholars' criticisms some comments of our own can now be added:

The first point that should be raised here concerns the status of *object suffixes* in O'Connor's system. In his explanation of what he meant by the category noun or *nomen* O'Connor (1980a, 68) specifically mentioned pronouns as being included in the class of nomina. Seeing that he then said that each verb or noun is a *unit* one would expect pronouns also to be units in his system. Moreover, since nominal phrases are *constituents* (1980a, 68) one would expect those pronouns which are nominal phrases to be counted as constituents. Collins (1978a, 30) regarded cases of the suffixation of the object pronoun to the verb as a "principal variation" on the line-types with object phrases and grouped them accordingly (e.g. 1978a, 90-91). In his classification O'Connor, however, completely ignored such object pronouns suffixed to verbs, as can be seen from his treatment of cola from Psalm 106.

Among cola of 1 predicator, 2 constituents, 2 units from Psalm 106 O'Connor listed 4b and 42a (1980a, 69), 8a and 47b (1980a, 71), and 27b (1980a, 72). His cola of 1 predicator, 2 constituents, 3 units included 10a, 10b, 41a and 43a (1980a, 70). As a colon of 1 predicator, 3 constituents, 3 units he mentioned 9b (1980a, 70).

He nowhere gives any explanation for his omission of these objects from his description of the colon, only a mere statement that they are not constituents (1980a, 404). Nor is it only for verse structure purposes that he ignored these pronominal objects, but also for

purely syntactical description, as his listing of Ps 106:4b, 10a, 10b, 41a
and 42a (1980a, 328) and 9b (1980a, 339) testifies. This is in sharp
contrast with his treatment of other objects, which he accorded both
unit and constituent status, including those pronominal objects consisting only of the sign of the accusative and a suffix, for example
אותם in Ps 106:26b and 46 (1980a, 72, 75). Furthermore, there are
no syntactical grounds for such discriminatory treatment of essentially
identical constructions. The chronologically varying preference for
the two possibilities among prose authors of the Old Testament was
examined by Polzin (1976, 28-31 and *passim*). Circumstances under
which the use of את before the suffix is obligatory were specified by
GKC (par. 117e), but these do not affect the unit and constituent
status of the suffix.

A second point relates to O'Connor's description of the *dominant
line form*, which he included at the end of his "restatement of the
constriction". It is followed by the statement: "A lineation which
yields lines of these constellations is preferred to other lineations"
(1980a, 87). Clearly O'Connor did not mean that the ancient Hebrew
poet preferred such cola, but rather that he himself did, and possibly
that other modern researchers of Hebrew verse did. The description
of the dominant line form, and especially the quoted statement is an
addition to his system rather than part of it. Seen thus, the statement,
indeed, hints at an inability of his constriction to lineate conclusively
in all cases.

Let us now take a closer look at O'Connor's description of the
dominant line form. It reads: "Most lines of Hebrew verse contain
one clause and either two or three constituents *of* two or three units"
(1980a, 87; emphasis added). As it stands, this description is misleading and incorrect. In the light of his statement that 57% of his
lines (cola) had three units and 25% had two units (1980a, 316) it
should read: "... *and* two or three units", thus specifying the number
of units per colon and not per constituent. From another formulation
of the dominant line form by O'Connor the figure *three* seems to have
dropped out before "... constituents (of 3 units); ..." (1980a, 138).

Thirdly, the close relation between *syntax and metre* poses the
question as to which is primary. This question is especially acute in
cases where syntactical constraints play a major role in the functioning of the versification system, or where such a major role is claimed

by a researcher, like O'Connor did. In our discussion of Collins' study
this question has already been touched upon and its importance
indicated. O'Connor's answer to the question was rather speculative,
but he seemed to give syntax the priority, both as to the origin of the
system and as to its repeated implementation (1980a, 69, 159-162).

Without going into the detail of this intricate problem here, it can
be said that one should keep the question of the origin of the metrical
system apart from the question of the repeated implementation
thereof. The metre - if it was not taken over from a different
language and verse system - imitates or is based upon the structure
of the language (Thompson, 1961, 167-169). The individual line of
verse on the other hand comes into being due to the influence of the
abstract metre on the language material (Zhirmunsky, 1966a, 21-23;
Thompson, 1961, 169-171; Tarlinskaja and Teterina, 1974, 63-64).
This influence is exercised on various parts of the language material,
that is on its phonological, grammatical (i.e. syntactical) or semantic
parts, differing in this respect from one language to the other
(Lotman, 1980). Thus it would seem that syntax could be primary to
the creation of metre in the case of specific languages and versification systems. Once the metre as abstraction exists, however, the
metre becomes primary to any line of verse, whether it is a metre in
which the syntactical component plays the major role or not. A poet
working in a metre in which the syntactic component plays the major
role, might easily have exploited certain syntactic structures, knowing
from experience - whether knowingly or not, probably not (cf. the
quotation from Jakobson in Ross, 1981, 281) - that such structures
produce rhythmic lines of metrical verse. As long as the syntactic
constraints which the poet takes into account are part of metre, and
not something in its stead, what the poet is "aiming" at is still the
metre and nothing else.

The problem just discussed will be familiar to anyone who knows
the various works on and methods of formula criticism, which has
been applied to various literatures, especially in connection with
theories of the oral origin of poetic works. A critical evaluation of the
application of these methods to Hebrew poetry has led to the following conclusion:

> We have indicated time and again that parallelism is *the*
> dominant characteristic of Hebrew poetry, and that the word pair

is the tool with which the poet constructs the parallelism. But we also said that there is even something more basic and essential to the poetry than the word pair, and that, for want of a better term, we must call 'meter'. The use of the word pairs in the verse seems to indicate that standardized patterns actually existed for the poet. And there are probably many more subtle and even more obvious rules which we have overlooked in our research. But the guidelines which we have found tell us that the organization of the words in the line is not haphazard. We suggest that work needs to be done in the area of 'meter'. We can only earnestly recommend that the work be done without dragging in the baggage of Classical Greek verse, and that we learn to deal with the poetry on its own terms (Watters, 1976, 149; cf. the extremely similar conclusion of Culley, 1967, 119).

To this need O'Connor responded, although he never completed his description of the metre by including a description of the phonological features of the metre, and thus in effect substituted syntax for metre. He regarded the phonological features as concomitant (1980a, 148), but if the nature of pure tonic metre is taken into account, that might prove not to be the case. O'Connor did, however, provide a theory to be further tested and refined. The main shortcoming of his description of the colon in Hebrew verse is, as was shown, some uncertainty as to the criteria for the delimitation of the cola.

3.3.6 Conclusion

The syntactical approach to versification systems appears to be theoretically acceptable in the light of the number of verse literatures to which it has been applied by scholars from various fields of study, as discussed in paragraph 3.2. This approach seems very likely to prove practically applicable to Hebrew verse when one takes into account the measure of success achieved in the studies just discussed, especially those of Collins and O'Connor.

The possibility has to be considered that there may have been attempts to apply this approach to Hebrew verse other than those discussed above. The name of Berlin has been mentioned in this regard (Hagstrom, 1982, 85) and it is likely that the grammatical aspects of parallelism which she treated (Berlin, 1979; 1985, 31-63) could in some cases help to determine the delimitation of cola. Her aim, however, was neither to delimit cola, nor to describe cola in

syntactical terms as in the case of these studies. No other studies of
Hebrew verse along these lines are known to exist.

Among the systems presented in the studies discussed in 3.3.2 -
3.3.5 those of Collins and O'Connor have the greatest merit. Van
Rensburg (1983) chose to follow the system of Collins, modifying it
mainly by the addition of detail as to the grammatical content of each
constituent, thereby trying to accommodate the criticism of Richter
(1980, 222 n.852) that Collins did not differentiate enough. The two
reasons given by Van Rensburg for his preferring Collins' system over
that of O'Connor have been dealt with. Unfortunately one has the
overall impression that Van Rensburg received O'Connor's book at a
late stage in his own research, when he was unable to study it
thoroughly or adapt his approach to it.

It is impossible to obtain reliable results in the study of the syntax
of Hebrew verse, and its word order in particular, before a valid
system for the description and delimitation of cola has been found.
This consideration determines our choice. In the discussion above
O'Connor's system of colon description and delimitation has proved
to be superior to any other suggested to date. It has the following
decided advantages over that of Collins:

1. It describes and delimits the colon (single line), thus clearly
    indicating where the colon boundary (line-break, or caesura)
    occurs.
2. Because it describes and delimits the colon, it is easily applica-
    ble to monocola, bicola, tricola and whatever other combi-
    nations of cola might occur.
3. It distinguishes three levels of description, thus offering more
    information as to the physical texture of the line than Collins'
    one level description.

It may be asked whether an improvement of the system of Collins like
that made by Van Rensburg might not be more suitable to our aims.
That is not the case, because in this study we are not trying to obtain
more detailed knowledge of the syntax itself, but rather in finding,
and improving if necessary, a valid system of colon delimitation. Our
approach here is similar to that of Parker (1974, 291) who, in terms
differing from ours, wrote:

> No note has been made of syntactic patterns, since although
> syntax is of importance in establishing parallelism it does not
> yield such regular patterns as may be thought to have formal
> prosodic significance.

By "syntactic patterns" Parker meant syntax and word order, whereas
we use the same term to refer to the versification system which exists,
or at the least exerts its influence, on the syntactic levels of the verse.

It has been pointed out that the system of colon delimitation
proposed by O'Connor is not without its problems, *inter alia* that of
the status of the constraints, and the question of the relation between
metre and the syntactic patterns as described by his matrix of the
constriction.

It will have to be established whether the syntactic patterns

1. are the *result* of metre in the usual, i.e. phonological, sense of
    the term, or
2. function as a *component* of metre in an expanded sense of the
    term, or
3. function as a *substitute* for metre in the usual, i.e. phonological,
    sense of the term.

If the latter proves to be the case, the question should be considered
whether these patterns themselves should be called a metre, i.e.
whether the term metre should be expanded in such a way as to
include the system of syntactic patterns as a distinct type of metre.

Chapter 4

The Role of Syntactical Constraints in the Colometry of Hebrew Verse

4.1 Scope and method

Within the broader aims of this study as stated in **1.6** an attempt will be undertaken in this chapter to formulate a valid and adequate description of the Hebrew colometric system, concentrating specifically on the role of syntactical constraints. In this attempt use will be made of the insights gained from the surveying of the various systems applied to Hebrew verse and from the criticisms that have been raised against them.

In the previous chapters it was established that the versification systems presently applied to Hebrew verse do not provide adequate means to reliably delimit cola. Indications were found that the system used by the Hebrew poets probably at least partially was of a syntactical rather than a phonological nature. Of the attempts to describe the colometric system of Hebrew in syntactical terms that of O'Connor (1980a) has proved to be the most accurate. Taking his description of the colometric system as a starting point, we shall in this chapter delimit the cola in our corpus, in an attempt to identify its inadequacies, for which the necessary adjustments or refinements will then be suggested and tested. With slight anticipation it can here be mentioned that the adjustments envisaged will concern his definitions, his formulation of the constraints, the role of main stresses, the syntactic integrity of the colon, and to some extent the syntactical status of colon ends.

Our description of the system will not entail a comprehensive description of the Hebrew colon, including detail such as the number of syllables or consonants, as there is no indication that these are significant in Hebrew colometry; cf. **2.4** and **2.5**. Nor will it be attempted to describe the system in all its details, aiming only at *validity* and *adequacy*. Indeed, the nature of the material is such that possibly some features of the system employed by the Hebrew poets may always elude the modern scholar. Nevertheless, if a description

which is both valid and adequate can be formulated, a new and useful
access to the art of the Hebrew poet will have been obtained.

As the *corpus* of text for examination were chosen those parts of
Jeremiah chapters 2 - 25 which are commonly considered to be verse.
Now this may seem too large a corpus for detailed research, but, as
will become clear in the following paragraphs, some of the
phenomena with which this study is concerned do not occur very
frequently. A relatively large corpus is, therefore, necessary so that
the number of examples will not be too small. Also, the corpus is
limited by the exclusion of any portion of text, however small, about
which reasonable doubt exists as to its being verse or prose, or which
is text critically uncertain in such a way that it would affect the
division into cola.

The *prose* portions of Jeremiah 2 - 25 are simply left out of our
representation of the text and their position is indicated by a blank
line space between the preceding and following cola. Among these
there are headings, messenger formulas and the like. The same
applies to those portions of text about which reasonable doubt exists
as to their being verse or prose. Such exclusions are rarely discussed.
Where part of a numbered verse is considered to be *prose or possibly
prose* such a part of the verse is indicated simply by inserting the word
prose on a line of its own between the preceding and following cola.
The reason or reasons for the presence of such small bits of prose in
the predominantly verse text lies beyond the scope of our study, but it
may be noted here that their presence may be due to factors in the
process of transmission and redaction through which the text eventu-
ally reached us, or may on the other hand be due to factors related to
the origin of the verse itself. That the latter possibility is not mere
speculation is proven by the fact that small prose fragments are also
to be found in some Ugaritic verse texts; cf. e.g. Cross (1974, 10-15).

The expression נאם־יהוה, as well as the two occurrences of
אמר יהוה, namely at the end of 6:15 and 8:12, are consistently
treated as extrinsic to the cola. This was also the view of Kosmala
(1964, 428 = 1978, 89), Bright (1965, cxxxiv) and Holladay (1966,
412), at least as far as נאם־יהוה is concerned. Both these expressions could be extrinsic to the verse, and could even be later additions
in some cases. They could also be cola on their own. In some cases
נאם־יהוה may also be part of a longer colon, although no certain

case was found. Probably more clarity on the problem could be obtained from a study of the strophic structures, which are beyond the scope of the present study. Our viewing these expressions as extrinsic to the cola is made visible formally in that they are set on their own lines, but are not alloted letter references as in the case of the cola.

It is impracticable to deal extensively with *text critical* problems within the scope of this study, but these problems cannot be totally avoided. Therefore a fairly simple policy towards text critical problems has been adopted, with admittedly rather uneven results. The text presented below is *not* to be seen as necessarily text critically correct. Text critical problems which do not affect our colon delimitation are usually ignored, except in cases where there is some specific reason to discuss them. Those text critical problems which do affect or which could perhaps affect our colon delimitation but to which the solution seems to us to be clear, are briefly discussed along with our grounds for the colon delimitation. All cases where we accept a reading different from that of the MT as represented in BHS is marked with an *asterisk* at the end of the specific colon. Text critical problems which could affect our colon delimitation and to which a solution does not seem to be at hand are avoided by simply leaving out the whole of the specific colon or cola and inserting instead the word *text* on a line of its own between the preceding and the following cola.

Keeping these limitations in mind the cola of the verse sections in Jeremiah 2 - 25 are set out in **4.2.1**, and sequential letter references allotted to each successive colon of every numbered verse. In **4.2.2** this is followed by the grounds for our colon delimitation, concentrating on those cases on which we differ from accepted delimitations and those on which divergent views have been advanced by commentators and translators. A systematic description of the colometric system as we understand it is offered in **4.3**. We do not claim that our description corresponds one hundred percent to the colometric system actually used by the Old Testament poets, but we do regard our description on the one hand as both valid and adequate, and on the other hand as a better approximation of that system than any other description of it known to us.

4.2   Colometric analysis of the verse sections in Jeremiah 2 - 25

4.2.1   The cola in Jeremiah 2 - 25

prose		2:1
prose		2
זכרתי לך חסד נעוריך	a	
אהבת כלולתיך	b	
לכתך אחרי במדבר	c	
בארץ לא זרועה	d	
קדש ישראל ליהוה	a	3
ראשית תבואתה	b	
כל־אכליו יאשמו	c	
רעה תבא אליהם	d	
נאם־יהוה		
שמעו דבר־יהוה בית יעקב	a	4
וכל־משפחות בית ישראל	b	
prose		2:5
מה־מצאו אבותיכם בי עול	a	
כי רחקו מעלי	b	
וילכו אחרי ההבל ויהבלו	c	
ולא אמרו איה יהוה	a	6
המעלה אתנו מארץ מצרים	b	
המוליך אתנו במדבר	c	
בארץ ערבה ושוחה	d	
בארץ ציה וצלמות	e	
בארץ לא־עבר בה איש	f	
ולא־ישב אדם שם	g	
ואביא אתכם אל־ארץ הכרמל	a	7
לאכל פריה וטובה	b	
ותבאו ותטמאו את־ארצי	c	
ונחלתי שמתם לתועבה	d	
הכהנים לא אמרו איה יהוה	a	8
ותפשי התורה לא ידעוני	b	
והרעים פשעו בי	c	
והנביאים נבאו בבעל	d	
ואחרי לא־יועילו הלכו	e	

לכן עד אריב אתכם	a	9
נאם־יהוה		
ואת־בני בניכם אריב	b	
כי עברו איי כתיים וראו	a	2:10
וקדר שלחו והתבוננו מאד	b	
וראו הן היתה כזאת	c	
ההימיר גוי אלהים	a	11
והמה לא אלהים	b	
ועמי המיר כבודו	c	
בלוא יועיל	d	
שמו שמים על־זאת	a	12
ושערו חרבו מאד	b	
נאם־יהוה		
כי־שתים רעות עשה עמי	a	13
אתי עזבו	b	
מקור מים חיים	c	
לחצב להם בארות	d	
בארת נשברים	e	
אשר לא־יכלו המים	f	
העבד ישראל	a	14
אם־יליד בית הוא	b	
מדוע היה לבז	c	
עליו ישאגו כפרים	a	2:15
נתנו קולם	b	
וישיתו ארצו לשמה	c	
עריו נצתה מבלי ישב	d	
גם־בני־נף ותחפנס	a	16
ירעוך קדקד	b	
הלוא־זאת תעשה־לך	a	17
עזבך את־יהוה אלהיך	b	
בעת מוליכך בדרך	c	
ועתה מה־לך לדרך מצרים	a	18
לשתות מי שחור	b	
ומה־לך לדרך אשור	c	
לשתות מי נהר	d	
תיסרך רעתך	a	19
ומשבותיך תוכחך	b	
ודעי וראי כי־רע ומר	c	

עזבך את־יהוה אלהיך	d
ולא פחדתי אליך	e
נאם־אדני יהוה צבאות	f
כי מעולם שברתי עלך	a 2:20
נתקתי מוסרתיך	b
ותאמרי לא אעבד	c
כי על־כל־גבעה גבהה	d
ותחת כל־עץ רענן	e
את צעה זנה	f
ואנכי נטעתיך שרק	a 21
כלה זרע אמת	b
ואיך נהפכת לסוריה *	c
גפן נכריה *	d
כי אם־תכבסי בנתר	a 22
ותרבי־לך ברית	b
נכתם עונך לפני	c
נאם אדני יהוה	d
איך תאמרי לא נטמאתי	a 23
אחרי הבעלים לא הלכתי	b
ראי דרכך בגיא	c
דעי מה עשית	d
בכרה קלה משרכת דרכיה	e
פרה למד מדבר	a 24
באות נפשו שאפה רוח	b
תאנתה מי ישיבנה	c
כל־מבקשיה לא ייעפו	d
בחדשה ימצאונה	e
מנעי רגלך מיחף	a 2:25
וגורנך מצמאה	b
ותאמרי נואש לוא	c
כי־אהבתי זרים	d
ואחריהם אלך	e
כבשת גנב כי ימצא	a 26
כן הבישו בית ישראל	b
המה מלכיהם שריהם	c
וכהניהם ונביאיהם	d
אמרים לעץ אבי אתה	a 27
ולאבן את ילדתני	b

כי־פנו אלי	c	
ערף ולא פנים	d	
ובעת רעתם יאמרו	e	
קומה והושיענו	f	
ואיה אלהיך	a	28
אשר עשית לך	b	
יקומו אם־יושיעוך	c	
בעת רעתך	d	
כי מספר עריך	e	
היו אלהיך יהודה	f	
למה תריבו אלי	a	29
כלכם פשעתם בי	b	
נאם־יהוה		
לשוא הכיתי את־בניכם	a	2:30
מוסר לא לקחו	b	
אכלה חרבכם נביאיכם	c	
כאריה משחית	d	
prose		31
המדבר הייתי לישראל	a	
אם ארץ מאפליה	b	
מדוע אמרו עמי רדנו	c	
לוא־נבוא עוד אליך	d	
התשכח בתולה עדיה	a	32
כלה קשריה	b	
ועמי שכחוני	c	
ימים אין מספר	d	
מה־תיטבי דרכך	a	33
לבקש אהבה	b	
לכן גם את־הרעות	c	
למדתי את־דרכיך	d	
גם בכנפיך נמצאו	a	34
דם נפשות אביונים נקיים	b	
לא־במחתרת מצאתים	c	
כי על־כל־אלה	d	
ותאמרי כי נקיתי	a	2:35
אך שב אפו ממני	b	
הנני נשפט אותך	c	
על־אמרך לא חטאתי	d	

מה־תזלי מאד	a	36
לשנות את־דרכך	b	
גם ממצרים תבושי	c	
כאשר־בשת מאשור	d	
גם מאת זה תצאי	a	37
וידיך על־ראשך	b	
כי־מאס יהוה במבטחיך	c	
ולא תצליחי להם	d	
prose		3:1
הן ישלח איש את־אשתו	a	
והלכה מאתו	b	
והיתה לאיש־אחר	c	
הישוב אליה עוד	d	
הלוא חנוף תחנף הארץ ההיא	e	
ואת זנית רעים רבים	f	
ושוב אלי	g	
נאם־יהוה		
שאי־עיניך על־שפים	a	2
וראי איפה לא שגלת	b	
על־דרכים ישבת להם	c	
כערבי במדבר	d	
ותחניפי ארץ	e	
בזנותיך וברעתך	f	
וימנעו רבבים	a	3
ומלקוש לוא היה	b	
ומצח אשה זונה היה לך	c	
מאנת הכלם	d	
הלוא מעתה קראתי לי אבי	a	4
אלוף נערי אתה	b	
הינתר לעולם	a	3:5
אם־ישמר לנצח	b	
הנה דברתי	c	
ותעשי הרעות ותוכל	d	
prose		12
שובה משבה ישראל	a	
נאם־יהוה		
לוא־אפיל פני בכם	b	

כי־חסיד אני c

נאם־יהוה

לא אטור לעולם d

אך דעי עונך a 13

כי ביהוה אלהיך פשעת b

prose

ואנכי אמרתי a 19

איך אשיתך בבנים b

ואתן־לך ארץ חמדה c

נחלת צבי צבאות גוים d

ואמר אבי תקראו־לי e

ומאחרי לא תשובו f

אכן בגדה אשה מרעה a 3:20

כן בגדתם בי בית ישראל b

נאם־יהוה

קול על־שפיים נשמע a 21

בכי תחנוני בני ישראל b

כי העוו את־דרכם c

שכחו את־יהוה אלהיהם d

שובו בנים שובבים a 22

ארפה משובתיכם b

הננו אתנו לך c

כי אתה יהוה אלהינו d

אכן לשקרם גבעות * a 23

המון הרים * b

אכן ביהוה אלהינו c

תשועת ישראל d

אם־תשוב ישראל a 4:1

נאם־יהוה

אלי תשוב b

ואם־תסיר שקוציך c

מפני ולא תנוד d

ונשבעת חי־יהוה באמת a 2

במשפט ובצדקה b

והתברכו בו גוים c

ובו יתהללו d

prose		3
נירו לכם ניר	a	
ואל־תזרעו אל־קוצים	b	
המלו ליהוה	a	4
והסרו ערלות לבבכם	b	
איש יהודה וישבי ירושלם	c	
פן־תצא כאש חמתי	d	
ובערה ואין מכבה	e	
מפני רע מעלליכם	f	
הגידו ביהודה	a	4:5
ובירושלם השמיעו ואמרו	b	
ותקעו שופר בארץ	c	
קראו מלאו ואמרו	d	
האספו ונבואה	e	
אל־ערי המבצר	f	
שאו־נס ציונה	a	6
העיזו אל־תעמדו	b	
כי רעה אנכי מביא מצפון	c	
ושבר גדול	d	
עלה אריה מסבכו	a	7
ומשחית גוים	b	
נסע יצא ממקמו	c	
לשום ארצך לשמה	d	
עריך תצינה מאין יושב	e	
על־זאת חגרו שקים	a	8
ספדו והילילו	b	
כי לא־שב אף־יהוה ממנו *	c	
prose		9
נאם־יהוה		
יאבד לב־המלך	a	
ולב השרים	b	
ונשמו הכהנים	c	
והנביאים יתמהו	d	
prose		4:10
אהה אדני יהוה	a	
אכן השא השאת	b	
לעם הזה ולירושלם	c	
לאמר שלום יהיה לכם	d	

ונגעה חרב עד־הנפש	e	
בעת ההיא יאמר	a	11
לעם־הזה ולירושלם	b	
רוח צח שפיים במדבר	c	
דרך בת־עמי	d	
לוא לזרות ולוא להבר	e	
רוח מלא יבוא לי *	a	12
עתה גם־אני אדבר	b	
משפטים אותם	c	
הנה כעננים יעלה	a	13
וכסופה מרכבותיו	b	
קלו מנשרים סוסיו	c	
אוי לנו כי שדדנו	d	
כבסי מרעה לבך ירושלם	a	14
למען תושעי	b	
עד־מתי תלין בקרבך	c	
מחשבות אונך	d	
כי קול מגיד מדן	a	4:15
ומשמיע און מהר אפרים	b	
הזכירו לגוים הנה	a	16
השמיעו על־ירושלם	b	
נצרים באים מארץ המרחק	c	
ויתנו על־ערי יהודה קולם	d	
כשמרי שדי היו עליה מסביב	a	17
כי־אתי מרתה	b	
נאם־יהוה		
דרכך ומעלליך	a	18
עשו אלה לך	b	
זאת רעתך כי מר	c	
כי נגע עד־לבך	d	
מעי מעי אחולה	a	19
קירות לבי המה־לי	b	
לבי לא אחריש	c	
כי קול שופר שמעתי נפשי	d	
תרועת מלחמה	e	
שבר על־שבר נקרא	a	4:20
כי שדדה כל־הארץ	b	
פתאם שדדו אהלי	c	

רגע יריעתי	d	
עד־מתי אראה־נס	a	21
אשמעה קול שופר	b	
כי אויל עמי	a	22
אותי לא ידעו	b	
בנים סכלים המה	c	
ולא נבונים המה	d	
חכמים המה להרע	e	
ולהיטיב לא ידעו	f	
ראיתי את־הארץ והנה־תהו *	a	23
ואל־השמים ואין אורם	b	
ראיתי ההרים והנה רעשים	a	24
וכל־הגבעות התקלקלו	b	
ראיתי והנה אין האדם	a	4:25
וכל־עוף השמים נדדו	b	
ראיתי והנה הכרמל המדבר	a	26
וכל־עריו נתצו	b	
מפני יהוה	c	
מפני חרון אפו	d	
prose		27
שממה תהיה כל־הארץ	a	
וכלה לא אעשה	b	
על־זאת תאבל הארץ	a	28
וקדרו השמים ממעל	b	
על כי־דברתי זמתי	c	
ולא נחמתי ולא־אשוב ממנה	d	
מקול פרש ורמה קשת	a	29
ברחת כל־העיר	b	
באו בעבים	c	
ובכפים עלו	d	
כל־העיר עזובה	e	
ואין־יושב בהן איש	f	
ואתי מה־תעשי *	a	4:30
כי־תלבשי שני	b	
כי־תעדי עדי־זהב	c	
כי־תקרעי בפוך עיניך	d	
לשוא תתיפי	e	
מאסו־בך עגבים	f	

נפשך יבקשו	g	
כי קול כחולה שמעתי	a	31
צרה כמבכירה	b	
קול בת־ציון תתיפח	c	
תפרש כפיה	d	
אוי־נא לי	e	
כי עיפה נפשי להרגים	f	
שוטטו בחוצות ירושלם	a	5:1
וראו־נא ודעו	b	
ובקשו ברחובותיה	c	
אם־תמצאו איש	d	
אם־יש עשה משפט	e	
מבקש אמונה	f	
ואסלח לה	g	
ואם חי־יהוה יאמרו	a	2
לכן לשקר ישבעו	b	
יהוה עיניך הלוא לאמונה	a	3
הכיתה אתם ולא־חלו	b	
כליתם מאנו קחת מוסר	c	
חזקו פניהם מסלע	d	
מאנו לשוב	e	
ואני אמרתי אך־דלים	a	4
הם נואלו	b	
כי לא ידעו דרך יהוה	c	
משפט אלהיהם	d	
אלכה־לי אל־הגדלים	a	5:5
ואדברה אותם	b	
כי המה ידעו דרך יהוה	c	
משפט אלהיהם	d	
אך המה יחדו שברו על	e	
נתקו מוסרות	f	
על־כן הכם אריה מיער	a	6
זאב ערבות ישדדם	b	
נמר שקד על־עריהם	c	
כל־היוצא מהנה יטרף	d	
כי רבו פשעיהם	e	
עצמו משבותיהם	f	
אי לזאת אסלוח־לך	a	7

בניך עזבוני	b	
וישבעו בלא אלהים	c	
ואשבע אותם וינאפו	d	
ובית זונה יתגדרו	e	
סוסים מיזנים משכים היו	a	8
איש אל־אשת רעהו יצהלו	b	
העל־אלה לוא־אפקד	a	9
נאם־יהוה		
ואם בגוי אשר־כזה	b	
לא תתנקם נפשי	c	
עלו בשרותיה ושחתו	a	5:10
וכלה אל־תעשו	b	
הסירו נטישותיה	c	
כי לוא ליהוה המה	d	
כי בגוד בגדו בי	a	11
בית ישראל ובית יהודה	b	
נאם־יהוה		
כחשו ביהוה	a	12
ויאמרו לא־הוא	b	
ולא־תבוא עלינו רעה	c	
וחרב ורעב לוא נראה	d	
והנביאים יהיו לרוח	a	13
והדבר אין בהם	b	
כה יעשה להם	c	
prose		14
יען דברכם את־הדבר הזה	a	
הנני נתן דברי	b	
בפיך לאש	c	
והעם הזה עצים	d	
ואכלתם	e	
הנני מביא עליכם	a	5:15
גוי ממרחק בית ישראל	b	
נאם־יהוה		
גוי איתן הוא	c	
גוי מעולם הוא	d	
גוי לא־תדע לשנו	e	
ולא תשמע מה־ידבר	f	
אשפתו כקבר פתוח	a	16

כלם גבורים	b	
ואכל קצירך ולחמך	a	17
יאכלו בניך ובנותיך	b	
יאכל צאנך ובקרך	c	
יאכל גפנך ותאנתך	d	
ירשש ערי מבצריך	e	
אשר אתה בוטח בהנה בחרב	f	
prose		18
prose		19
הגידו זאת בבית יעקב	a	5:20
והשמיעוה ביהודה לאמר	b	
שמעו־נא זאת	a	21
עם סכל ואין לב	b	
עינים להם ולא יראו	c	
אזנים להם ולא ישמעו	d	
האותי לא־תיראו	a	22
נאם־יהוה		
אם מפני לא תחילו	b	
אשר־שמתי חול גבול לים	c	
חק־עולם ולא יעברנהו	d	
ויתגעשו ולא יוכלו	e	
והמו גליו ולא יעברנהו	f	
ולעם הזה היה	a	23
לב סורר ומורה	b	
סרו וילכו	c	
ולא־אמרו בלבבם	a	24
נירא נא את־יהוה אלהינו	b	
text		
עונותיכם הטו־אלה	a	5:25
וחטאותיכם מנעו הטוב מכם	b	
כי־נמצאו בעמי רשעים	a	26
ישור כשך יקושים	b	
הציבו משחית	c	
אנשים ילכדו	d	
ככלוב מלא עוף	a	27
כן בתיהם מלאים מרמה	b	
על־כן גדלו ויעשירו	c	
שמנו עשתו	a	28

גם עברו דברי־רע	b	
דין לא־דנו	c	
דין יתום ויצליחו	d	
ומשפט אביונים לא שפטו	e	
העל־אלה לא־אפקד	a	29
נאם־יהוה		
אם בגוי אשר־כזה	b	
לא תתנקם נפשי	c	
שמה ושערורה נהיתה בארץ	a	5:30
הנביאים נבאו־בשקר	a	31
והכהנים ירדו על־ידיהם	b	
ועמי אהבו כן	c	
ומה־תעשו לאחריתה	d	
העזו בני בנימן	a	6:1
מקרב ירושלם	b	
ובתקוע תקעו שופר	c	
ועל־בית הכרם שאו משאת	d	
כי רעה נשקפה מצפון	e	
ושבר גדול	f	
הנוה והמענגה	a	2
דמיתי בת־ציון	b	
אליה יבאו רעים ועדריהם	a	3
תקעו עליה אהלים סביב	b	
רעו איש את־ידו	c	
קדשו עליה מלחמה	a	4
קומו ונעלה בצהרים	b	
אוי לנו כי־פנה היום	c	
כי ינטו צללי־ערב	d	
קומו ונעלה בלילה	a	6:5
ונשחיתה ארמנותיה	b	
prose		6
כרתו עצה	a	
ושפכו על־ירושלם סללה	b	
היא העיר הפקד	c	
כלה עשק בקרבה	d	
כהקיר בור מימיה	a	7
כן הקרה רעתה	b	
חמס ושד ישמע בה	c	

עַל־פְּנֵי תָמִיד חלי וּמַכָּה	d	
הוסרי יְרוּשָׁלַם	a	8
פֶּן־תֵּקַע נַפְשִׁי מִמֵּךְ	b	
פֶּן־אֲשִׂימֵךְ שְׁמָמָה	c	
אֶרֶץ לוֹא נוֹשָׁבָה	d	
prose		9
עוֹלֵל יְעוֹלְלוּ	a	
כַּגֶּפֶן שְׁאֵרִית יִשְׂרָאֵל	b	
הָשֵׁב יָדְךָ	c	
כְּבוֹצֵר עַל־סַלְסִלּוֹת	d	
עַל־מִי אֲדַבְּרָה	a	6:10
וְאָעִידָה וְיִשְׁמָעוּ	b	
הִנֵּה עֲרֵלָה אָזְנָם	c	
וְלֹא יוּכְלוּ לְהַקְשִׁיב	d	
הִנֵּה דְבַר־יְהוָה	e	
הָיָה לָהֶם לְחֶרְפָּה	f	
לֹא יַחְפְּצוּ־בוֹ	g	
וְאֵת חֲמַת יְהוָה מָלֵאתִי	a	11
נִלְאֵיתִי הָכִיל	b	
שְׁפֹךְ עַל־עוֹלָל בַּחוּץ	c	
וְעַל סוֹד בַּחוּרִים יַחְדָּו	d	
כִּי־גַם־אִישׁ עִם־אִשָּׁה יִלָּכֵדוּ	e	
זָקֵן עִם־מְלֵא יָמִים	f	
וְנָסַבּוּ בָתֵּיהֶם לַאֲחֵרִים	a	12
שָׂדוֹת וְנָשִׁים יַחְדָּו	b	
כִּי־אַטֶּה אֶת־יָדִי	c	
עַל־יֹשְׁבֵי הָאָרֶץ	d	
נְאֻם־יְהוָה		
כִּי מִקְּטַנָּם וְעַד־גְּדוֹלָם	a	13
כֻּלּוֹ בּוֹצֵעַ בָּצַע	b	
וּמִנָּבִיא וְעַד־כֹּהֵן	c	
כֻּלּוֹ עֹשֶׂה שָּׁקֶר	d	
וַיְרַפְּאוּ אֶת־שֶׁבֶר עַמִּי	a	14
עַל־נְקַלָּה לֵאמֹר	b	
שָׁלוֹם שָׁלוֹם	c	
וְאֵין שָׁלוֹם	d	
הֹבִישׁוּ כִּי תוֹעֵבָה עָשׂוּ	a	6:15
גַּם־בּוֹשׁ לֹא־יֵבוֹשׁוּ	b	

גם־הכלים לא ידעו	c	
לכן יפלו בנפלים	d	
בעת־פקדתים יכשלו	e	
אמר יהוה		
prose		16
עמדו על־דרכים וראו	a	
ושאלו לנתבות עולם	b	
אי־זה דרך הטוב ולכו־בה	c	
ומצאו מרגוע לנפשכם	d	
ויאמרו לא נלך	e	
והקמתי עליכם צפים	a	17
הקשיבו לקול שופר	b	
ויאמרו לא נקשיב	c	
לכן שמעו הגוים	a	18
text		
שמעי הארץ	a	19
הנה אנכי מביא רעה	b	
אל־העם הזה	c	
פרי מחשבותם	d	
כי על־דברי לא הקשיבו	e	
ותורתי וימאסו־בה	f	
למה־זה לי	a	6:20
לבונה משבא תבוא	b	
וקנה טוב מארץ מרחק *	c	
עלותיכם לא לרצון	d	
וזבחיכם לא־ערבו לי	e	
prose		21
הנני נתן	a	
אל־העם הזה מכשלים	b	
וכשלו בם	c	
אבות ובנים יחדו	d	
שכן ורעו יאבדו	e	
prose		22
הנה עם בא	a	
מארץ צפון	b	
וגוי גדול יעור	c	
מירכתי־ארץ	d	
קשת וכידון יחזיקו	a	23

אכזרי הוא ולא ירחמו	b	
קולם כים יהמה	c	
ועל־סוסים ירכבו	d	
ערוך כאיש למלחמה	e	
עליך בת־ציון	f	
שמענו את־שמעו	a	24
רפו ידינו	b	
צרה החזיקתנו	c	
חיל כיולדה	d	
אל־תצאי השדה	a	6:25
ובדרך אל־תלכי	b	
כי חרב לאיב	c	
מגור מסביב	d	
בת־עמי חגרי־שק	a	26
והתפלשי באפר	b	
אבל יחיד עשי לך	c	
מספר תמרורים	d	
כי פתאם יבא השדד עלינו	e	
בחון נתתיך בעמי מבצר	a	27
ותדע ובחנת את־דרכם	b	
text		28
text		29
לשוא צרף צרוף	a	
ורעים לא נתקו	b	
כסף נמאס קראו להם	a	6:30
כי־מאס יהוה בהם	b	
גזי נזרך והשליכי	a	7:29
ושאי על־שפים קינה	b	
כי מאס יהוה	c	
ויטש את־דור עברתו	d	
prose		8:4
היפלו ולא יקומו	a	
אם־ישוב ולא ישוב	b	
מדוע שובב העם הזה *	a	5
ירושלם משובה נצחת	b	
החזיקו בתרמית	c	

מאנו לשוב	d	
הקשבתי ואשמע	a	6
לוא־כן ידברו	b	
אין איש נחם על־רעתו	c	
לאמר מה עשיתי	d	
כלה שב במרצותם	e	
כסוס שוטף במלחמה	f	
גם־חסידה בשמים ידעה מועדיה	a	7
ותר וסוס ועגור	b	
שמרו את־עת באנה	c	
ועמי לא ידעו את משפט יהוה	d	
איכה תאמרו חכמים אנחנו	a	8
ותורת יהוה אתנו	b	
אכן הנה לשקר עשה	c	
עט שקר ספרים	d	
הבישו חכמים	a	9
חתו וילכדו	b	
הנה בדבר־יהוה מאסו	c	
וחכמת־מה להם	d	
לכן אתן את־נשיהם לאחרים	a	8:10
שרותיהם ליורשים	b	
כי מקטן ועד־גדול	c	
כלה בצע בצע	d	
מנביא ועד־כהן	e	
כלה עשה שקר	f	
וירפו את־שבר בת־עמי	a	11
על־נקלה לאמר	b	
שלום שלום	c	
ואין שלום	d	
הבשו כי תועבה עשו	a	12
גם־בוש לא־יבשו	b	
והכלם לא ידעו	c	
לכן יפלו בנפלים	d	
בעת פקדתם יכשלו	e	
אמר יהוה		
אסף אסיפם	a	13
נאם־יהוה		
אין ענבים בגפן	b	

ואין תאנים בתאנה	c	
והעלה נבל	d	
ואתן להם יעברום	e	
על־מה אנחנו ישבים	a	14
האספו ונבוא	b	
אל־ערי המבצר	c	
ונדמה־שם	d	
כי יהוה אלהינו הדמנו	e	
וישקנו מי־ראש	f	
כי חטאנו ליהוה	g	
קוה לשלום ואין טוב	a	8:15
לעת מרפה והנה בעתה	b	
מדן נשמע נחרת סוסיו	a	16
מקול מצהלות אביריו	b	
רעשה כל־הארץ	c	
ויבואו ויאכלו ארץ ומלואה	d	
עיר וישבי בה	e	
כי הנני משלח בכם	a	17
נחשים צפענים	b	
אשר אין־להם לחש	c	
ונשכו אתכם	d	
נאם־יהוה		
text		18
הנה־קול שועת בת־עמי	a	19
מארץ מרחקים	b	
היהוה אין בציון	c	
אם־מלכה אין בה	d	
מדוע הכעסוני בפסליהם	e	
בהבלי נכר	f	
עבר קציר	a	8:20
כלה קיץ	b	
ואנחנו לוא נושענו	c	
על־שבר בת־עמי השברתי	a	21
קדרתי שמה החזקתני	b	
הצרי אין בגלעד	a	22
אם־רפא אין שם	b	
כי מדוע לא עלתה	c	
ארכת בת־עמי	d	

מי־יתן ראשי מים	a	23
ועיני מקור דמעה	b	
ואבכה יומם ולילה	c	
את חללי בת־עמי	d	
מי־יתנני במדבר	a	9:1
מלון ארחים	b	
ואעזבה את־עמי	c	
ואלכה מאתם	d	
כי כלם מנאפים	e	
עצרת בגדים	f	
וידרכו את־לשונם קשת *	a	2
משקר ולא לאמונה גברו בארץ *	b	
כי מרעה אל־רעה יצאו	c	
ואתי לא־ידעו	d	
נאם־יהוה		
איש מרעהו השמרו	a	3
ועל־כל־אח אל־תבטחו	b	
כי כל־אח עקוב יעקב	c	
וכל־רע רכיל יהלך	d	
ואיש ברעהו יהתלו	a	4
ואמת לא ידברו	b	
למדו לשונם דבר־שקר	c	
text		
text		9:5
prose		6
הנני צורפם ובחנתים	a	
כי־איך אעשה מפני בת־עמי	b	
חץ שוחט לשונם	a	7
מרמה דבר בפיו	b	
שלום את־רעהו ידבר	c	
ובקרבו ישים ארבו	d	
העל־אלה לא־אפקד־בם	a	8
נאם־יהוה		
אם בגוי אשר־כזה	b	
לא תתנקם נפשי	c	
על־ההרים אשא בכי ונהי	a	9
ועל־נאות מדבר קינה	b	
כי נצתו מבלי־איש עבר	c	

d	ולא שמעו קול מקנה
e	מעוף השמים ועד־בהמה
f	נדדו הלכו
a 9:10	ונתתי את־ירושלם לגלים
b	מעון תנים
c	ואת־ערי יהודה אתן שממה
d	מבלי יושב
prose 11	
a	על־מה אברה הארץ
b	נצתה כמדבר מבלי עבר
prose 9:16	
text	
text 17	
a	ותשנה עלינו נהי
b	ותרדנה עינינו דמעה
c	ועפעפינו יזלו־מים
a 18	כי קול נהי
b	נשמע מציון
c	איך שדדנו
d	בשנו מאד
e	כי־עזבנו ארץ
f	כי השליכו משכנותינו
a 19	כי־שמענה נשים דבר־יהוה
b	ותקח אזנכם דבר־פיו
c	ולמדנה בנותיכם נהי
d	ואשה רעותה קינה
a 9:20	כי־עלה מות בחלונינו
b	בא בארמנותינו
c	להכרית עולל מחוץ
d	בחורים מרחבות
prose 21	
a	ונפלה נבלת האדם
b	כרמן על־פני השדה
c	וכעמיר מאחרי הקצר
d	ואין מאסף
prose 22	
a	אל־יתהלל חכם בחכמתו

b	ואל־יתהלל הגבור בגבורתו
c	אל־יתהלל עשיר בעשרו
a 23	כי אם־בזאת יתהלל המתהלל
b	השכל וידע אותי
c	כי אני יהוה עשה חסד
d	משפט וצדקה בארץ
e	כי־באלה חפצתי
	נאם־יהוה

prose 10:2	
a	אל־דרך הגוים אל־תלמדו
b	ומאתות השמים אל־תחתו
c	כי־יחתו הגוים מהמה
a 3	כי־חקות העמים הבל הוא
b	כי־עץ מיער כרתו
c	מעשה ידי־חרש במעצד
a 4	בכסף ובזהב ייפהו
b	במסמרות ובמקבות
c	יחזקום ולוא יפיק
a 10:5	כתמר מקשה המה ולא ידברו
b	נשוא ינשוא כי לא יצעדו
c	אל־תיראו מהם כי־לא ירעו
d	וגם־היטיב אין אותם
a 6	מאין כמוך יהוה
b	גדול אתה
c	וגדול שמך בגבורה
a 7	מי לא יראך
b	מלך הגוים
c	כי לך יאתה
d	כי בכל־חכמי הגוים
e	ובכל־מלכותם
f	מאין כמוך
a 8	ובאחת יבערו ויכסלו
b	מוסר הבלים עץ הוא
a 9	כסף מרקע
b	מתרשיש יבוא
c	וזהב מאופז
d	מעשה חרש וידי צורף

תכלת וארגמן לבושם	e	
מעשה חכמים כלם	f	
ויהוה אלהים אמת הוא־	a	10:10
אלהים חיים ומלך עולם	b	
מקצפו תרעש הארץ	c	
ולא־יכלו גוים זעמו	d	
aramaic		11
עשה ארץ בכחו	a	12
מכין תבל בחכמתו	b	
ובתבונתו נטה שמים	c	
לקול תתו המון מים בשמים	a	13
ויעלה נשאים מקצה ארץ	b	
ברקים למטר עשה	c	
ויוצא רוח מאצרתיו	d	
נבער כל־אדם מדעת	a	14
הביש כל־צורף מפסל	b	
כי שקר נסכו	c	
ולא־רוח בם	d	
הבל המה	a	10:15
מעשה תעתעים	b	
בעת פקדתם יאבדו	c	
לא־כאלה חלק יעקב	a	16
כי־יוצר הכל הוא	b	
וישראל שבט נחלתו	c	
יהוה צבאות שמו	d	
text		17
prose, text		18
אוי לי על־שברי	a	19
נחלה מכתי	b	
ואני אמרתי	c	
אך זה חלי ואשאנו	d	
אהלי שדד	a	10:20
וכל־מיתרי נתקו	b	
בני יצאני ואינם	c	
אין־נטה עוד אהלי	d	
ומקים יריעותי	e	
כי נבערו הרעים	a	21
ואת־יהוה לא דרשו	b	

על־כן לא השכילו	c	
וכל־מרעיתם נפוצה	d	
קול שמועה הנה באה	a	22
ורעש גדול מארץ צפון	b	
לשום את־ערי יהודה שממה	c	
מעון תנים	d	
ידעתי יהוה	a	23
כי לא לאדם דרכו	b	
לא־לאיש הלך	c	
והכין את־צעדו	d	
יסרני יהוה אך־במשפט	a	24
אל־באפך פן־תמעטני	b	
שפך חמתך	a	10:25
על־הגוים אשר לא־ידעוך	b	
ועל משפחות אשר בשמך לא קראו	c	
כי־אכלו את־יעקב ויכלהו *	d	
ואת־נוהו השמו	e	
מה לידידי בביתי	a	11:15
עשותה המזמתה	b	
text		
זית רענן יפה תאר *	a	16
קרא יהוה שמך	b	
לקול המולה גדלה	c	
הצית אש עליה	d	
ורעו דליותיו	e	
ויהוה צבאות שפט צדק	a	11:20
בחן כליות ולב	b	
אראה נקמתך מהם	c	
כי אליך גליתי את־ריבי	d	
צדיק אתה יהוה	a	12:1
כי אריב אליך	b	
אך משפטים אדבר אותך	c	
מדוע דרך רשעים צלחה	d	
שלו כל־בגדי בגד	e	
נטעתם גם־שרשו	a	2

ילכו גם־עשו פרי	b	
קרוב אתה בפיהם	c	
ורחוק מכליותיהם	d	
ואתה יהוה ידעתני *	a	3
ובחנת לבי אתך	b	
התקם כצאן לטבחה	c	
והקדשם ליום הרגה	d	
עד־מתי תאבל הארץ	a	4
ועשב כל־השדה ייבש	b	
מרעת ישבי־בה	c	
ספתה בהמות ועוף	d	
כי אמרו לא יראה את־אחריתנו	e	
כי את־רגלים רצתה וילאוך	a	12:5
ואיך תתחרה את־הסוסים	b	
ובארץ שלום אתה בוטח	c	
ואיך תעשה בגאון הירדן	d	
כי גם־אחיך ובית־אביך	a	6
גם־המה בגדו בך	b	
גם־המה קראו אחריך מלא	c	
אל־תאמן בם	d	
כי־ידברו אליך טובות	e	
עזבתי את־ביתי	a	7
נטשתי את־נחלתי	b	
נתתי את־ידדות נפשי	c	
בכף איביה	d	
היתה־לי נחלתי	a	8
כאריה ביער	b	
נתנה עלי בקולה	c	
על־כן שנאתיה	d	
העיט צבוע נחלתי לי	a	9
העיט סביב עליה	b	
לכו אספו כל־חית השדה	c	
התיו לאכלה	d	
רעים רבים שחתו כרמי	a	12:10
בססו את־חלקתי	b	
נתנו את־חלקת חמדתי	c	
למדבר שממה	d	
שמה לשממה	a	11

אבלה עלי שממה	b	
נשמה כל־הארץ	c	
כי אין איש שם על־לב	d	
על־כל־שפים במדבר	a	12
באו שדדים	b	
prose		
זרעו חטים	a	13
וקצים קצרו	b	
נחלו לא יועלו	c	
ובשו מתבואתיכם	d	
מחרון אף־יהוה	e	
שמעו והאזינו אל־תגבהו	a	13:15
כי יהוה דבר	b	
תנו ליהוה אלהיכם כבוד	a	16
בטרם יחשך	b	
ובטרם יתנגפו רגליכם	c	
על־הרי נשף	d	
וקויתם לאור	e	
ושמה לצלמות	f	
ישית לערפל	g	
ואם לא תשמעוה	a	17
במסתרים תבכה־נפשי	b	
מפני גוה	c	
ודמע תדמע	d	
ותרד עיני דמעה	e	
כי נשבה עדר יהוה	f	
אמר למלך ולגבירה	a	18
השפילו שבו	b	
כי ירד מראשותיכם	c	
עטרת תפארתכם	d	
ערי הנגב סגרו	a	19
ואין פתח	b	
הגלת יהודה כלה	c	
גלת שלמה *	d	
שאי עיניך *	a	13:20
וראי הבאים מצפון	b	
איה העדר נתן־לך	c	

צאן תפארתך	d	
מה־תאמרי כי־יפקד עליך	a	21
ואת למדת אתם	b	
עליך אלפים לראש	c	
הלוא חבלים יאחזוך	d	
כמו אשת לדה	e	
וכי תאמרי בלבבך	a	22
מדוע קראני אלה	b	
ברב עונך נגלו שוליך	c	
נחמסו עקביך	d	
היהפך כושי עורו	a	23
ונמר חברברתיו	b	
גם־אתם תוכלו להיטיב	c	
למדי הרע	d	
ואפיצם כקש־עובר	a	24
לרוח מדבר	b	
זה גורלך	a	13:25
מנת־מדיך מאתי	b	
נאם־יהוה		
אשר שכחת אותי	c	
ותבטחי בשקר	d	
וגם־אני חשפתי	a	26
שוליך על־פניך	b	
ונראה קלונך	c	
נאפיך ומצהלותיך	a	27
זמת זנותך	b	
על־גבעות בשדה	c	
ראיתי שקוציך	d	
אוי לך ירושלם	e	
לא תטהרי אחרי *	f	
עד מתי עד *	g	
אבלה יהודה	a	14:2
ושעריה אמללו	b	
קדרו לארץ	c	
וצוחת ירושלם עלתה	d	
ואדריהם שלחו צעוריהם למים	a	3
באו על־גבים	b	

לא־מצאו מים	c	
שבו כליהם ריקם	d	
בשו והכלמו	e	
וחפו ראשם	f	
בעבור האדמה חתה	a	4
כי לא־היה גשם בארץ	b	
בשו אכרים	c	
חפו ראשם	d	
כי גם־אילת בשדה ילדה ועזוב	a	14:5
כי לא־היה דשא	b	
ופראים עמדו על־שפים	a	6
שאפו רוח כתנים	b	
כלו עיניהם	c	
כי־אין עשב	d	
אם־עונינו ענו בנו	a	7
יהוה עשה למענך *	b	
כי־רבו משובתינו	c	
לך חטאנו	d	
מקוה ישראל	a	8
מושיעו בעת צרה	b	
למה תהיה כגר בארץ	c	
וכארח נטה ללון	d	
למה תהיה כאיש נדהם	a	9
כגבור לא־יוכל להושיע	b	
ואתה בקרבנו יהוה	c	
ושמך עלינו נקרא	d	
אל־תנחנו	e	

	prose	14:17
תרדנה עיני דמעה	a	
לילה ויומם ואל־תדמינה	b	
כי שבר נשברה בת־עמי *	c	
מכה נחלה מאד	d	
אם־יצאתי השדה	a	18
והנה חללי־חרב	b	
ואם באתי העיר	c	
והנה תחלואי רעב	d	
כי־גם־נביא גם־כהן	e	

סחרו אל־ארץ לא ידעו *	f	
המאס מאסת את־יהודה	a	19
אם־בציון געלה נפשך	b	
מרוע הכיתנו	c	
ואין לנו מרפא	d	
קוה לשלום ואין טוב	e	
ולעת מרפא והנה בעתה	f	
ידענו יהוה רשענו	a	14:20
עון אבותינו	b	
כי חטאנו לך	c	
אל־תנאץ למען שמך	a	21
אל־תנבל כסא כבודך	b	
זכר אל־תפר בריתך אתנו	c	
היש בהבלי הגוים מגשמים	a	22
ואם־השמים יתנו רבבים	b	
text		
prose		

prose		15:2
אשר למות למות	a	
ואשר לחרב לחרב	b	
ואשר לרעב לרעב	c	
ואשר לשבי לשבי	d	

כי מי־יחמל עליך ירושלם	a	5
ומי ינוד לך	b	
ומי יסור	c	
לשאל לשלם לך	d	
את נטשת אתי	a	6
נאם־יהוה		
אחור תלכי	b	
ואט את־ידי *	c	
ואשחיתך	d	
נלאיתי הנחם	e	
ואזרם במזרה	a	7
בשערי הארץ	b	
שכלתי אבדתי את־עמי	c	
מדרכיהם לוא־שבו	d	

עצמו־לי אלמנתו	a	8
מחול ימים	b	
הבאתי על־אם בחור *	c	
שדד בצהרים	d	
הפלתי עליה פתאם	e	
עיר ובהלות	f	
אמללה ילדת השבעה	a	9
נפחה נפשה	b	
באה שמשה בעד יומם	c	
בושה וחפרה	d	
ושאריתם לחרב אתן	e	
לפני איביהם	f	
נאם־יהוה		
אוי־לי אמי כי ילדתני	a	15:10
איש ריב ומדון לכל־הארץ *	b	
לא־נשיתי ולא־נשו־בי	c	
כלהם קללוני *	d	
text		11
הירע ברזל	a	12
ברזל מצפון ונחשת	b	
cf. 17:3-4		13-14
אתה ידעת יהוה	a	15:15
זכרני ופקדני	b	
והנקם לי מרדפי	c	
אל־לארך אפך תקחני	d	
דע שאתי עליך חרפה	e	
נמצאו דבריך ואכלם	a	16
ויהי דבריך לי לששון	b	
ולשמחת לבבי	c	
כי־נקרא שמך עלי	d	
יהוה אלהי צבאות	e	
לא־ישבתי בסוד־משחקים ואעלז	a	17
מפני ידך בדד ישבתי	b	
כי־זעם מלאתני	c	
למה היה כאבי נצח	a	18
ומכתי אנושה	b	
מאנה הרפא	c	
היו תהיה לי כמו אכזב	d	

מים לא נאמנו	e	
prose		19
אם־תשוב ואשיבך	a	
לפני תעמד	b	
ואם־תוציא יקר מזולל	c	
כפי תהיה	d	
ישבו המה אליך	e	
ואתה לא־תשוב אליהם	f	
ונתתיך לעם הזה	a	15:20
לחומת נחשת בצורה	b	
ונלחמו אליך	c	
ולא־יוכלו לך	d	
כי־אתך אני	e	
להושיעך ולהצילך	f	
נאם־יהוה		
והצלתיך מיד רעים	a	21
ופדיתיך מכף ערצים	b	
יהוה עזי ומעזי	a	16:19
ומנוסי ביום צרה	b	
אליך גוים יבאו	c	
מאפסי־ארץ ויאמרו	d	
אך־שקר נחלו אבותינו	e	
הבל ואין־בם מועיל	f	
היעשה־לו אדם אלהים	a	20
והמה לא אלהים	b	
לכן הנני מודיעם	a	21
בפעם הזאת אודיעם	b	
את־ידי ואת־גבורתי	c	
וידעו כי־שמי יהוה	d	
חטאת יהודה כתובה	a	17:1
בעט ברזל	b	
בצפרן שמיר חרושה	c	
על־לוח לבם	d	
ולקרנות מזבחותיכם	e	
prose		2
prose		3
חילך וכל־אוצרותיך *	a	

לבז אתן	b	
במחיר בכל־חטאותיך *	c	
בכל־גבוליך	d	
ושמטתה ידך מנחלתך *	a	4
אשר נתתי לך	b	
והעבדתיך את־איביך	c	
בארץ לא־ידעת *	d	
כי־אש קדחה באפי *	e	
עד־עולם תוקד	f	
prose		17:5
ארור הגבר	a	
אשר יבטח באדם	b	
ושם בשר זרעו	c	
ומן־יהוה יסור לבו	d	
והיה כערער בערבה	a	6
ולא יראה כי־יבוא טוב	b	
ושכן חררים במדבר	c	
ארץ מלחה ולא תשב	d	
ברוך הגבר	a	7
אשר יבטח ביהוה	b	
והיה יהוה מבטחו	c	
והיה כעץ שתול על־מים	a	8
ועל־יובל ישלח שרשיו	b	
ולא ירא כי־יבא חם	c	
והיה עלהו רענן	d	
ובשנת בצרת לא ידאג	e	
ולא ימיש מעשות פרי	f	
עקוב הלב מכל	a	9
ואנש הוא	b	
מי ידענו	c	
אני יהוה חקר לב	a	17:10
בחן כליות	b	
ולתת לאיש כדרכו	c	
כפרי מעלליו	d	
קרא דגר ולא ילד	a	11
עשה עשר ולא במשפט	b	
בחצי ימו יעזבנו	c	
ובאחריתו יהיה נבל	d	

כסא כבוד מרום מראשון	a	12
מקום מקדשנו	b	
מקוה ישראל יהוה	a	13
כל־עזביך יבשו	b	
יסורי בארץ יכתבו	c	
כי עזבו מקור מים־חיים *	d	
רפאני יהוה וארפא	a	14
הושיעני ואושעה	b	
כי תהלתי אתה	c	
הנה־המה אמרים אלי	a	17:15
איה דבר־יהוה יבוא נא	b	
ואני לא־אצתי מרעה אחריך	a	16
ויום אנוש לא התאויתי	b	
אתה ידעת מוצא שפתי	c	
נכח פניך היה	d	
אל־תהיה־לי למחתה	a	17
מחסי־אתה ביום רעה	b	
יבשו רדפי	a	18
ואל־אבשה אני	b	
יחתו המה	c	
ואל־אחתה אני	d	
הביא עליהם יום רעה	e	
ומשנה שברון שברם	f	

prose		18:13
שאלו־נא בגוים	a	
מי שמע כאלה	b	
שערות עשתה מאד	c	
בתולת ישראל	d	
היעזב מצור שדי	a	14
שלג לבנון	b	
אם־ינתשו מים זרים	c	
קרים נוזלים	d	
כי־שכחני עמי	a	18:15
לשוא יקטרו	b	
ויכשלום בדרכיהם	c	
שבילי עולם	d	
ללכת נתיבות	e	

דרך לא סלולה	f	
לשום ארצם לשמה	a	16
שרוקת עולם	b	
כל עובר עליה ישם	c	
ויניד בראשו	d	
כרוח־קדים אפיצם	a	17
לפני אויב	b	
ערף ולא־פנים אראם	c	
ביום אידם	d	
prose		18
הקשיבה יהוה אלי	a	19
ושמע לקול יריבי	b	
הישלם תחת־טובה רעה	a	18:20
כי־כרו שוחה לנפשי	b	
זכר עמדי לפניך	c	
לדבר עליהם טובה	d	
להשיב את־חמתך מהם	e	
לכן תן את־בניהם לרעב	a	21
והגרם על־ידי־חרב	b	
ותהינה נשיהם שכלות ואלמנות	c	
ואנשיהם יהיו הרגי מות	d	
בחוריהם מכי־חרב במלחמה	e	
תשמע זעקה מבתיהם	a	22
כי־תביא עליהם גדוד פתאם	b	
כי־כרו שיחה ללכדני	c	
ופחים טמנו לרגלי	d	
ואתה יהוה ידעת	a	23
את־כל־עצתם עלי למות	b	
אל־תכפר על־עונם	c	
וחטאתם מלפניך אל־תמחי	d	
והיו מכשלים לפניך	e	
בעת אפך עשה בהם	f	
פתיתני יהוה ואפת	a	20:7
חזקתני ותוכל	b	
הייתי לשחוק כל־היום	c	
כלה לעג לי	d	
כי־מדי אדבר אזעק	a	8

חמס ושׁר אקרא	b	
כי־היה דבר־יהוה לי לחרפה	c	
ולקלס כל־היום	d	
ואמרתי לא־אזכרנו	a	9
ולא־אדבר עוד בשׁמו	b	
והיה בלבי כאשׁ בערת	c	
עצר בעצמתי	d	
נלאיתי כלכל	e	
ולא אוכל לשׂאת *	f	
כי שׁמעתי דבת רבים	a	20:10
מגור מסביב	b	
הגידו ונגידנו	c	
כל אנושׁ שׁלומי	d	
שׁמרי צלעי	e	
אולי יפתה ונוכלה לו	f	
ונקחה נקמתנו ממנו	g	
ויהוה אותי כגבור עריץ	a	11
על־כן רדפי יכשׁלו ולא יכלו	b	
בשׁו מאד כי־לא השׂכילו	c	
כלמת עולם לא תשׁכח	d	
ויהוה צבאות בחן צדיק	a	12
ראה כליות ולב	b	
אראה נקמתך מהם	c	
כי אליך גליתי את־ריבי	d	
שׁירו ליהוה	a	13
הללו את־יהוה	b	
כי הציל את־נפשׁ אביון	c	
מיד מרעים	d	
ארור היום	a	14
אשׁר ילדתי בו	b	
יום אשׁר־ילדתני אמי	c	
אל־יהי ברוך	d	
ארור האישׁ	a	20:15
אשׁר בשׂר את־אבי לאמר	b	
ילד־לך בן זכר	c	
שׂמח שׂמחהו	d	
והיה האישׁ ההוא כערים	a	16
אשׁר־הפך יהוה ולא נחם	b	

ושמע זעקה בבקר	c
ותרועה בעת צהרים	d
אשר לא־מותתני מרחם	a 17
ותהי־לי אמי קברי	b
ורחמה הרת עולם	c
למה זה מרחם יצאתי	a 18
לראות עמל ויגון	b
ויכלו בבשת ימי	c

prose	21:12
דינו לבקר משפט	a
והצילו גזול מיד עושק	b
פן־תצא כאש חמתי	c
ובערה ואין מכבה	d
text	
הנני אליך ישבת העמק	a 13
צור המישר	b
נאם־יהוה	
האמרים מי־יחת עלינו	c
ומי יבוא במעונותינו	d
text, prose	14
והצתי אש ביערה	a
ואכלה כל־סביביה	b

גלעד אתה לי	a 22:6
ראש הלבנון	b
אם־לא אשיתך מדבר	c
ערים לא נושבה	d
וקדשתי עליך משחתים	a 7
איש וכליו	b
וכרתו מבחר ארזיך	c
והפילו על־האש	d

אל־תבכו למת	a 22:10
ואל־תנדו לו	b
בכו בכו להלך	c
כי לא ישוב עוד	d
וראה את־ארץ מולדתו	e

הוי בנה ביתו בלא־צדק	a	13
ועליותיו בלא משפט	b	
ברעהו יעבד חנם	c	
ופעלו לא יתן־לו	d	
האמר אבנה־לי בית מדות	a	14
ועליות מרוחים	b	
וקרע לו חלוני *	c	
ספון בארז *	d	
ומשוח בששר	e	
התמלך כי אתה מתחרה בארז	a	22:15
אביך הלוא אכל ושתה	b	
ועשה משפט וצדקה	c	
אז טוב לו	d	
דן דין־עני ואביון	a	16
text		
הלוא־היא הדעת אתי נאם־יהוה	b	
כי אין עיניך	a	17
ולבך כי אם־על־בצעך	b	
ועל דם־הנקי לשפוך	c	
ועל־העשק ועל־המרוצה לעשות	d	
prose		18
לא־יספדו לו	a	
הוי אחי	b	
והוי אחות	c	
לא־יספדו לו	d	
הוי אדון	e	
והוי הרה	f	
קבורת חמור יקבר	a	19
סחוב והשלך	b	
מהלאה לשערי ירושלם	c	
עלי הלבנון וצעקי	a	22:20
ובבשן תני קולך	b	
וצעקי מעברים	c	
כי נשברו כל־מאהביך	d	
דברתי אליך בשלותיך	a	21
אמרת לא אשמע	b	

זה דרכך מנעוריך	c	
כי לא־שמעת בקולי	d	
כל־רעיך תרעה־רוח	a	22
ומאהביך בשבי ילכו	b	
כי אז תבשי ונכלמת	c	
מכל רעתך	d	
ישבתי בלבנון	a	23
מקננתי בארזים	b	
מה־נחנת בבא־לך חבלים	c	
חיל כילדה	d	
text		22:28
ארץ ארץ ארץ	a	29
שמעי דבר־יהוה	b	
prose		30
כתבו את־האיש הזה ערירי	a	
גבר לא־יצלח בימיו	b	
כי לא יצלח מזרעו איש	c	
ישב על־כסא דוד	d	
ומשל עוד ביהודה	e	
הנה ימים באים	a	23:5
נאם־יהוה		
והקמתי לדוד צמח צדיק	b	
ומלך מלך והשכיל	c	
ועשה משפט וצדקה בארץ	d	
בימיו תושע יהודה	a	6
וישראל ישכן לבטח	b	
וזה־שמו אשר־יקראו	c	
יהוה צדקנו	d	
נשבר לבי בקרבי	a	9
רחפו כל־עצמותי	b	
הייתי כאיש שכור	c	
וכגבר עברו יין	d	
מפני יהוה	e	
ומפני דברי קדשו	f	
כי מנאפים מלאה הארץ	a	23:10

כי מפני אלה אבלה הארץ	b	
יבשו נאות מדבר	c	
ותהי מרוצתם רעה	d	
וגבורתם לא־כן	e	
כי־גם־נביא גם־כהן חנפו	a	11
גם־בביתי מצאתי רעתם	b	
נאם־יהוה		
לכן יהיה דרכם להם	a	12
כחלקלקות באפלה	b	
ידחו ונפלו בה	c	
כי־אביא עליהם רעה	d	
שנת פקדתם	e	
ובנביאי שמרון ראיתי תפלה	a	13
הנבאו בבעל	b	
ויתעו את־עמי את־ישראל	c	
ובנביאי ירושלם ראיתי שערורה	a	14
נאוף והלך בשקר	b	
וחזקו ידי מרעים	c	
לבלתי־שבו איש מרעתו	d	
היו־לי כלם כסדם	e	
וישביה כעמרה	f	
prose		23:15
הנני מאכיל אותם לענה	a	
והשקתים מי־ראש	b	
כי מאת נביאי ירושלם	c	
יצאה חנפה לכל־הארץ	d	
prose		16
אל־תשמעו על־דברי הנבאים	a	
הנבאים לכם	b	
מהבלים המה אתכם	c	
חזון לבם ידברו	d	
לא מפי יהוה	e	
אמרים אמור למנאצי דבר יהוה *	a	17
שלום יהיה לכם	b	
וכל הלך בשררות לבו אמרו	c	
לא־תבוא עליכם רעה	d	
הנה סערת יהוה חמה יצאה	a	19

וסער מתחולל	b	
על ראש רשעים יחול	c	
לא ישוב אף־יהוה עד־עשתו	a	23:20
ועד־הקימו מזמות לבו	b	
באחרית הימים תתבוננו בה *	c	
לא־שלחתי את־הנבאים	a	21
והם רצו	b	
לא־דברתי אליהם	c	
והם נבאו	d	
ואם־עמדו בסודי	a	22
וישמעו דברי את־עמי	b	
וישבום מדרכם הרע	·c	
ומרע מעלליהם	d	
האלהי מקרב אני	a	23
נאם־יהוה		
ולא אלהי מרחק	b	
אם־יסתר איש במסתרים	a	24
ואני לא־אראנו	b	
נאם־יהוה		
הלוא את־השמים ואת־הארץ	c	
אני מלא	d	
נאם־יהוה		

prose		23:28
מה־לתבן את־הבר	a	
נאם־יהוה		
הלוא כה דברי כאש	a	29
נאם־יהוה		
וכפטיש יפצץ סלע	b	

prose		25:30
יהוה ממרום ישאג	a	
וממעון קדשו יתן קולו	b	
שאג ישאג על־נוהו	c	
הידד כדרכים יענה	d	
אל כל־ישבי הארץ	e	
בא שאון עד־קצה הארץ	a	31
כי ריב ליהוה בגוים	b	

נשפט הוא לכל־בשר c
הרשעים נתנם לחרב d
נאם־יהוה

prose 32

הנה רעה יצאת a
מגוי אל־גוי b
וסער גדול יעור c
מירכתי־ארץ d

הילילו הרעים וזעקו a 34
והתפלשו אדירי הצאן b
כי־מלאו ימיכם לטבוח c

text

ונפלתם ככלי חמרה d
ואבד מנוס מן־הרעים a 25:35
ופליטה מאדירי הצאן b
קול צעקת הרעים a 36
יללת אדירי הצאן b
כי־שדד יהוה את־מרעיתם c
ונדמו נאות השלום a 37
מפני חרון אף־יהוה b
עזב ככפיר סכו a 38
כי־היתה ארצם לשמה b
מפני חרון היונה c
ומפני חרון אפו d

4.2.2 Grounds for our colon delimitation

2:4a cannot be subdivided in 3 + 2 units, producing a count of 2 + 1 main stresses, for then 4b would have to be divided as well. Such subdivision of 4b is impossible, seeing that it consists of only one constituent, namely a threefold construct relation.

2:5a cannot be subdivided in 3 + 2 units, for the first and the last unit in this colon belong to the same constituent. All the consulted sources are in agreement with this delimitation.

2:5c was treated as a prose addition by Cornill (1901, 1) and Loretz (1970, 114), because the exact words also occur in 2 Kg 17:15. Giesebrecht (1905, 2) regarded וילכו as part of 5b and deleted the rest of the verse. Our colon 2:5c cannot be subdivided before the last verb, as in BHS and by commentators generally, because that would produce a fourth colon of only one unit. We have no indication that such cola existed in biblical verse, unless we assume the existence of incomplete cola in Hebrew verse, used for expressive purposes (Van Selms, 1972, 44). The supposed incomplete cola are not to be confused with Fohrer's (1967) *Kurzvers* which is a monocolon and which can be quite long. The examples of such incomplete or "truncated" cola cited by Collins (1978a, 253-255) are not convincing, because they are either delimited incorrectly or must be regarded as cola of two units. To our mind 5c is rather a case where action and result are both described in one and the same colon, as in 4:24a, 4:25a, and 4:26a; cf. Thompson (1980, 165).

2:8a should not be subdivided as in BHS because of its clear parallelism to 8b and 8c which are indivisible. The only difference between it and 2:6a is the presence of an explicit subject. This subject, being only one unit, does not provide any reason to subdivide into two cola.

2:10 was not delimited into cola by Duhm, Collins, EÜ and ANV. After deleting the first וראו Cornill (1901, 2), Rudolph (1968, 14), JB and DLB read the verse as a double 3 + 2, with colon boundaries before וקדר and הן. Loretz (1970, 115) deleted both the first וראו and מאד, dividing the remainder as we do. It is significant that Rudolph in both BHK and BHS delimited the same three cola as we do, in contrast with the view expressed in his commentary. The same colon delimitation also was made by Giesebrecht (1905, 3), Wambacq

(1957, 35), Bright (1965, 11), Thompson (1980, 166), Weiser (1981, 12), RSV, NEB and NIV. Our colon 10a clearly cannot be subdivided. It is paralleled syntactically and semantically by 10b, which also, therefore, is indivisible, the only difference being that in 10b each verb has a nominal argument. We note that 10c begins by repeating the last word of 10a. Repetition of last word as first word is not unusual, and is an aid in colon delimitation, although it might be unusual to find an intervening colon as here; cf. 4:5bcd.

2:11d is an apparent one unit colon, seeing that neither the preposition nor the negation normally counts as a unit. Here, however, the word בלוא counts as a unit. The colon is a prepositional phrase, dependent on the verb in 11c and containing an embedded clause. From it a nominal element has been suppressed (GKC, par. 155n). Such suppression or ellipsis of the nominal element gives the negation a quasi-nominal status.

2:14ab could conceivably have been taken together as one colon. Had that been the intention of the poet, however, he would have done better without the then syntactically and metrically unnecessary הוא which only makes the supposed long colon even longer. In fact the presence of the pronoun indicates clearly that we have three questions in parallel in verse 14, of which the first and second are syntactically and semantically parallel, while the third provides the reason for asking the first and second. Cf. Van Selms (1972, 272-273) and Watson (1984, 340-341).

2:18a in spite of its length should not be subdivided. The strongly repetitive parallelism of verse 18 makes it quite clear that 18a is parallel to 18c, and that subdivision both of 18c and 18a is uncalled for.

2:21c and 21d we have emended, accepting, like all the commentaries consulted, the emendation suggested by Duhm (1901, 25). Similar, though not identical, emendations were suggested by Cornill (1901, 2) and Giesebrecht (1905, 4) in their delimitations of the cola. The cola are within accepted limits either way.

2:27a cannot be divided 2 + 2 in spite of the prominent syntactic boundary, due to its parallel 27b being indivisible.

2:27cd was usually divided after ערף as in BHS, but 27d then is abnormally short whether measured in terms of stresses or of units. Another possibility would be to take 27c and 27d together as one

colon, which, however, seems too long for this context. Our delimitation was suggested as a possibility, but not preferred, by Collins
(1978a, 291). In 18:17c עֶרֶף וְלֹא פָנִים indubitably occur together in
one colon. An additional advantage of our delimitation is that it more
forcibly contrasts פָנִים not only with עֶרֶף, as would otherwise have
been the case, but also with its cognate פְּנוּ.

2:28 was divided into four cola in BHS, two long followed by two
short, which to our mind is wrong. It would be possible to combine
BHS's last two cola, producing a third long colon for the verse. It is
striking, however, that the most prominent syntactic boundaries
within each of these supposed three long cola are all immediately
preceded by the same suffix, forming a kind of rhyme. We, therefore,
divide according to these boundaries, as did RSV, producing six cola,
all twos and threes. For 28a-d this was also the colon delimitation of
DLB and of Duhm (1901, 29) as indicated by the use of capitals in his
translation. The fact that the last colon of the verse has the suffix at
its second last word does not detract from the significance of its
previous occurrences at syntactic boundaries.

2:31cd we divide like all the consulted commentaries and translations except JB and ANV, which incorrectly regarded רְדֶנּוּ as a
separate colon. O'Connor (1980a, 304, 323) counted מַדּוּעַ as a
predicator because of its etymology and its length. Accordingly our
colon 31c would then have three major clause predicators as well as a
dependent nominal phrase, which combination is not allowed in one
and the same colon by O'Connor's (1980a, 87) theory or ours. He
would, therefore, be forced to divide 31cd before רְדֶנּוּ or its text
critical substitute, which could only be another verb (Bright, 1965, 16;
Rudolph, 1968, 20) and which would, thus, not make any difference to
the delimitation of cola. Such division would create two very unequal
cola and destroy the parallelism. We regard 31cd as proof that מַדּוּעַ
in spite of its etymology (cf. GKC, 99e; HAL, 520), cannot have
predicator status within the colometric system.

3:1e was treated as two cola in BHS, which places unwarranted
emphasis on הָאָרֶץ הַהִיא and is unnecessary in terms of colon
length. Wambacq (1957, 41) and Weiser (1981, 24) translated it as
one colon.

3:2ab was divided after וּרְאִי in BHS, i.e. into two unequal cola of
4 + 2 units with both verbs in 2a. Our division lets each colon begin

with a verb - they are morphologically identical - followed by its direct object. In 2:10c the same root, also in the Qal imperative, begins the colon, its direct object being, as here, an embedded clause which completes the colon. Cf. also 2:23c and especially 13:20ab.

3:5cd was usually divided 3 + 2 as in BHS. Wambacq (1957, 42) regarded only the last word as 5d. We divide at the most prominent syntactical boundary. As this is the end of a section of text, a colon longer than the preceding ones is not out of place here.

3:12a-15 was taken as verse by Thompson (1980, 198). Others thought that the poetry ended with 14 (DLB), or with 13 (JB; NEB; BHS). Wambacq (1957, 44) took only up to 13b as verse. We follow him in order not to include any possible prose.

3:23a in the MT is syntactically difficult. Cornill (1901, 4) deleted the מ from מגבעות. Duhm (1901, 43), Rudolph (168, 28) and Weiser 1981, 25) replaced the מ with the definite article. We follow Bright and Van Selms in redividing the second and third words, i.e. adding the מ to לשקר. This leaves two possible interpretations, namely that the מ is enclitic (Bright, 1965, 20; Thompson, 1980, 204 n.7) or that it is the plural ending written defectively (Van Selms, 1972, 81). All four views could be claimed to be in agreement with the Septuagint, the Peshitta and the Vulgate. There is no uncertainty on the delimitation of the cola.

3:23b we have changed the first vowel so as to have a construct relation between the two nouns, again in agreement with the Septuagint, Peshitta and Vulgate, as well as a number of Hebrew manuscripts. This emendation was accepted by all the commentaries consulted.

3:24-25 seems to be a mixture of prose and verse. Wambacq (1957, 47) took the whole of these two verses as prose. Possibly it is a prose reworking of a verse passage. Note that the same expression is used towards the end of 25 as at the end of 3:13 and that there also prose and verse are difficult to distinguish.

4:1d in spite of the presence of the waw - which is absent in some manuscripts and not reflected in the ancient versions - begins with the prepositional phrase, which belongs syntactically to this colon and not to the preceding (GKC, par. 143d).

4:4ab we divide one word earlier than BHS in accordance with the most prominent syntactical boundary and with semantic parallelism,

producing cola of 2 + 3 units. Note that also 4:5 begins with cola of
2 + 3 units, as does 14:18.

4:5 twice contains the verb ואמרו, and both occurrences have been
doubted, e.g. by Rudolph (1968, 32). In the light of the chiastic
arrangement of constituents in 5a and 5b the occurrence in 5b does at
first sight seem intrusive. Althann (1983, 39) tried to resolve the
seeming intrusiveness by assuming both occurrences to be "interspersed imperatives" which do belong to the text, but not to any
colon. The objection to the first occurrence on the grounds that it
refers to an action which should chronologically follow rather than
precede the blowing of the trumpet, is mistaken, for chronologically
the blowing of the trumpet should precede all the actions of 5a and
5b. Rather than describing chronological sequence the poet gives a
vivid impression of the tumult and confusion. Parallelistic verse lends
itself well to such use, because of its inherent repetitive nature. After
proceeding in 5b to the word which would normally precede the
direct speech, the poet returns to the event which would chronologically take place first. Parallelistic verse sometimes does repeat the
last word of a colon as the last word of a later colon (Watson, 1984,
276-277). Here one colon intervenes; cf. 2:10. We, therefore, regard
both occurrences of ואמרו as possibly original, although the first
might be intrusive. Either way it would not influence our colon
delimitation.

4:5ab was divided as a bicolon of 3 + 2 units by Van Selms (1972,
87) on the grounds that the following two bicola are such. To our
mind the fact that the two prepositional phrases as well as the two
verbs are morphologically similar and that these four are in chiastic
order urges us to divide between the two prepositional phrases as in
BHS, although there this division was coupled with the deletion of
ואמרו from 5b. For other cases of 2 + 3 cf. 4:4 and 14:18.

4:5d in our delimitation differs from that of BHS and some
commentators in including the second ואמרו. There are two reasons
for this. The three imperative verbs which form our 5d are a syntactic
and semantic unity, are addressed to the same audience and are
followed by a prominent syntactical boundary, namely the beginning
of direct speech; cf. the use of ואמרו as the third of three imperatives
in one colon in 31:7c. The fact that Duhm (1901, 48) deleted the
second ואמרו and Rudolph (1968, 32) accepted a proposal of Volz to

read another verb in its place, is a direct result of its not being suited to 5e. Secondly, 5ef also appear as 8:14bc, and thus are very likely to be complete cola on their own.

4:5ef could conceivably be understood as one colon, as did Weiser (1981, 35). However, Weiser (1981, 73) did not treat 8:14bc in the same way. To our mind the cola of a passage of verse that occurs more than once should be delimited identically at every occurrence, unless there are very convincing reasons not to do so. Among the views we consulted, only Wambacq (1957, 49, 79), Bright (1965, 28, 61), Thompson (1980, 217, 301), Loretz (1970, 118, 126), JB and EÜ seem to have realised this principle. There are two reasons for dividing 5ef. The construction Imperative + וֹ + Cohortative forms a very firm unity, with the result that the syntactic boundary after it becomes more prominent. Also, the prepositional phrase here is to be seen as a somewhat independent cry, semantically almost equivalent to the preceding two verbs. Duhm (1901, 48), Bright (1965, 28), Loretz (1970, 118) and RSV delimited 5ef as we do. Giesebrecht (1905, 7), Rudolph (1968, 32), Thompson (1980, 217) and NEB also recognised the colon boundary between 5e and 5f.

4:6cd was divided as 3 + 3 units by Rudolph (1968, 32) and by Althann (1983, 39-40), who explicitly called this a case of enjambement. The only argument in favour of such a division is the more equal cola so produced. Our division into 4 + 2 units produces two quite normal cola, is based on the most prominent syntactic boundary in the bicolon, and is accepted generally by commentators and translators, significantly also by Rudolph himself in BHS.

4:7b and *7c* as divided in BHS are both semantically parallel to 7a. However, this division results in 7b being long (three units) and 7c being short (two units). One would rather expect 7b to be short after the long 7a, and 7c to be long, as is 7d. Like the Massoretes, Duhm (1901, 49) and NEB we divide before the two verbs, placing both verbs together as a ballast variant in parallelism with the very generic עלה in 7a, providing more specific and vivid meaning, נסע referring to the striking of tents (HAL, 665) and יצא to the departure of the army (HAL, 406). That the parallelism involved is between 7a and 7c, rather than between 7a and 7b, is clear from the morphologically identical prepositional phrases at the ends of both 7a and 7c. The short 7b is in the same relationship to אריה in 7a as 6d is to רעה in

6c. The occurrence of two verbs in the suffix conjugation in direct sequence in the same colon is attested elsewhere, e.g. in 9:9f, 15:17c and Jdg 5:27.

4:7e was subdivided by BHK and Van Selms (1972, 88). We see no reason to do so. Bright (1965, 28), Collins (1978a, 185), Thompson (1980, 217) and Weiser (1981, 35) treated it as one colon.

4:8c in the MT has five units and four stresses, and was treated as one colon by Weiser (1981, 35), who also incorrectly treated 8ab as one colon. Cornill (1901, 5), Duhm (1901, 49), Giesebrecht (1905, 8) and all the other commentaries consulted transposed מִמֶּנּוּ to stand after שָׁב, leaving the double construct relation as their colon 8d. There is no text critical evidence for such a transposition, and the only argument in favour of it is the argument *metri causa*. Loretz (1970, 119) and Althann (1983, 51-55) divided between חֲרוֹן and אַף, a division which requires either the revocalisation of חֲרוֹן as being in the absolute state or the acceptance of enjambement. Although the syntactically indivisible colon 4:8c in the MT is not too long in terms of the colon level constraints which we accept, it would stand out as an unusually long colon in its context. The best Greek witnesses have no equivalent for חֲרוֹן here (Ziegler, 1976, 167). Therefore, we delete חֲרוֹן, leaving 4:8c as a four unit colon with three stresses.

4:11c must syntactically include בַּמִּדְבָּר, which can only be excluded from this colon if it is emended as in BHS, for which there is no evidence. Althann (1983, 63) took בַּמִּדְבָּר as a separate one unit colon, one of five such cola which he found in verses 11-12, based on syllable count. His concept of what a colon is, is quite different from ours, his being defined solely in terms of the number of syllables and thus allowing one unit cola; cf. also Hauser (1980, 29, 34).

4:12a is an indivisible four unit colon. The word מֵאֵלֶּה, which has no equivalent in the best Greek witnesses (Ziegler, 1976, 168), probably resulted from dittography, for which reason we delete it; cf. Duhm (1901, 50), Rudolph (1968, 34), Loretz (1970, 119) and Thompson (1980, 223 n.3).

4:12bc was treated as one colon by Wambacq (1957, 50), Weiser (1981, 36), NEB, EÜ and DLB. This cannot be correct, as the supposed colon would have too many main stresses and too many constituents. Althann's (1983, 63) decision to divide both before and after the verb produces a middle colon consisting of only the verb

אדבר, which also cannot be correct. One might consider dividing before the verb so that 12c would be syntactically complete, i.e. a "core line" in the terms of O'Connor (1980a, 412-420), leaving 12b as an example of a colon consisting of an extended subject. We divide only after the verb, taking the two direct objects as the final colon of the verse, because we are of the opinion that our colon 12b can be regarded as a core colon. Our colon delimitation is the same as that of Cornill (1901, 5), Giesebrecht (1905, 8), Bright (1965, 29), Rudolph (1968, 34), Loretz (1970, 119), Collins (1978a, 78), Thompson (1980, 223) and JB. Other examples where a colon boundary occurs between the verb and its direct object are 5:15ab, 6:21ab, 8:17ab, 13:26ab, 18:23ab.

4:17a is an indivisible five unit colon with four main stresses, following two cola of four units and three main stresses each. On syntax alone it would have been allowable to subdivide after the second unit, but this would produce a first colon of only one main stress which would be out of place here.

4:17b might well include the following נאם־יהוה if we take the preceding long cola into account. We kept the phrase separate here, only to treat it consistently.

4:19bc was usually divided into three cola as in BHS. We interpret each of the first three cola of this verse as consisting of two parts. In every case the first part is a cry of pain, couched as a nominal phrase referring to an organ of the body with which the pain is associated, and the second part is a clause, syntactically independent of the preceding phrase. This is the pattern commonly accepted as regards 19a and we contend that it fits well for the rest. Note how the first part, the cry, becomes progressively shorter - in 19a it consists of two nouns, in 19b the two nouns are in a construct relationship, and in 19c there is only one noun - as if the speaker becomes quite out of breath with pain. None of the sources consulted had this delimitation of the cola. Althann (1983, 87-88) did notice the correspondence of the nouns and of the verbs.

4:23a as it stands in the MT is an unusually long colon, having five units and five main stresses. It is indivisible, however, in the light of the seven cola following it. The best Greek witnesses have only one word here for תהו ובהו. Of the two Hebrew words only תהו occurs alone elsewhere in the OT, and it is rendered by the same Greek word in 1 Sm 12:21, Job 26:7 and Is 40:23. We, therefore, reject the proposal to delete תהו ו (Rudolph, 1968, 36), deleting rather ובהו; cf. Cornill (1901, 6) and Van Selms (1972, 92).

4:30a in the MT has one word more, namely שרור, which is in the wrong gender and is not represented in the best Greek witnesses (Ziegler, 1976, 171). Efforts to retain שרור have led to wild speculation, e.g. by Duhm (1901, 55) and Althann (1983, 109). Following Cornill (1901, 6), Rudolph (1968, 36), Loretz (1970, 120) and Van Selms (1972, 93) we have deleted it.

4:31ef was treated as one colon by Wambacq (1957, 54) and Weiser (1981, 37). The division 3 + 2 as in BHS was preferred by Duhm (1901, 55), Rudolph (1968, 36) and Thompson (1980, 232). Althann (1983, 112) took the last word as a separate colon, having placed his first division as we do. Our division is the same as that of Loretz (1970, 120), although he doubts whether the last word belongs to the original poem, and Bright (1965, 32) seems to have had the same division in mind with his paraphrase. It is in accord with the Massoretic verse division and produces a case of 2 + 3, whether counting stresses or units. In terms of units the cola are similar to 4:26cd. Our main consideration is the most prominent syntactical boundary.

5:3a was subdivided as in BHS by Bright (1965, 35), Rudolph (1968, 38), Thompson (1980, 233), and Althann (1983, 118), the latter of whom also subdivided our 3b and 3c. Loretz (1970, 121) regarded it as one colon, but he removed יהוה as he did in most cases. There is no reason to do so. In the light of the length of 3b and 3c, both having four words, we keep 3a as one colon, as did BHK, Wambacq (1957, 55), Weiser (1981, 41), JB, NEB, and EÜ. Again it is clear from the very short cola delimited by Althann (1983, 118) that his concept of colon differs from ours.

5:14bc and *14de* were treated as one colon each by Wambacq (1957, 57), Weiser (1981, 42), Loretz (1970, 122) and NEB. In the light of 14e being only one word, this might seem advisable, but 14bc together would have five constituents, i.e. one too many, and five main stresses. Therefore, we divide 14bc as well as its parallel 14de, as did Duhm (1901, 61), Rudolph (1968, 38), Bright (1965, 37) and Thompson (1980, 241). The one word colon 14e can be recognised as a colon if verbs with suffixed objects are counted as two units and two constituents.

5:15b could be taken as two cola, but since בֵּית יִשְׂרָאֵל corresponds to עֲלֵיכֶם and since the following three cola starting with גּוֹי like 15b all have three main stresses, it is more likely that 15b should not be subdivided.

5:17f is a longer colon than those preceding it. The word בַּחֶרֶב was perceived as "nachhinkend und störend" and thus deleted (Rudolph, 1968, 40), or regarded as an explanation added to the verse (Van Selms, 1972, 103). There are two problems. The first is the length of the colon, which in itself could be quite legitimate, seeing that it has five units, four constituents and four main stresses. Extra length can be a method of closure for a section of verse (Gordis, 1971, 70-71). The second problem is the fact that בַּחֶרֶב has been understood to be far removed from the verb of which it is an argument. If the word has its usual meaning of "with the sword" here, it can only be dependent on יִרְשׁוּ in 17e. If it were dependent on בּוֹטֵחַ in 17f, which would be normal syntax in Hebrew verse, a meaning like "in war" would be well suited to the context. In Arabic a cognate noun means "Krieg" (HAL, 335) and in Ancient South Arabic a cognate verb meant "to wage war" (Gordon, 1965, 398). Indeed, in Biblical Hebrew prisoners of war are called "captives of the sword" in Gn 31:26 and surely some of those called "slain by the sword" were actually killed by other weapons in battle. In the combination of חֶרֶב, רָעָב and דֶּבֶר, which occurs a number of times in the book of Jeremiah, the word also means, or at the least refers to "war" or "battle". So, possibly, 17f is an unharmed colon after all. We find no reason to regard 17ef as an "unsegmented line" as did Yoder (1972, 52-53), for the relative אֲשֶׁר would be preceded by a fairly prominent syntactic boundary and a pause.

5:23ab was taken as one colon by Wambacq (1957, 59), Weiser (1981, 43), Thompson (1980, 246), NEB and EÜ. Such a colon would be abnormally long in terms of any system of measurement. The problem is that the only prominent syntactical boundary within 23ab is after the second word. It would be possible to divide there, as did JB, but such division produces a 2 + 4 bicolon, which is very unusual. Another possibility would be to divide as in BHS, between the verb and its subject, taking the prepositional phrase and the verb as the first colon. Then we have to keep in mind, however, that this would be a clear case of enjambement, the two cola both being syntactically incomplete, and, therefore, interdependent; cf. the translation of Bright (1965, 38). Enjambement is a very rare technique in Hebrew verse, and it is used here to aid the expression of the content. The verse is as stubborn as the people and does not acknowledge the rules for its own existence.

5:26b had been regarded as textually corrupt due to its grammatical problems. As a result it had been suggested that יקושים belongs to 26c, cf. BHS. In spite of the problems Cooper (1976, 94-101) in his treatment of 5:26-27, succeeded in proving that the correct colon delimitation is as we have it. Cf. also Bright (1965, 38) and Thompson (1980, 246).

5:30 is usually regarded as two cola as in BHS. Collins (1978a, 218) regarded all sentences with היה as verb to be bicola. To our mind this is highly unlikely in the case of sentences with three units, e.g. his example from Jl 2:2. Cases with four units are, of course, more difficult to decide, but we should in every case ask whether we have any reason to subdivide it. Here in 5:30 there is no reason for subdivision. Wambacq (1957, 60), Weiser (1981, 43) and EÜ did not subdivide. Indeed, 5:30 is the beginning of a new section, as recognised by Bright (1965, 39), Weiser (1981, 43) and NEB. The other cola of the new section have three units each, so an introductory colon of four units is well suited.

6:1ab could be taken together as one colon of five units (Wambacq, 1957, 61) if we take into consideration only the parallelism and the three root plays, namely בני/בנימן, בתקוע/תקעו and שאו/משאת. A count of the main stresses would seem to confirm this impression, for 1ab would have three main stresses, 1c, 1d and 1e three each and 1f two. If, however, units and not stresses are decisive, it is better to regard 1ab as two cola and divide it 3 + 2 as in BHS. There are two factors in favour of this. If the poet had wanted 1ab to be one colon, he would have done better in terms of length without the semantically unnecessary קרב, for then his first colon would have had four units like his third. Secondly, 1b can be regarded as a second shout, semantically just about equivalent to 1a; cf. the relationship between 4:5e and 5f. Also, given the fact that verse sometimes - also for structural purposes - is based

on older forms of the language concerned, one might wonder whether
בנימן was still regarded as a compound noun, counting two units and
causing a preceding noun in the construct state to receive its own
main stress. This we will probably never know.

6:3a was subdivided as in BHS by Duhm (1901, 65), Bright (1965,
43), Rudolph (1981, 42) and Thompson (1980, 252). Such subdivision
is based on two assumptions, namely that ועריהם carries two
stresses, and that parallelism works in twos. The first assumption
cannot be proved and the second is wrong. Parallelism in verse 3 is
primarily between 3a and 3b, and is then extended by 3c. Neither are
there any grounds for subdividing both 3a and 3b as cases of 2 + 2, as
did Althann (1983, 199), creating unnecessary cases of enjambement.
Our delimitation of 3a and 3b is the same as that of Cornill (1901, 8),
Wambacq (1957, 61) and Weiser (1981, 50).

6:6ab we have divided according to the most prominent syntactical
boundary, as did Wambacq (1957, 62), Collins (1978a, 173), JB and
EÜ.

6:9 would have a stress pattern of 3 + 1, 3 + 1, if we were to follow
the colon delimitation of BHS, which is accepted by commentators
and translators generally. There are alternatives, however. It would
be possible to regard 9ab as one colon of five units and four stresses,
and 9cd as its parallel, which indeed it is, of four units and four
stresses. But the supposed long cola so produced are not indivisible.
The most prominent syntactical boundary in 9cd is before the two
prepositional phrases, producing 2 + 2 with short words in 9c and
long ones in 9d. In the light of this division the correct division of 9ab
becomes clear, namely before the preposition כ, again producing
2 + 2 stresses with the second colon being the longer. In addition to
the equal number of stresses per colon this delimitation has the
advantage of letting the second and fourth colon start with the same
preposition. Cola 9a and 9c contain the action, while in 9b and 9d the
comparisons are followed by the objects to which the actions are
applied.

6:10efg was regarded as two long cola by BHS and some commentators, although they differ on the exact division of the cola. Bright
(1965, 44) and Thompson (1980, 255) took the words after לחרפה as
an asyndetic relative clause dependent on that noun. That clearly
cannot be the case, for then the suffix would have had to be feminine.

The syntactical boundary after לחרפה, therefore, is a major one, as realised by Duhm (1901, 68), Wambacq (1957, 63), Loretz (1970, 123) and Weiser (1981, 51). There is no way BHS's last colon can be a colon, unless one accepts both enjambement and a syntactical break within the colon. On the other hand לא יחפצו־בו is an acceptable colon by any standard. Seeing, further, that there is no uncertainty as to the end of 10d, we are left with six words, which Wambacq (1957, 63) and Weiser (1981, 51) treated as one colon. Such a colon would be longer than any other known to us and we would prefer to divide it. Those who do so differ. Their uncertainty is illustrated by the fact that Rudolph divided after להם in BHS, but before it in his commentary (1968, 44). Our division (cf. also Althann, 1983, 220) has the advantage that 10f could syntactically stand on its own, whilst 10e contains its explicit subject. In terms of stresses this yields 2 + 3 + 2, and in terms of units it produces 3 + 3 + 2.

6:14 is one of the verses on the colon delimitation of which even BHK and BHS disagree. It should be acknowledged forthwith that the difference between 6:14 and 8:11 is so small - one monosyllabic word בת which makes no difference in terms of the number of stresses - that there can be no difference between the colon delimitation of these verses. Nevertheless, Thompson (1980, 256, 297), Weiser (1981, 51, 70), EÜ and ANV treated the two verses differently. The different treatment of 8:11 in BHS as against that of 6:14 must surely be a slip on Rudolph's behalf, in that BHK's treatment was retained for 8:11, whereas 6:14 was brought in line with Rudolph's commentary (1968). Rudolph (1968, 44, 60) surely was correct in placing both words שלום in the same colon, but wrong in including also ואין שלום in that colon (Althann, 1983, 232-233). The latter expression is not part of the quotation like the former, and is semantically in contrast with 14c. The prepositional phrase על־נקלה is syntactically dependent on the verb in 14a, but so is לאמר, and both describe the manner (cf. GKC, par. 114o) in which the so-called healing is done. These two prepositional phrases form the second colon. Just as there is a contrast between 14c and 14d, which is syntactically dependent on 14c, so there is an ironical contrast between 14a and 14b, which is dependent on 14a. In terms of stresses the cola have a decreasing pattern, namely 3 + 2 + 2 + 1.

Our cola are exactly the same as those delimited by Bright (1965, 45, 61) and Loretz (1970, 124, 126).

6:16c we delimit as in BHS. In a certain sense six words can be identified in it and it would seem to be too long (Althann, 1983, 241). But in the light of וראו at the end of 16a we cannot place a colon boundary before ולכו־בה as Althann and EÜ would have it. The solution must be that אי־זה was counted as one unit, because זה in such combinations serves only to emphasise the interrogative (HAL, 37, 254); cf. also the orthography of מזה in Ex 4:2 and our discussion of 6:20. We regard 16c as one colon with five units, four constituents and four stresses.

6:20 is problematic in various respects in spite of the fact that its last two cola cannot be delimited in any other way than that in BHS. The MT's קנה הטוב is rendered by only one word in the best Greek witnesses. Nevertheless, we should not delete הטוב, as suggested by Duhm (1901, 71) and Cornill (1901, 9), for the Greek word κιννάμωμον should be understood as a translation of both the noun and the adjective. In the light of the related Akkadian expression quoted by Van Selms (1972, 117 n.25) and HAL (1040) there is nothing late about the expression except the article, which we delete as a dittography with Van Selms, Rudolph (1968, 46) and HAL. Commentators generally, and also EÜ and NIV, took 20ab as one colon. Such a colon would have five constituents and five stresses, and should be subdivided. This, however, raises the question whether 20c should also be subdivided. Rudolph (1968, 46) and JB did so, and accordingly divided 20ab after לבונה. Their fourth colon would then have one main stress only. We prefer to regard 20abc as three cola, each longer than its predecessor, with syntactic and semantic parallelism between 20b and 20c. In 20a there are two units and two stresses, in 20b three units and three stresses and in 20c four units and three stresses. As in 16c זה in 20a adds emphasis and length but neither a unit nor a stress.

6:21 has four cola according to the commentaries and the translations consulted, except NIV which delimited only three cola. The translations JB, NEB, EÜ, DLB, ANV all placed their first division after מכשלים, i.e. at the first prominent syntactical boundary, producing two very unequal cola of which the first has five units and five stresses. Such a colon would be acceptable in terms of units and of constituents, e.g. in a system such as that of O'Connor, in which stresses play no role. The commentaries consulted as well as Loretz (1970, 124) and Althann (1983, 250) regarded מכשלים as the first word of the second colon, a division which produces cola of 4 + 3 units or stresses, but with enjambement and with a very prominent syntactical break after the first word of the second colon. There would then also be two references - the suffix and the noun - to the stumbling blocks in the same colon, which is unusual in parallelistic verse. One way in which the unusual relation between the supposed colon boundary and the syntax could be explained, would be to regard it as expressive of the disruptive effect of the מכשלים, an agreement between verse form and content, but none of the commentaries mentioned this explanation. To our mind the use of the root כשל in two directly successive words with a strong syntactic boundary between them is an aid in the delimitation of cola, and not indicative that the two words belong to the same colon. The last two cola should also be taken into account when deciding on the delimitation of their predecessors, and indeed their 3 + 3 pattern seems to have added to the conviction that 4 + 3 would be correct for 21abc. We note that 21cd could in all respects be regarded as one colon, except in terms of its five stresses, which force us to divide 2 + 3. Syntactically 21c belongs to 21d at least as much as to 21b, if not more. Taking that into account we see no reason not to divide 21ab as 2 + 3 as well, a division we claim better accords with the syntax than any other would. Thus, we regard 6:21 to follow the pattern 2 + 3, 2 + 3 + 3.

6:22 was treated as two cola of five units and four stresses each by Wambacq (1957, 66), Loretz (1970, 124), Collins (1978a, 99), Weiser (1981, 52), as well as in BHK, BHS, RSV, JB, NEB and DLB. A similar delimitation was made by Cornill (1901, 9) after deleting מארץ and גדול. Giesebrecht (1905, 15) placed another colon boundary before יעור, while EÜ and ANV placed one after יעור. We agree with Duhm (1901, 72), Bright (1965, 46), Rudolph (1968, 43, 46), Thompson (1980, 263), Althann (1983, 255) and NIV in delimiting four cola, of which the second and fourth are one stress prepositional phrases. The difference between 6:22 and 25:32 is too small - one stress and one constituent - to warrant two different treatments of these two verses; cf. also 31:8 and 50:41. The 3 + 2 pattern here functions on the level of units.

6:24 was taken as two cola by Rudolph (1968, 46); also in BHS. But in BHK and the other commentaries consulted it was regarded as four short cola of two units each, to our mind correctly so. The verbs in 24a and 24b have different subjects and each verb has its own nominal phrase. The whole of 24d is in apposition to צרה in 24c. Thus, in terms of both syntax and semantics the verse is divided into four parts, grouped in pairs, i.e. parallel, if we use the term as vaguely as is usually done in biblical studies.

6:25 also was taken as two cola by Rudoplh (1968, 43, 46) and in BHS. In BHK he treated the verse as four cola, as was done in all the other commentaries and translations consulted. The parallelism and chiasm of 25a and 25b are quite clear. The last two cola are best understood as two separate brief cries, as described by Van Selms (1972, 118), who aptly referred to Jdg 7:20 to explain the construction of 25c.

6:26e was subdivided by BHS and most commentators, Wambacq (1957, 67) and Weiser (1981, 52) being the exceptions. For the subdivision neither syntax nor parallelism affords reason, and we presume it was based on the number of stresses. Now 26a has four stresses, and 26c has three. Thus, it is more likely that the verse will end with a four stress colon than with two two stress cola. Furthermore, both 26a and 26c have four units, just like 26e. That 26e is longer in terms of syllables or consonants than those two cola, is no objection, since extra length is a means of closure for a section of verse.

7:29cd was divided as 3 + 2 by BHS and most commentators. Van Selms (1972, 134) specifically mentioned that this is a case of the normal lament rhythm. In terms of both parallelism and syntax, however, the colon boundary should be placed one word earlier. We have divided 2 + 3, as did Thompson (1980, 291).

8:5a in the MT has the word שובבה of which we have deleted the last consonant, which probably was the result of dittography. Cornill (1901, 12), Giesebrecht (1905, 18) and all the commentaries consulted, except Wambacq (1957, 78, 313), deleted the ה in order to have agreement between the subject and the verb. This does not affect the delimitation of cola.

8:7a has four units and four stresses and was regarded as one colon by Weiser (1981, 70), but as two cola by commentators generally.

Taken on its own this sentence neither in terms of parallelism nor in terms of syntax contains any reason for subdivision. The cause of its being divided by scholars seems to lie in 7b and 7c, which indisputably are two cola. But the counterpart of 7a is 7d, as is indicated by its having the same number of units and by its use of the same verb. The cola 7b and 7c are rather an expansion of 7a. Therefore, the decision whether 7a should be subdivided depends on 7d, which is a four unit colon with three stresses and which should not be subdivided (Wambacq, 1957, 78; Weiser, 1981, 70; NEB). It follows that 7a should be regarded as one colon. To summarise: 7a has four units and four stresses, has its counterpart in 7d, which has four units and three stresses, and between them there is a bicolon of 3 + 3 units and 3 + 2 stresses.

8:8a is a type of colon not allowed by O'Connor (1980a, 87), seeing that it contains nominal phrases dependent on both its predicators. It should, however, not be subdivided, as realised by commentators and translators generally.

8:11 we have treated as 6:14; cf. our discussion above.

8:14a is delimited quite naturally by the end of the interrogative sentence, as in BHK. The fact that 8:14bc also occurs as 4:5ef makes it highly likely that 14bc are complete cola.

8:14b and *14c* we have delimited as 4:5e and 5f; cf. our discussion above. We can only add that our cola for 8:14 are identical with those of Bright (1965, 61), Loretz (1970, 126) and Thompson (1980, 301). The colon boundary between 14b and 14c was also recognised by Cornill (1901, 13).

8:15 was regarded as four cola by Bright (1965, 62), Loretz (1970, 126), Thompson (1980, 301), NIV and EÜ. Division into two cola only was preferred by Cornill (1901, 13), Wambacq (1957, 80), Weiser (1981, 73), JB and NEB; cf. also Rudolph (1968, 100) on 14:19. We are well aware of the syntactical boundary in the middle of both 15a and 15b, but we prefer to see these cola as further examples of the type in which the action and its result are described in one and the same colon; cf. 2:5c and 4:23-26.

8:16abc was treated as only two parallel cola by Weiser (1981, 73), NEB and EÜ. In terms of stresses only this would be possible, but such a combination of 16bc would have too many units, and would be too long in any other terms as well. This fact led to the subdivision of

16a by BHS and most commentators and to emendation in some cases (e.g. Duhm, 1901, 91). The parallelism between 16a and 16bc is very superficial, however, and does not warrant subdivision of 16a. Not only does 16b begin with the same preposition as 16a, but it also ends with the same suffix as 16a. This repetition of both morphology and sound confirms the unity of 16a as the counterpart of the indivisible 16b. We also note the decreasing patterns in 16a-c, namely in terms of units 4 + 3 + 3 and in terms of stresses 4 + 2 + 2, paralleled partially in 16de.

8:20ab was usually taken together as in BHS. This was done for the wrong reasons, however, namely to have a pair of cola and, secondly to have a long colon followed by a shorter. In the case of Loretz (1970, 126) the decisive factor was different, for he tried to delimit cola of roughly equal length in terms of the number of consonants. There can be no question about the parallelism between 20a and 20b. Neither can it be doubted that such cola do exist in Hebrew verse. Yet these two very brief cola seem to be in imbalance with the long 20c. We contend that this contrast in length is exactly what the poet wanted, in order to emphasise that so much time had passed already, and still the dreaded situation dragged on. Each colon in 8:20 is a complete sentence, containing a subject and a verb, and in the case of 20c a negation. In terms both of stresses and of units the cola scan as 2 + 2 + 2. This delimitation of cola was also preferred by Cornill (1901, 13), Bright (1965, 62), Collins (1978a, 223-224), Thompson (1980, 303) and NIV.

9:1 was treated as three long cola by Wambacq (1957, 81), Rudolph (1968, 64) and Weiser (1981, 76), but as six cola by Cornill (1901, 13), Duhm (1901, 93), Bright (1965, 67), Loretz (1970, 127) and Thompson (1980, 307). There should be no doubt that 1c and 1d are two separate parallel cola (cf. Collins, 1978a, 172) of two units and two stresses each. Similarly 1e and 1f have a prominent syntactical boundary between them, 1f being in apposition to the last word of 1e, and these two cola each have two units. Like 1f our colon 1b also has only one main stress. Nevertheless, 1ab should not be taken as one colon, for such a very long colon would be singularly out of place in the context of the following four cola. It would also be too long in terms of both units and constituents if suffixed objects are counted as units and constituents. According to our division 1a is the

only colon in this verse that has more than two units, and still the
verse seems to consist of a clear pattern of three times short-long.

9:2ab is generally considered to be textually corrupt, a problem
already influencing the Septuagint, which reflects neither a suffix with
קשׁת, nor prepositions with שׁקר and אמונה. The simplest emendation which makes perfect sense of the consonantal text is to take the
ם as a preposition with שׁקר. There is no reason to subdivide 2b as in
BHS, and among the commentators consulted only Rudolph (1968,
64) did so.

9:4d and 5 are generally emended in such a way that a delimitation
of cola different from that required by the MT is necessary. NIV followed the MT. To avoid the uncertainty it is best for our purposes to
leave out the passage like a number of others.

9:18 was treated as three cola by NEB, which cannot be correct. In
the light of the clear semantic and syntactic parallelism between 18e
and 18f these definitely are two separate cola of two units each. The
same applies to 18c and 18d, in which אין and מאד are corresponding terms, although this division was not recognised by Loretz (1970,
128), Thompson (1980, 315) and Weiser (1981, 78). The most difficult
decision on this verse is whether 18ab is one colon. This was the view
of the commentators already mentioned, as well as of Duhm (1901,
96), BHK, Wambacq (1957, 84) and the translations consulted. If
קול נהי is taken as a construct relation 18ab is likely to be one
clause and one colon of four units and three stresses. However, such
a long colon seems to be out of place before the following four cola
of two units each. Syntactically there is another possibility, namely
that קול was intended as an interjection calling the attention to a
sound which follows (HAL, 1015), in this case the נהי. Then 18b is a
complete clause, separate from 18a, and קול has a stress of its own.
The verse is seen to consist of six cola of two units and two stresses
each. Like Cornill (1901, 15), Bright (1965, 69), Rudolph (1968, 68)
and BHS we prefer this division.

10:4bc was divided after יחזקום in BHK, followed by commentators and translations generally, producing a colon 4b syntactically
equivalent to 4a, and their colon 4c then has only one unit, unless a
verb is added on meagre textual evidence (cf. BHK and Ziegler, 1976,
200). Such a colon delimitation also involves the change of either the
suffix in יחזקום to singular or the verb יפיק to plural. Rudolph

(1968, 70) preferred to delimit as we do, producing cola of more equal length, but understood יחזקום as syntactically belonging to the prepositional phrases of 4b, i.e. as a case of enjambement, and then still had to change יפיק to plural. We regard 4b as syntactically dependent on ייפהו in 4a, and quite ironic in sense. Our colon 4c begins a new sentence, in which the suffix refers to the masculine noun מסמרות (cf. Ec 12:11). It is not clear from the formulation of Van Selms (1972, 161 n.7) whether he took the suffix to refer to the two metals or to the nails. The verb חזק Pi. has "tent-pegs" as object in Is 54:2, so there is no reason why it cannot have "nails" as object here. This interpretation obviates emendation, enjambement and unusual colon length, and has the further advantage that all references to the idol in verse 4 are in the singular.

10:5 has been divided into cola in a number of different ways by commentators and the translations consulted. Our colon delimitation is in agreement with that of Bright (1965, 76), Rudolph (1968, 70), Weiser (1981, 85), JB and NEB. The translations RSV, NIV and DLB subdivided 5a, 5b and 5c. Wambacq (1957, 88) and Thompson (1980, 323) subdivided only 5a and 5b. EÜ subdivided only 5a and 5c. It is significant that all recognised 5d. In fact it provides the clue to the correct delimitation of the verse, for 5d follows - at least superficially - the construction in two parts of the preceding three verses, of which the second part is consistently couched as a negation. In addition we must point out that these second parts could not stand alone as cola, consisting of only one unit as they do. The cola are admittedly of a long type, but the mould for this was provided by 5a, which is closely related to the usually fairly long action-result colon (cf. 4:23-26), and which can be described as a statement-consequence colon. This logical relation between the two parts of the colon is reversed in 5b and 5c. We find two complementary decreasing patterns in the verse, for the first colon has four units and the following three have three each, whilst the number of stresses is three in the first three cola and two in the last.

10:6ab was taken as one colon by Wambacq (1957, 88) and Weiser (1981, 86). On the other hand Thompson (180, 323), RSV, NEB, EÜ, DLB and ANV took 6bc as one colon. Both these treatments we consider to be extremely unlikely in any terms. Our division of the verse into three cola is in agreement with that of Bright (1965, 76), Rudolph (1968, 72), JB and NIV.

10:7 is closely related to 10:6, also in terms of verse structure. Nevertheless, there is difference of opinion on the colon delimitation of 10:7 even between BHK and BHS, namely as regards 7ef. The only colon in this verse recognised by all sources consulted is 7c. The recognition of this short colon immediately rules out the possibility of combining 7d and 7e, as did Wambacq (1957, 89), NEB and DLB. It also casts serious doubt on the combining of 7a and 7b, as did Wambacq (1957, 89), Thompson (1980, 323), Weiser (1981, 86), RSV, JB, NEB, EÜ and DLB. Such combining of 7a and 7b is based solely on the premise that cola with only one main stress do not exist. Treating 7ef as one colon, as did Rudolph (1968, 72), Weiser (1981, 86) and EÜ, is little more likely. Taking into account the whole of verses 6 and 7, specifically the length of their other cola and the wording of 6a opening the passage, it is by far the best to follow BHK, Bright (1965, 76), Thompson (1980, 323), RSV, JB and NIV in taking 7e and 7f as separate cola.

10:9abc was treated as one colon by Wambacq (1957, 89) and EÜ. Weiser (1981, 85) and the other translations consulted took 9ab as one colon. To our mind Bright (1965, 76) and Rudolph (1968, 70) correctly delimited three cola of two units and two stresses each. There are two facts in the text that confirm this view. Firstly, it has become clear that מאופז in 9c is not a prepositional phrase corresponding to מתרשיש in 9b, but is rather a passive verb form, corresponding to מרקע in 9a (Van Selms, 1972, 162), a possibility pointed out already by Duhm (1901, 100); cf. also HAL (22, 870). Secondly, the three verb forms with which the cola end are phonologically similar, each having as its last two vowels u-a.

10:10ab was treated as three cola by Bright (1965, 76-77), Rudolph (1968, 72) and JB, taking the words ומלך עולם as the third colon. Such a short colon seems to be out of place, however, and both in BHK and in BHS Rudolph took 10ab to be two cola. The latter view was accepted also by Wambacq (1957, 89), Thompson (1980, 324), Weiser (1981, 86), RSV, NEB, NIV, DLB and ANV. The length of 10b as divided by them is within bounds, but does stand out somewhat. We suggest that הוא syntactically belongs to 10a. The maqqeph is a much later addition, based on the Massoretes' interpretation of the syntax. The personal pronoun at the beginning of 10b would be out of place, seeing that the subject has been introduced already in 10a, where ויהוה, in the pendens construction, is contrasted with the idols previously described. Thus, the whole of 10b is in apposition to אלהים אמת of 10a. Possibly this was the interpretation of EÜ. In addition to the advantage of the better syntactical motivation for the presence of הוא, our interpretation produces cola more equal in length than those accepted by commentators and translators. We may add that this division would also be correct if ויהוה originally belonged to 12a as in the Septuagint.

10:13a has long been recognised as problematic and various solutions have been suggested. The words לקול תתו have no equivalent in the best Greek witnesses to this verse, but are represented in their rendering of the doublet in 51:16 (Ziegler, 1976, 201, 294). We may, therefore, assume that the translators did have our Hebrew text before them, but left out the two words because they failed to make sense of them. In view of the lack of evidence for a longer text, it is highly unlikely that any words were lost, as supposed by Bright (1965, 77). At first sight our 13a, having five units and four stresses, might seem to be too long a colon for this context. However, it is followed by 13b, which indisputably is one colon and which has four units and three stresses, i.e. exactly one unit and one stress less than 13a. The relationship of one less is a widely acknowledged feature of consecutive cola in Hebrew verse. With this in mind let us return to the interpretation of 13a. One possibility is to assume a sort of metathesis by which a supposed original לתתו קול[ו] had become לקול תתו (Ackroyd, 1963, 388-389, following BHK and Weiser). To our mind the best solution is to assume that the poet had the expression נתן קול "to raise the voice" in mind, but left out the direct object, firstly, because it would be tautological after לקול, and secondly, in order to keep the length of the colon within limits. Such ellipsis of a well-known component of a fixed expression is common in Hebrew as well as in other languages. Wambacq (1957, 90) and Rudolph (1968, 72) understood the text in this way, although the latter preferred to accept an emendation suggested by Duhm.

10:14cd was taken as one colon by Cornill (1901, 34), Bright (1965, 77), Rudolph (1968, 72) and Weiser (1981, 86). The supposed colon then consists of two clauses and four units, has four stresses and a semantic parallelism within itself. Cola of two clauses, four units and four stresses with the clause boundary between the second and third unit do exist, as can be seen from 8:8a. However, in the case of 8:8a the second clause is a subordinate clause embedded into the first and there is no trace of parallelism within the colon. Our colon 10:14d is semantically equivalent to 14c and clearly meant as its parallel. Wambacq (1957, 90), Thompson (1980, 325) and the translations consulted also took 14c and 14d as separate cola. The brevity of the two cola apparently was meant to be expressive of the nothingness of the idols.

10:15a and *15b* are similar very brief cola of two units each, and 15b has only one main stress, due to which 15ab was treated as one colon by the commentaries and translations. Following 14c and 14d, however, two brief cola with the same illustrative effect are more likely. The syntactical boundary between the two is quite prominent, 15b being in apposition to הבל in 15a and thus semantically repetitive. The poet used הבל as a parallel term for שקר as in 16:19ef. Interestingly in 14d רוח, which can have the same negative connotation (cf. Is 41:29), is used in a positive sense but negated by לא to make it correspond in meaning to שקר and הבל. In 14c-15b, then, we find four brief cola of two units each, the last having only one main stress, even the rhythm ridiculing the idols.

10:18 has generally been treated as verse, but it might very well be prose, for which reason we choose to exclude it. Parts of it are also text critically uncertain.

10:19cd has been treated variously. Wambacq (1957, 91) and NEB took it to be one colon, but such a colon would be too long, whether in terms of units, constituents or stresses. Bright (1965, 70), Rudolph (1968, 74) and Weiser (1981, 86) divided after זה, which resulted in a doubtful case of enjambement. Duhm (1901, 104), Thompson (1980, 333), RSV, DLB and ANV divided after חלי, making 19c rather long and 19d very short, a division of 4 + 1 in terms of main stresses. Apparently to resolve this inequality of the cola EÜ then placed another division after אמרתי, producing three fairly equal cola. It is doubtful, however, whether ואשאנו was intended as a separate colon. To our mind 10:19d is a further example of the statement-consequence type of colon (cf. 10:5a) and we follow JB and NIV in dividing only after אמרתי.

10:20ab was taken as one colon by Wambacq (1957, 91), Rudolph (1968, 74) and NEB. The explicit parallelism within the supposed colon combined with its length clearly shows that this cannot be. We agree with Bright (1965, 70), Thompson (1980, 333), Weiser (1981, 86), JB, NIV, EÜ and DLB that 20a and 20b are separate cola.

10:20c was subdivided by Bright (1965, 70), Thompson (1980, 333) and EÜ, apparently to bring it in line with their division of 20ab. This, however, is unnecessary and incorrect. Colon 20c is an action-result colon with three stresses. Our treatment accords with that of Wambacq (1957, 91), Rudolph (1968, 74), Weiser (1981, 86), JB, NIV and DLB.

10:22cd was taken to be one colon by Weiser (1981, 87) and NEB, but divided before שממה by Duhm (1901, 105), Wambacq (1957, 91), Bright (1965, 71) and JB, as well as by Rudolph (1968, 75) in his summary of the number of stresses and in BHK and BHS. In his translation of the verse, however, Rudolph (1968, 74) divided after שממה as did also Thompson (1980, 333), RSV, NIV, EÜ, DLB and ANV. In terms of the approximate equality of cola the division before שממה would seem preferable, but in terms of the content the inequality of cola might be deliberate. The most prominent syntactical boundary is after שממה, to which מעון תנים is appositional, and without שממה 22c would be an incomplete clause. Furthermore, in 9:10 we find cola not only similar in formulation, but also having the same syntactical and rhythmical pattern. Yet of all the works consulted not one proposed dividing 9:10ab before גלים or 9:10cd before שממה. Taking all these factors into account we cannot but divide after שממה in 10:22cd.

10:25abc and its doublet in Ps 79:6 have been treated variously by commentators and translators. Weiser (1981, 87), RSV and ANV regarded 25ab as one colon, as did BHK and NEB with Ps 79:6ab. The most common view, adhered to by Wambacq (1957, 92), Bright (1965, 71), Rudolph (1968, 74), BHS, JB and EÜ, is that 25ab is to be divided after הגוים and 25c likewise after משפחות. BHS, RSV, JB, NIV and ANV did the same for Ps 79:6. However, BHK, Thompson (1980, 333), NEB and NIV did not divide after משפחות, and similarly EÜ for Ps 79:6. Indeed, there is no reason to suppose that ועל משפחות can on its own be a complete colon. On the other hand 25ab would be very long for a single colon, irrespective of the chosen system of measurement. The only possibility then is to let 25b start with the phrase עַל־הַגּוֹיִם corresponding with the first phrase of 25c, in which we agree with DLB; cf. also Dahood (1968, 249) on Ps 79:6. Our division may be objected to because it regards 25a, the first colon, as the shortest of the cola concerned. However, the syntactical similarity between 25b and 25c argues strongly for this division, and we have already seen that shorter cola can precede longer ones. Moreover, the colon boundary before עַל־הַגּוֹיִם may well have created some tension and thus facilitated the concentration of the hearers.

10:25d we have emended by deleting וְאָכְלֻהוּ, which is not represented in the best Greek witnesses (Ziegler, 1976, 204). The word probably originated through dittography of וַיְכַלֻּהוּ; cf. Duhm (1901, 106), Wambacq (1957, 92), Bright (1965, 71), Rudolph (1968, 74) and Weiser (1981, 87).

11:16a has one word more in the MT, namely פְּרִי, which is not represented in the best Greek witnesses (Ziegler, 1976, 207) and which we have for that reason deleted. All the commentaries consulted except Wambacq (1957, 95) accepted either this deletion or a proposal that יְפֵה פְרִי originally was one noun, which as one unit would for our purposes have the same effect.

12:3a in the MT contains also the verb תְּרָאֵנִי, which is not represented in the best Greek witnesses (Ziegler, 1976, 209), semantically fits badly between יָדַע and בָּחַן and which we have, therefore, deleted; cf. also Cornill (1901, 11), Duhm (1901, 115) and Van Selms (1972, 182).

12:6 was regarded as prose by Rudolph (1968, 80), Weiser (1981, 94), Wambacq (1957, 98) and JB. There is no reason for doing so, however. Cornill (1901, 11), Duhm (1901, 116), Bright (1965, 83-84), Thompson (1980, 348) and the other translations consulted treated it as verse. Although 12:6 at first sight might seem to be no high quality poetry, it is verse nevertheless, as is clear from the repetitive use of גַּם and גַּם־הֵמָּה at the beginning of the first three cola. The similarity in construction between בָּגְדוּ בָךְ in 6b and תַּאֲמִן בָּם in 6d is used to emphasise their contrast in meaning. The same technique is employed as to the last three words of 6c and 6e respectively. The double and interweaved use of this technique corroborates not only our judgement of 12:6 as verse, but also our delimitation of its cola,

which is in agreement with that of Cornill (1901, 11; deleting 6c),
Bright (1965, 83-84), Collins (1978a, 172, 275, cf. 60-61), Thompson
(1980, 348), Longman (1982, 247), RSV, NIV and DLB. Cola 6a and
6b were combined by NEB and EÜ, as were cola 6d and 6e by Duhm
(1901, 116) and NEB. Duhm also took גַּם־הֵמָּה from 6c as part of
6b, and deleted אֵלֶיךָ from 6e. Once the correspondences between
the cola of this verse are recognised the unequal lengths of cola 6c
and 6d become quite acceptable.

   12:8d is a colon of a type not encountered by O'Connor (1980a) in
his corpus, which did not include any example with the adverbial
עַל־כֵּן. If עַל־כֵּן is regarded as only a particle, not counting as a
unit, this would be our second case of a one word colon. There is
unanimity among the sources consulted - with the sole exception of
NEB - that indeed 8d is a separate colon. For a colometric system in
terms of units there are two possibilities of accounting for this colon.
Firstly כֵּן may be regarded as an adjective, meaning "so" (cf. HAL,
459-460) and functioning here as a one member nominal sentence,
and thus having unit status. In that case עַל functions as a conjunction, meaning "because" (cf. HAL, 782), and עַל־כֵּן could be translated as "because it is so". Secondly we may here, as we did concerning 5:14e, regard the suffixed object as a unit and constituent separate
from the verb to which it is suffixed. These possibilities are not
mutually exclusive.

   12:11 was treated as two cola by NEB, which cannot be correct
seeing that both the supposed cola would be extremely long. In spite
of 11c being longer than 11d the commentaries and the other translations are unanimous as to their division. Yet no concensus exists
concerning 11ab. Duhm (1901, 117), Wambacq (1957, 100), Rudolph
(1968, 86), Weiser (1981, 101), JB and EÜ divided after אֲבֵלָה. On
the other hand Cornill (1901, 23), Bright (1965, 85), Thompson (1980,
356), RSV, NIV and DLB divided before אֲבֵלָה, producing another
case of short colon before long colon. There are some factors which
indicate that the latter view is correct. In verse 11 the poet exploits
the noun שְׁמָמָה from verse 10, using it again and adding four similar
sounding words, namely שַׁמָּה, שְׁמֵמָה (the adjective), נָשַׁמָּה and שָׁם.
It would then not be strange to find שְׁמָמָה in the very prominent
colon final position again as in 10d. In 11b it is the cognate adjective
שְׁמֵמָה which concludes the colon and in 11a the noun שְׁמָמָה does so

if the natural syntactical boundary is not allowed to be overridden by a supposed preference for a rhythm of 3 + 2. Rudolph's suggestion that we should either regard אבלה as an asyndetic relative clause or change its punctuation to that of an adjective and Duhm's enjambed translation are both dictated by such a supposed preference. If אבלה is taken as part of 11a and enjambement is not accepted, 11b becomes the only colon in verse 11 without a verb and one is forced to supply a verb like "lies", as did Wambacq, Rudolph and Weiser. We, therefore, maintain that the correct division is before אבלה and that we have an example here of two successive cola ending with the same word and a third ending with a related and very similar word.

12:13ab was taken as one colon by all sources consulted except DLB. Apparently the supposed colon was interpreted as an action-result colon in the light of 13c. Two further factors probably also played a role in the decision not to divide 13ab, namely the preference for bicola, and the preference for long-short sequence rather than for short-long. There are, however, other factors to be taken into account. Each colon in the rest of the verse has only two main stresses and the only colon with more than two units is 13e, which as the last colon of the section may well be lengthened to effect closure. It would then be strange to have a colon of four stresses to begin with. Moreover, the supposed long colon consists of two clearly parallel parts, each consisting of a verb and an object, and these are chiastically arranged. We, therefore, contend that this is not an action-result colon, but an antithetical bicolon, and that 13c is less of a parallel to 13ab than to 13d and 13e.

13:16ef was taken as one colon by Duhm (1901, 123), Bright (1965, 92), Rudolph (1968, 92) and Weiser (1981, 109). The supposed colon would then have four units and four stresses, and would be internally antithetically parallel. It would be followed by a colon exactly identical in structure and length to either of the supposed colon's halves, and which is parallel synonymously to the second half and antithetically to the first. We, therefore, agree with Wambacq (1957, 104), Thompson (1980, 368), RSV, JB, NIV and EÜ that 16e, 16f and 16g are separate parallel cola.

13:17abc was divided in BHS on three assumptions, namely that cola should occur in pairs, that the longer of the pair should precede the shorter, and that במסתרים is textually corrupt; cf. Rudolph

(1968, 92). For the latter assumption there is no evidence and for the former two we have already found clear counter-examples. Also for the rearrangement suggested by Van Selms (1972, 196) there is no support. Our division of the cola is in agreement with that of Giesebrecht (1905, 27; deleting 17d), BHK, Wambacq (1957, 104), Bright (1965, 92) and NIV. On the other hand Thompson (1980, 368), Weiser (1981, 109), RSV and EÜ combined 17b with 17c and 17d with 17e. JB deleted 17d, but also combined 17b with 17c. We consider these combinations unacceptable because they produce cola of five units each, with four and five main stresses respectively, and with prominent syntactical boundaries within them at which the supposed long cola could be divided. We are aware of the textual problem concerning 17d, but have not deleted it as its presence or absence does not affect the delimitation of its neighbouring cola. Colon 17a is a further example of an unallowable one unit colon in terms of O'Connor's system. We allow it, counting the suffixed object as a second unit. The word מְּנִי has unit status; cf. 4:26c, 23:9e and our discussion of לִפְנֵי in 15:9f and 18:17b.

13:19ab could easily in terms of main stresses have been taken as one colon. Yet not one of the commentaries and translations consulted did so. The preference for bicola by scholars may have played a part in this. We regard the prominent syntactic boundary and the number of units as the deciding factors as far as the poet was concerned. Incidentally 19c and 19d also have 3 + 2 units. The cola 9:21c and 21d are quite similar in form to 19a and 19b.

13:19d we have emended as is generally done by commentators, following the versions, although Bright (1965, 93-94) and Van Selms (1972, 197) did not mention the emendation; cf. also GKC (par. 118q) and HAL (184, 185). This emendation does not affect our colon delimitation.

13:20a in the MT has the plural suffix, which is in disagreement with the verbs and the other suffixes in the verse. The emendation is based on Greek evidence, is generally accepted by commentators and does not affect our colon delimitation. However, the addition of יְרוּשְׁלַם to 20a on the basis of the Septuagint does seem to have influenced Bright (1965, 93), Weiser (1981, 109) and EÜ in their decision to divide before וּרְאִי, as did Rudolph's (1968, 92; and BHS) decision to add צִיּוֹן before עֵינַיִךְ, for those commentators and translations which did not add a word to 20a, divided after וראי. They are Duhm (1901, 125), Cornill (1901, 23), Giesebrecht (1905, 27), Wambacq (1957, 105), Thompson (1980, 371), BHK, RSV, JB, NEB and NIV. Now one could argue, as we have done in the case of 4:5e, that the two verbs belong closely together, and that they therefore should be in the same colon. Here, however, the two verbs do not belong so closely together as in the construction used in 4:5e. Indeed the same two verbs occur together but one more time in our corpus, namely in 3:2ab, where we have argued that their morphological similarity indicates rather that the two verbs are the first words of two successive cola. In 20ab there are two further factors in favour of this view. The two cola are syntactically similar, both having direct objects after the morphologically similar verbs. A colon boundary between a verb and its direct object where this could be avoided, also seems very unlikely. Again we have found a case of 2 + 3.

13:21 is generally considered to be textually corrupt, although the versions seem to have read essentially the same text (Van Selms, 1972, 198). Suggested emendations vary and have no support from textual evidence, except for the possibility of reading יפקדו in 21a. We have retained the MT and divided the cola according to the prominent syntactic boundaries. All the cola are of acceptable length, and to our mind they all make perfect sense. BHS excluded the first עליך from 21a, a decision facilitated by the transposition of a word from 21d. We agree with Wambacq (1957, 105) and Weiser (1981, 109) that the first עליך is part of 21a. We understand 21a and 21c as a single rhetorical question, the word עליך being repeated by the poet after 21b, which is an interjected circumstantial clause. On the one hand the repetition enables the poet to continue his sentence and still be understood, and on the other the interjection as well as the repetition serves to emphasise the irony of the appointment as against previous relations.

13:25ab was regarded as one colon by Wambacq (1957, 106), but the supposed colon would have five main stresses. That 25a and 25b are two separate cola was realised by Cornill (1901, 23) and Giesebrecht (1905, 27), but they transposed מאתי to the end of 25a, for which there are no grounds excepting the supposed preference of the order long-short. The most popular approach has been to place the first colon boundary after מדיך, as did Duhm (1901, 126), Bright

(1965, 93), Rudolph (1968, 94), Thompson (1980, 372), JB, NEB and EÜ. The prepositional phrase מֵאִתִּי is then taken with נְאֻם־יְהוָה as the second colon of the verse. This is wrong for two reasons. It fails to recognise that מְנָת־מִדַּיִךְ is semantically a repetition of זֶה גּוֹרָלֵךְ, and it separates the prepositional phrase from the expression on which it is syntactically dependent, to become a one word nominal clause, used with the one constituent nominal clause נְאֻם־יְהוָה to form a colon. Like Weiser (1981, 110), RSV and NIV we regard the cola as 2 + 3 and the expression נְאֻם־יְהוָה as falling outside the system of cola.

13:26ab was treated as one colon by Wambacq (1957, 106), Rudolph (1968, 96), Collins (1978a, 169), Thompson (1980, 372), Weiser (1981, 110), RSV, JB and NIV. Having four units and four constituents the supposed colon would not be too long to exist, but it would have twice the length of any neighbouring colon and would thus stand out in this context. It would be possible to argue that the extra length was chosen for expressive purposes, namely to express the violence of the action described. But one could just as well argue that a colon boundary in an unusual place, e.g. between verb and direct object, could express the same violence. Collins (1978a, 235-236) also claimed that there is special emphasis on the subject, which is probably true, seeing that the first person verb is preceded by both גַּם and the personal pronoun. However, the unusual length of the supposed colon would tend rather to emphasise its latter part, the direct object and the prepositional phrase, thus creating a tension within the colon. For these reasons we have divided 26ab between the verb and its direct object, as did also Duhm (1901, 126), Bright (1965, 94) and EÜ. It is worthy of note that none of the sources consulted divided verse 26 into two equal cola by placing their colon boundary before עַל־פָּנָיִךְ. This fact is a testimony to the conviction amongst scholars that cola do have syntactic integrity.

13:27ab was treated as one colon by Wambacq (1957, 107), but as two divided as we did by all other sources consulted. The colon boundary is the syntactic boundary between two expressions with similar meaning.

13:27efg was divided before לֹא by Bright (1965, 94) and NIV, while EÜ made לֹא תִטְהֲרִי a colon on its own. If one retains MT, one is forced to divide as in BHS, as is witnessed by Cornill (1901,

23), Wambacq (1957, 107), Rudolph (1968, 96), Thompson (1980, 372), Weiser (1981, 110), JB and NEB. Duhm (1901, 126) divided as BHS did, but deleted ירושלם. Obviously the length of the MT's 27e creates some doubt as to the correctness of the text. This doubt is strengthened by the occurrence of אחרי before מת׳. We have reconstructed the Hebrew text on the basis of the Greek (Ziegler, 1976, 218) and we believe it makes both normal cola and perfect sense. Our emendation not only has the Greek text as witness in its favour, but is also less drastic than the proposals of both HAL (618) and NEB (cf. Brockington, 1973, 204). The phrase אחרי (preposition plus suffix first person singular) we take to imply cultic loyalty to Yahweh. A colon similar to our 27e occurs in 48:46a.

14:2 was treated as two cola by Giesebrecht (1905, 28), Thompson (1980, 375) and Weiser (1981, 119), the two supposed cola having internal parallelism and according to our count four and five units respectively, and four main stresses each. Curiously Wambacq (1957, 108) and NEB treated 2ab as one colon but 2c and 2d as two separate cola. Duhm (1901, 127) and Rudolph (1968, 98) recognised four cola, but found the short first colon lacking, Duhm putting 2d first and Rudolph adding to 2a the phrase על־בצרת which he regarded to have been lost by haplography. Although a longer colon is sometimes used to introduce a section of poetry this was not necessary. It seems unlikely that a poem would have started with a prepositional phrase and the chiastic placing of the verbs also refute such a view. At the end of a strophe a longer colon is not out of place, since it is one way of effecting closure. Guided by the clear parallelism, the prominent syntactic boundaries, the use of chiasm and accepted limits as to length, we concur with Cornill (1901, 20), Bright (1965, 97), RSV, JB, NIV, EÜ and DLB in our delimitation of the cola.

14:3a was subdivided as 2 + 2 by Duhm (1901, 127), Bright (1965, 97) and Collins (1978a, 78). On the other hand Giesebrecht (1905, 28), Wambacq (1957, 108), Thompson (1980, 375), Weiser (1981, 119) and NEB took 3bc as one colon. To our mind the structure and meaning of the cola 3b, 3c and 3d clearly show that they belong together as a tricolon. Therefore 3b is not to be taken together with 3c as one colon, nor yet to be regarded as some sort of parallel to 3a, which is "a self-sufficient unit" (Collins, 1978a, 275). We would term 3a an introductory monocolon (cf. Watson, 1984, 171), not finding any reason here to posit a colon boundary between the verb and the direct object. On the delimitation of 3a-d we are in agreement with Cornill (1901, 20), Rudolph (1968, 98), RSV, JB, NIV and EÜ.

14:3ef was deleted by Duhm (1901, 127), Cornill (1901, 20), Rudolph (1968, 98), Weiser (1981, 119), JB and NEB, and placed in brackets by EÜ as a secondary addition because it is not represented in the best Greek witnesses. The alliteration of שֹׁב and כֹל in 3d with בֹשׁ and כֹל in 3e might indicate otherwise. Giesebrecht (1905, 28), Wambacq (1957, 108) and Thompson (1980, 376 n.3) took 3ef as one colon. It is clear, however, that the third verb in 3ef is closely associated with its object ראשֹׁם, which is not true of בֹשׁו והכלמו. These two verbs form a semantic unity, corresponding in meaning to וחפו ראשֹׁם. The similarity with 4c and 4d as well as the alliteration we have referred to corroborate this interpretation. We thus agree with Bright (1965, 97), Collins (1978a, 275), Thompson (1980, 375, against 376 n.3), RSV, NIV, EÜ and DLB that 3e and 3f are two separate cola.

14:4cd was treated as one colon by Giesebrecht (1905, 28), Wambacq (1957, 108) and Weiser (1981, 119). All the other sources consulted recognised 4c and 4d as separate parallel cola. The prominent syntactic boundary between the second and the third main stress, as well as the correspondence between the two verbs as to form and position, indicate this to be correct.

14:5 could conceivably have been divided differently. A division before ועזוב would have produced two cola very equal in length and contrasting in meaning. Yet this view was not chosen by any of our sources, and with good reason. The infinitive absolute in the function of a finite verb (GKC, par.113y,z) is strongly dependent upon the previous finite verb and the second action follows directly on the first. Of crucial importance here is the fact that the particle גֹם at the beginning of 5a causes us to expect some unusual action from the אילת, which ילדה is not. Had the two verbs been in successive cola, the contrast in their meaning would have excluded the possibility of גֹם doing double duty and so being effective also for עזוב. In spite of the unanimity on the two verbs being in the same colon, there is difference of opinion as to the number of cola in this verse. Cornill (1901, 20), Duhm (1901, 128), Wambacq (1957, 108), Bright (1965, 97), Thompson (1980, 376), Weiser (1981, 119), NEB, NIV and EÜ subdivided 5a after בשרה. The colon boundary would then separate the subject from its verb. There are cases in which we have to accept such a position for the colon boundary, e.g. 2:16ab and 9:9ef. The present case is very similar to 8:7a, however, more so than to those just mentioned. There is no objection to 5a being one colon in terms of stresses (cf. 14:3a), units or constituents, the colon having four of each. It is also true that the semantic relation between גם and its expected unusual action in ועזוב is clearest when both occur in the same colon. Therefore, we agree with Giesebrecht (1905, 28), Rudolph (1968, 98), RSV, JB and DLB that 5a is a single long colon. Possibly it introduces a new section of verse, as in the case of 3a.

14:6cd was treated as one colon by Giesebrecht (1905, 28), Wambacq (1957, 108), Rudolph (1968, 97-98), Thompson (1980, 376), Weiser (1981, 119) and DLB. In both BHK and BHS, however, Rudolph distinguished two cola, as did also Cornill (1901, 20), Bright (1965, 97), Collins (1978a, 217), Watson (1984, 308), RSV, JB, NIV and EÜ. This latter view we regard as correct. There is a prominent syntactic boundary between 6c and 6d, and 6d is closely related to 5b, although slightly shorter. It might have only one main stress, but that would suit the content, for it could then be interpreted as an expression on the level of rhythm of the shortage described.

14:7ab could conceivably be divided after the vocative יהוה, especially in view of יהוה and שם being used in successive cola in 14:9cd. This option, which would produce a case of 4 + 3, was preferred by Giesebrecht (1905, 28) and DLB. All other sources consulted are unanimous that the division should be before יהוה, excepting Duhm (1901, 128) who deleted both יהוה and שם. For the former deletion there are no grounds, but the latter is based on reliable Greek witnesses (Ziegler, 1976, 219) and the reading in MT may be due to later theological speculation, for which reasons we have deleted שם. As to colon length either reading would be possible, but a colon of three units seems more appropriate after the three units of 7a.

14:9e is another example of a one word colon, not recognised within O'Connor's (1980a, 87) system because he does not allow cola of one unit and he does not count the suffixed object as a unit. We regard the suffix as both a unit and a constituent and therefore recognise this type of colon. Among the commentaries consulted only

Thompson (1980, 376) did not regard 9e as a separate colon. Fohrer (1967, 69) and Watson (1984, 171) recognised it as a closing monocolon.

14:17c in the MT contains two more words, גדול and בתולת, which are not represented in the best Greek text (Ziegler, 1976, 219). They seem to be later additions conditioned by the words שבר and בת already in the text. We have deleted them, following Van Selms (1972, 206). The noun בתולת only was deleted by Bright (1965, 99), Rudolph (1968, 100), Thompson (1980, 384) and Weiser (1981, 120). We see no reason to treat the two words in two different ways. The word גדול is tautological and unnecessary where the cognate object is already used with the verb.

14:18ab and *18cd* were translated as one colon each by Wambacq (1957, 111) and Weiser (1981, 120), while NEB inconsistently distinguished three cola, namely 18a, 18b and 18cd. Giesebrecht (1905, 29) divided before the first והנה, but after the second. All the other sources consulted recognised the same four cola as we did. If 18ab and 18cd were treated as only two cola, each of the supposed cola would have five units and four main stresses, which in itself would be acceptable. These lengths combined with the quite prominent syntactic boundary near the middle of each of the supposed long cola indicate, however, that we do have four cola. It will be noted that these action-result bicola are in fact each one unit longer than the action-result cola we found in 4:23a, 24a, 25a and 26a.

14:18ef was divided only after ארץ by RSV, which quite obviously produces cola not only of unequal length, but both unacceptable, their 18e being too long and their 18f having only one unit. Only EÜ took the verb סחרו or its text critical replacement as part of 18e. If one thinks in terms of 3 + 2 this would have been the obvious division, yet no other consulted source did so, and we should try to establish why not. Even arguing in terms of syntax one could have taken the verb with its subject and have left the prepositional phrase for the second colon. However, there are a number of cases where an extended subject stands as a colon on its own before the core colon, which then need not contain an explicit subject; cf. 2:16ab and 9:9ef. There are two reasons to regard this as a similar case. The subject is extended, and there seems to be a strong bond between the verb and its prepositional phrase as if the latter is obligatory when the verb has this meaning. Unfortunately the exact combination of verb and preposition occurs only here in the Old Testament and we are unable to test this impression. We do agree with the overwhelming majority of sources that 18f and not 18e is the core colon. In 18f we have deleted a וֹ, taking לֹא יְדָעוֹ as an asyndetic relative clause as in a large number of Hebrew manuscripts, the Septuagint, Codex Reuchlinianus and the Vulgate; cf. BHS.

14:19c-f were treated in various ways. Fohrer (1967, 83), Rudolph (1968, 100), Weiser (1981, 120), JB and NEB took 19cd as one colon, probably due to its similarity with 19e and 19f. On the other hand Bright (1965, 99), Thompson (1980, 384), NIV and EÜ subdivided 19e and 19f, again probably due to the similarity with 19cd. DLB is clearly inconsistent in subdividing 19e but not 19f, for these two cola are so similar in form that they have to be treated in the same way. However, that does not apply to 19cd, which in spite of some similarity to 19e and 19f is different from them, even superficially, having five words in comparison with their four each. The difference does go deeper. If we accept that אֵין does not carry its own stress, 19cd would have four stresses as against the three each of 19e and 19f. We do not follow O'Connor (1980a, 304, 323) in counting מַרְפֵּא as a predicator; cf. our discussion of 2:31cd above. We do, however, count suffixed objects as units and constituents. Taken together 19cd would have six units and five constituents, one too many of each. Both Cornill's (1901, 21) deletion of לָנוּ and Giesebrecht's (1905, 29) division of 19cd bear witness to their conviction that 19cd cannot be one colon. All the factors which indicate that 19c and 19d are separate cola are absent in 19e and 19f, which therefore should not be subdivided; cf. 8:15. Our delimitation of the cola is in agreement with that of Wambacq (1957, 112) and RSV.

14:20bc was regarded as one colon by Wambacq (1957, 112), Fohrer (1967, 83), Rudolph (1968, 100) and Weiser (1981, 120). This was probably due to metrical considerations as indicated by Rudolph (1968, 97) where he described this verse as 3 + 3. We count 3 + 2 + 2 units and the same pattern of main stresses, עָוֹן having its own stress due to the suffix in אֲבוֹתֵינוּ. Our delimitation is in accordance with that of Cornill (1901, 21), Bright (1965, 99), Thompson (1980, 384) and all the translations consulted. Both the colon boundaries in the verse are very prominent syntactic boundaries.

14:21c was subdivided by Bright (1965, 100), EÜ and DLB. Such a colon boundary between the verbs and their direct object is highly unlikely in the absence of any indications that it was intended. The longer colon, which caused Duhm (1901, 131) to delete זכר, can be understood as closure, the more so in the light of the set pattern of rhetorical questions with which the next verse begins; cf. Watson (1984, 340-342).

15:5cd was taken as one colon in NEB and NIV. This cannot be correct, however, as the supposed colon would have five constituents and five stresses. Had the poet wanted to create one long colon with the same meaning he could have attached the suffix to לשלום instead of using לך. Rudolph (1968, 102) preferred to divide 5cd after לשאל, which would be in keeping with the supposed preference of 3 + 2. Unless לשלום לך is interpreted as direct speech, which is unlikely in the light of the preposition before שלום, the most prominent syntactic boundary must be before לשאל. All other sources consulted divided 5cd in accordance with this syntactic boundary.

15:6cd was treated as one colon by all commentaries and translations consulted except EÜ which divided as we do. We have followed Cornill (1901, 21), Duhm (1901, 133) and Giesebrecht (1905, 30) in deleting עליך from 6c in accordance with the best Greek witnesses (Ziegler, 1976, 224). Even though we do so 6cd would be a colon far longer than any other in this verse. We have found that verbs with object suffixes can stand as complete cola on their own; cf. 5:14e and 14:9e. The other cola in this verse are short, even if עליך were to be retained in 6c. Therefore, we judge 6d to be another case of the one word colon, with one main stress, but two units and two constituents.

15:7ab was divided by all sources consulted, and apparently all would agree with Rudolph (1968, 103) that this is a case of 2 + 2. Strictly, however, 7b has only one main stress and the syntactic boundary exploited for colon end is not very prominent, so that 7ab could just as well have been regarded as a monocolon with three stresses. The deciding factor seems to have been the supposed preference of the poet for bicola. There is another possible colometry for this verse, namely if one takes שכלתי from 7c as part of 7b. Tradition that שכלתי belongs with אברתי is strong, however, being represented in both the Massoretic accents and the Greek text.

Semantically the two verbs fit well in their sequence and with their direct object in 7c. We have already noted that it is possible in Hebrew verse to have two verbs in the suffix conjugation in direct sequence in the same colon; cf. our discussion of 4:7c. Therefore, we prefer to keep שכלתי in 7c as in all our consulted sources. Returning to the division of 7a and 7b we want to suggest two reasons which we believe have probably contributed to this generally accepted division, but which have not received the necessary attention. The first is the presence of the suffixed object in 7a, which when counted as a unit and as a constituent would give 7ab taken together the maximum length on both the unit and constituent level, namely five and four respectively. We surmise that a colon of such length would be out of the ordinary and would be used only for conscious expressive purposes and then only in the context of other fairly long cola. Secondly, although the syntactical boundary between 7a and 7b is not in itself as prominent as for instance that preceding an appositional phrase, its prominence is enhanced by two factors, namely the double use of the preposition ב and the fact that בשערי הארץ as a non-obligatory prepositional phrase of place adds vividness to the image already called to mind by the two preceding words, and thus is repetitious in effect.

15:8 is textually in doubt in several places. We have deleted להם from 8c in accordance with the Septuagint, as was also done by Wambacq (1957, 115) and Bright (1965, 104). The plural masculine suffix does not fit the context and the word להם could have originated through a "slip of the ear" during dictation. On the colon delimitation there is unanimity.

15:9f is a separate colon according to all sources consulted, excepting JB and DLB which offer free translations and do not adhere to the Hebrew cola. As 9f is a very short colon some may claim that נאם־יהוה should be part of it. However, the commentators generally indicated that they regarded נאם־יהוה as separate from 9f, as Collins (1978a, 238) also did. Duhm (1901, 133) deleted it, stating that it was superfluous after verse 6, lacked in the Septuagint and did not fit in the metre. The two words לפני איביהם are therefore to be regarded as a complete colon on their own. This is understandable when one takes into account not the meaning of לפני, but rather its origin. For the purposes of colon structure לפני

is to be counted as a preposition plus a noun in the construct state. The uncertainty left by O'Connor (1980a, 75, 300) on the possible unit status of לפני and מפני is resolved. Cf. 18:17b and מפני in 4:26c, 13:17c and 23:9e.

15:10b in MT has one unit too many, although if main stresses only were to be counted, it would pass as an acceptable colon. We have deleted איש before מרון on the authority of the witnesses cited in BHS, namely a few Hebrew manuscripts and the recension of Symmachus, with reference also to the Septuagint. The same was done by Cornill (1901, 21), Rudolph (1968, 104) and Weiser (1981, 104). There is no textual support nor any need for deleting with Duhm (1901, 134), Giesebrecht (1905, 30) and Van Selms (1972, 213) the whole of איש מרון. While there is some difference of opinion as to the grammaticality of the construction (Williams, 1976, par.29), it does occur a number of times (Davidson, 1901, 37-38), e.g. in 2:6d, 11:20b and 20:12b.

15:10d we have emended by redividing the words כלה מקללוני, as did Cornill (1901, 21), Giesebrecht (1905, 30) and all the commentators consulted.

15:12 cannot, if its text is at all reliable, be taken as one colon like Thompson (1980, 391) did, nor even if ונחשת is deleted as in NEB. There are five units, five constituents and five stresses in the verse. The repetition of ברזל is an indication of colon boundary, for it would be the repetition of the last word of a colon as the first of the next colon. Thus we have a rhetorical question in 12a, extended in 12b, and a case of 2 + 3 whether in terms of units or of stresses. Both Wambacq (1957, 116) and Rudolph (1968, 104-105) accepted this interpretation, but curiously kept the verse as one colon in their translations. Our delimitation was also that of JB, NIV and EÜ.

15:13-14 we have deleted as a misplaced doublet of 17:3-4.

15:15ab has been delimited variously by commentators and translators. Taking 15a to include זכרני as in EÜ, is obviously wrong since 15a would then be far too long in comparison with the one word colon 15b. It is more difficult to decide whether יהוה belongs in 15a or in 15b. If one shares the view of Van Selms (1972, 214) that אתה ידעת are Yahweh's words to Jeremiah, the case is settled that יהוה is part of 15b. But in the whole context there is no indication that Yahweh is speaking, except of course in the intruding verses 13-

14. The words אתה ידעת were left out by the Septuagint, probably due to the intrusion of verses 13-14 which caused them to seem out of context (Duhm, 1901, 135). This in turn seems to have facilitated the division of 15ab before יהוה by Cornill (1901, 21), in JB, NEB and all the commentaries consulted except that of Duhm (1901, 135); cf. Giesebrecht (1905, 31). Among the translations RSV and NIV divided 15ab after יהוה; cf. also EÜ and DLB. If we apply O'Connor's (1980a, 86-87) system of counting units, constituents and predicators to 15b as delimited in the commentaries, with the modification that we count also suffixed objects as units and constituents, we find that the supposed colon 15b is one constituent too long and has two dependent nominal phrases not allowed in a colon with three predicators. For this reason we have taken יהוה as part of 15a.

15:16a was subdivided by EÜ alone of all sources consulted. Purely in terms of the length of single cola such subdivision would be possible. In view of the other long cola in this context, however, a colon of three stresses fits better. Our colon 16a is a typical action-result colon, emphasising by its very nature the relation between the two actions.

15:16bc was taken as one colon by Wambacq (1957, 116), Bright (1965, 106, deleting דבריך), NEB, NIV and EÜ. Even with the deletion 16bc would have 5 main stresses. Therefore 16bc must be divided. Those that did so, namely Cornill (1901, 21), Duhm (1901, 135), Giesebrecht (1905, 31), Rudolph (1968, 104), Thompson (1980, 394), Weiser (1981, 130), RSV and JB, included לששון in 16b. This would mean that 16c is semantically a repetition of לששון in 16b. Another possibility would be to include לששון in 16c. In that case 16b would correspond to נמצאו דבריך in 16a, the verb היה being used for the act of revelation, whilst 16c would correspond very vaguely to ואכלם in 16a. The latter possibility is much less likely than the former, in spite of the resultant contrast in length between 16b and 16c. Colon 16c is indeed a semantically repetitious extension of לששון in 16b, a ballast variant to it. In this case the ballast variant is the whole colon, whereas it usually is only part of a colon; cf. Watson (1984, 343-346).

15:17a seems to be a rather long colon within its context. For that reason BHK, Cornill (1901, 22), Giesebrecht (1905, 31) and Van Selms (1972, 215) have suggested textual changes, but these have no evidence in their favour. Wambacq (1957, 117), Bright (1965, 106), Collins (1978a, 171), RSV, NEB, NIV and DLB preferred to sub-divide 17a. In the case of Duhm (1901, 136) the suggested subdivision is made possible by first changing the word order. Duhm realised that with the word order as it is, subdivision is impossible. But for a change in the word order we have again no evidence. A closer look at 17a reveals that it is not too long. It has four words like 16b and 17b, and three main stresses like 16d and 16e. We therefore agree with Rudolph (1968, 104), Thompson (1980, 394), Weiser (1981, 130), JB and EÜ that 17a is only one colon.

15:18c was regarded as an addition by Duhm (1901, 136) and Van Selms (1972, 215). All the other commentaries consulted as well as JB, NEB and NIV took 18bc as one colon. The supposed colon would have four units and four stresses, internal parallelism on the semantic level and a very prominent syntactic boundary dividing it into equal halves. The interrogative particle למה does triple duty. All these factors indicate that RSV and EÜ were correct in regarding 18b and 18c as separate cola. The pattern of 4 + 2 + 2 words which we find in 18a-c, is corroborated by the preceding 4 + 4 + 2 and the following 4 + 2.

15:19ab would have five units and all sources consulted divided it. Rudolph (1968, 104) and Weiser (1981, 130) understood ואשיבך as a semantically incomplete verb having תעמד as its complement. This interpretation would to our mind be incompatible with the generally accepted division of the cola after ואשיבך, and would favour rather the division before ואשיבך as in JB. Of course that would leave only אם תשוב as 19a, which cannot be correct. So we have a case here in which the colon delimitation disproves an interpretation of the syntax that would otherwise have been possible.

15:20cd was taken as one colon by Giesebrecht (1905, 31 with emendation), Thompson (1980, 395), NEB and DLB. The other sources consulted unanimously divided as we do. The division is based on the clear syntactic and antithetic semantic parallelism of these cola and the resultant prominent syntactic boundary between them.

15:20ef was divided after להושיעך by Cornill (1901, 22 with emendation), Thompson (1980, 395) and NEB. The other sources consulted divided as we do, except Giesebrecht (1905, 31) who

regarded this part of the verse as a prose addition. Our delimitation
produces two cola of two main stresses each. In 20f we have a clear
internal parallelism. A subdivision of 20f is not advisable, in spite of
its having four units as against the two units of 20e, as such subdivision would produce two successive cola with only one stress each.

16:19de was divided before ויאמרו by EÜ. Collins (1978a, 68, 146)
found these two cola problematical, for he ended 19d with ארץ, but
began 19e with אך, somehow losing ויאמרו along the way. Except
for Duhm (1901, 141) who provided no translation of the verse, all
consulted sources divided 19de as we do. O'Connor (1980a, 87) would
also have experienced difficulty with 19d, seeing that according to him
a colon containing a clause predicator may not contain a nominal
phrase dependent on a predicator outside that colon. That is exactly
what is generally accepted to be the case here. The concensus on the
delimitation of these cola is quite amazing, considering the number of
possible solutions. There need be no doubt that מאפסי־ארץ, a two
unit expression with one main stress, should fall outside 19c, which is
a three unit colon with three stresses; cf. 9:10ab, 12:10cd, 13:16cd. A
first possible solution would be to take our cola 19d and 19e as three
short cola, the proposed 19d consisting only of מאפסי־ארץ, 19e
being ויאמרו אך־שקר, and 19f being נחלו אבותינו. The weak
point of this solution is that the supposed 19f would have to be
regarded as an asyndetic relative clause in order to have a prominent
syntactic boundary between 19e and 19f. This seems very unlikely. A
second possibility would be to regard ויאמרו as an anacrusis,
external to the limits of the neighbouring cola. Our theory does not
allow for such an anacrusis. Thirdly one could take ויאמרו as the
first word of 19e without subdividing 19e. In this case 19e would be a
long colon of four stresses following directly upon 19d with its one
main stress. This solution also seems very unlikely. The only probable
solution is to take ויאמרו as the last word of 19d. This is the
generally accepted view, but it poses a question, namely whether the
concept of the syntactic integrity of a colon is still valid. To our mind
it is, but not in the simple form suggested by O'Connor. It seems as if
a colon can in certain cases contain nominal phrases not dependent
on its own predicator. In such cases a prominent syntactic boundary
would occur within the colon, but the end of such a colon must also
coincide with a very prominent syntactic boundary. A similar case

occurs in Jon 2:3b. There is also some measure of similarity between
19d and 6:14b (= 8:11b). The rhyming of 19cde may be intentional.

17:1ab has only three main stresses. In spite of that all commentaries consulted divided the cola as we do. Here, then, not the
number of stresses, but rather the number of units per colon is
decisive, in this case 3 + 2.

17:1cd also has five units, and it would be easy to interpret
בצפרן שמיר as an appositional expression to בעת ברזל in 1b,
taking חרושה as the verb of a new clause. This was the way in which
the Massoretes understood it, as can be seen from their placing the
'atnach under שמיר. If we were to divide the cola according to this
interpretation, however, 1c would have only one main stress and 1d
would have three stresses. Taking חרושה as the last word of 1c
produces two cola of two stresses each, but again with a 3 + 2 pattern
of units. Our delimitation is in agreement with all the consulted
commentaries.

17:3-4 has a doublet in 15:13-14, which we have deleted, but from
which important information as to the correct reading of 17:3-4 can
be obtained. In spite of the textual corruption of both passages the
pairing of long plus short cola is a conspicuous feature of both. There
remain small differences of opinion between some commentators as
to the exact reading of these verses, but they do not affect the colon
delimitation. Our cola 4a and 4b were discarded as prose by Duhm
(1901, 143), who also left out כל in 3a. Like Duhm we have deleted
the prosaic אשר in 4d in accordance with 15:14. For the rest our
reconstructed text and colon delimitation are the same as that of
Wambacq (1957, 124), Bright (1965, 114), Rudolph (1968, 104, 114),
Thompson (1980, 417, but cf. 391) and Weiser (1981, 142). Brief but
clear descriptions of the textual changes made to obtain this text and
the reasons for them were given by Bright (1965, 118) and Rudolph
(1968, 114). These two verses follow a pattern of 3 + 2 throughout,
both in terms of main stresses and of units. The colon boundaries are
all prominent syntactical boundaries, though slightly less so in the
case of 3ab and 3cd.

17:5ab as well as its equal in *17:7ab* was treated as one colon by
Giesebrecht (1905, 33), Wambacq (1957, 125), Bright (1965, 114-115),
Thompson (1980, 419), Weiser (1981, 142), BHK, BHS and all the
translations consulted. Both were divided into two cola each by

Cornill (1901, 33) and Rudolph (1968, 114-115) as we do. Although Duhm (1901, 144-145) offered no translation or colon delimitation of these verses, he referred to both 5-6 and 7-8 as "Achtzeiler", having deleted our colon 7c. This can only mean that he too distinguished two cola in both 5ab and 7ab. To solve the problem we have to take into account similar verses in the book of Jeremiah. Of those 48:10 can be discounted immediately, seeing that it is generally regarded as a later prose addition, in spite of its presentation as verse in BHK and BHS and its translation as verse by Wambacq (1957, 270) and Weiser (1981, 392, cf. 398), both of whom explicitly referred to it as an addition. Bright (1965, 314, 320) and Thompson (1980, 700, 704) treated 48:10 as a prose comment. More important for our purposes than the origin of 48:10 is the fact that it is formulated differently, with the result that, even if it were verse, its colon delimitation might be quite different from that of 17:5ab and 7ab. The only other comparable cases within the book of Jeremiah are in 20:14ab and 15ab, on the colon delimitation of which there are divergent views, but both of which we have seen fit to divide before אֲשֶׁר. In the light of their similarity with 17:5ab and 7ab as well as the fact that each of these consists of two clauses, each clause having at least one finite verb and one dependent nominal phrase, and with a prominent syntactic boundary between them, we have divided 17:5ab and 7ab at that syntactic boundary, i.e. before אֲשֶׁר.

17:9 has been treated in three different ways. Duhm (1901, 146), Giesebrecht (1905, 33), Wambacq (1957, 126) and EÜ took 9ab as one colon. The supposed colon would have five stresses and five constituents with a clause boundary dividing it between the third and the fourth. On the other hand Rudolph (1968, 114), Weiser (1981, 143), JB and NEB took 9bc as one colon. This supposed colon would have four stresses, but again five constituents and a clause boundary between the second and third words. According to the third view, held by Cornill (1901, 33), Bright (1965, 115), Thompson (1980, 421), RSV and NIV, verse 9 consists of three cola, divided as we have done. The verse consists of three clauses and we regard their boundaries to be the boundaries of the cola. In each clause, and thus in each colon, one constituent refers to the לֵב. It can also be said that each of our cola is parallel to the other two, 9c being a rhetorical question and thus a statement like 9a and 9b.

17:10a could be interpreted as two clauses as in DLB. In such a case it might be argued that 10a should be read as two cola. However, all other sources consulted regarded יהוה אני as appositional and treated 10a as one colon. We agree with this view. It should be pointed out that 10a, which has three main stresses, is followed by 10b with only one main stress. Still it would be wrong to take 10ab as one colon, as did Weiser (1981, 143), for בחן כליות is clearly equivalent to חקר לב and 10ab would have too many units for one colon.

17:12a was subdivided after כבוד by Bright (1965, 115). His supposed first colon would have only one main stress because כסא is in the construct. Cornill (1901, 33), Duhm (1901, 147) and Giesebrecht (1905, 33) did not provide a delimitation of cola for this verse, the latter only stating that it has six stresses, which cannot be correct. The other commentaries and translations consulted were unanimous in dividing it as a case of 3 + 2 main stresses. To our mind this case and other similar ones show that not only the number of words or units play a role in the versification system, but also the number of main stresses.

17:13d in the MT ends with את־יהוה to which even the Septuagint bears witness and which was retained by Wambacq (1957, 127). The resultant colon would be rather long in this context, but it would be allowable in terms of the number of stresses, units and constituents. Its extra length may be viewed as effecting closure, seeing that 17:14 is the beginning of a new section. Another possibility would be to change the word order so as to include את־יהוה in 13d directly after the verb and to regard מקור מים־חיים as a separate colon, as was done by Cornill (1901, 33), RSV, NIV and EÜ. We have deleted את־יהוה like Duhm (1901, 147), Giesebrecht (1905, 33), Bright (1965, 116), Rudolph (1968, 116), Thompson (1968, 423), Weiser (1981, 143), JB and NEB. It may be a gloss, unnecessarily making explicit what was clear already from the mention of יהוה in 13a, or it may be the result of a misreading of אתה at the end of verse 14. Even without את־יהוה 13d would effect closure, being longer than the preceding three cola.

17:14bc was regarded as one colon with four stresses by Rudolph (1968, 116-117); cf. also Giesebrecht (1905, 34). This cannot be correct. There is clear semantic and syntactical parallelism between

14a and 14b, in the light of which the inclusion of an extra nominal clause in 14b would be highly unlikely. We should also note that 14a and 14b are examples of the so-called "plea and response" colon, in which the active and the passive of the same verb are used in the same colon; cf. Watson (1984, 280 and n.31). One would hardly expect an additional clause within the second of two cola following such a fixed scheme. All the other commentaries and translations consulted were in agreement with this delimitation.

17:15b was subdivided by Bright (1965, 116), RSV, NIV, EÜ and DLB in such a way that יבוֹא נא becomes a separate colon, but that expression has only one unit and carries only one stress, נא being an enclitic particle. Such a subdivision therefore cannot be accepted, the more so as the supposed 15b would then have three units and two stresses only, whereas one might rather expect it to have at least three stresses after the indivisible 15a with its four units and either three or four stresses. Even more unlikely is the delimitation of Thompson (1980, 424) and NEB, who took איה דבר־יהוה as part of 15a, leaving only יבוֹא נא as 15b. Thompson here seems to have been misled by Bright and NEB. In its syntactical structure our colon 15b is somewhat similar to 2:10a, 6:16a and 6:16c. Our delimitation of the cola is in agreement with that of Cornill (1901, 22), Wambacq (1957, 128), Rudolph (1968, 116), Weiser (1981, 143) and JB.

17:16a was subdivided by Duhm (1901, 148), Giesebrecht (1905, 34) and Weiser (1981, 143). There is no reason to do so, and the indivisibility of its counterpart 16b proves our decision to be correct. All the other sources consulted agree with our delimitation.

17:16cd was a problem to translators and to some commentators. The problem is an old one as is clear from the placing of the *'atnach* under ידעת and from the division of sentences in the Greek rendering. The main question is whether ידעת is the end of a colon or not. Among the commentators only Duhm (1901, 148) and Giesebrecht (1905, 34) thought so. Like them RSV and EÜ took 16c to be two separate and complete cola, whereas JB, NIV and DLB took the second half of 16c to be part of 16d. NIV even took the first half of 16c to be part of 16b, which makes that colon far too long and gives it five stresses. On the other hand, if one takes only אתה ידעת as 16c, the words מוֹצא שפתי as a two unit subject of the following colon can hardly stand on its own as a complete colon. But taking it as part of 16d would give that colon five main stresses. It is far better to take מוֹצָא שְׂפָתֶי as the direct object of יֶרַעת and therefore as part of 16c, whilst at the same time understanding it as the implied subject of הָיָה in 16d. Each colon in the verse is a complete clause. In terms of units and stresses 16cd is a 4 + 3 just like 16ab. Cornill (1901, 22) and all the newer commentaries consulted, i.e. from Wambacq (1957, 128) onwards, as well as NEB preferred this delimitation of the cola.

17:18ab and 18cd were each treated as one colon by Bright (1965, 116), Rudolph (1968, 116), Weiser (1981, 143), JB and NEB, as well as by Thompson (1980, 425) in his translation of the verse. However, in a note Thompson (1980, 425 n.3) reproduced the four cola which he perceived in the Hebrew text. Wambacq (1957, 128), RSV, NIV, EÜ and DLB also translated 18a-d as four cola. At least three factors support this view. The syntactical boundary between 18a and 18b as well as that between 18c and 18d are clause boundaries and thus very prominent. There is an explicit strong contrast in meaning between the cola in each pair of cola. The cola in each pair make use of the same verb in the same verbal theme, and the subjects, which function as corresponding terms, are contrasted, being third person plural as against first person singular.

18:13d is a one stress colon of two units like 15b, 16b and 17b. This type of colon is generally recognised by scholars and we have come across it repeatedly, cf. 9:10b, 13:24b, 15:8b, 17:1b as a few random examples. From the translations provided by Thompson (1980, 436) and Weiser (1981, 151), however, one could get the impression that they do not recognise this type of colon. Such an impression would be incorrect. These commentators have unfortunately not always distinguished between a colon and a bicolon in the printed layout of their translations. This is clear from e.g. their treatment of 13a, which cannot but be two cola, but which they presented as one printed line without any indication of the colon boundary. For other examples which illustrate their inconsistence in this respect one can compare their translations of 18:13-17 with BHS and Thompson's (1980, 438) setting out of the cola of verse 16.

18:14 presents some text critical problems and its syntax and exact meaning is uncertain. There does exist a concensus on the general import of the verse, as well as the delimitation of its cola, as is clear from the commentaries consulted. This is true in spite of the printing of undivided bicola in Wambacq (1957, 132), Thompson (1980, 436) and Weiser (1981, 151); cf. the point made above with reference to 18:13d. We have accepted the concensus delimitation which produces quite normal cola, and have left the MT unemended, regarding the possible emendation of the verse as beyond the scope of the present study.

18:17ab was printed undivided by Weiser (1981, 151), as did Thompson (1980, 437) with both 17ab and 17cd. NEB and NIV divided our cola 17ab before the verb. Collins (1978a, 90, 256, 260) had difficulty in deciding whether to divide 17ab and 17cd before or after the verbs. All the other commentators consulted as well as RSV and JB divided after the verbs in both cases, as did Weiser (1981, 151) with 17cd. On לפני cf. our discussion of 15:9f. Division after the verbs is more likely not only in terms of rhythm but also in terms of syntax, the dependent phrases in 17b and 17d being extra circumstantial information. Those in 17a and 17c seem to be obligatory with the verbs.

18:21c was subdivided as a 2 + 2 by Rudolph (1968, 122), JB and EÜ. Excepting for Duhm (1901, 159) who did not provide a colon delimitation, all other commentators and RSV, NEB, NIV and DLB treated 21c as one colon. We also take this view, noting that each colon in verse 21 has four units and that the stress pattern is 4 + 3, 4 + 3 + 3. The syntactical boundary in the middle of 21c is not very prominent. The corresponding subjects and verbs in 21c and 21d indicate that these cola were meant to be a pair, with 21e as a further extension of the thought. It would therefore be wrong to subdivide 21c.

18:23ab was divided before ידעת by JB and EÜ, but after עצתם by DLB. Both delimitations produce very unequal cola and are in fact impossible, since one of the cola would then have five stresses, unless כל - unlike other nouns - does not have its own stress when followed by a noun with suffix. We would prefer a consistent versification system. One possibility would be to regard 23ab as prose, a view which could claim the support of Cornill (1901, 12) and perhaps Duhm (1901, 159) who called all of 18:21-23 "Halbprosa". But Giesebrecht (1905, 35) and all the more recent commentators unanimously treated the passage including 23ab as verse, and although 23ab completely lacks parallelism it fits its context well. The commentaries which did provide colon delimitations and RSV, NEB and NIV were unanimous in dividing after ירעת. We concur, but we are aware that the colon boundary between the verb and its direct object may seem unacceptable. It would seem that exactly this fact contributed to the rather unusual delimitations represented in JB, EÜ and DLB. One possible solution would be to delete את־ from 23b, surmising that it was either due to dittography or was a later addition to the text for syntactical clarification. On the latter assumption one might even delete the whole of את־כל־; cf. Würthwein (1957, 74). Our colon 23b could then be understood as a verbless clause and there would be a very prominent syntactic boundary preceding it. The translations given by Rudolph (1968, 124) and Weiser (1981, 152) tend somewhat in this direction, although these commentators did not object to the את־. Another possible interpretation would be that the colon boundary has its unusual position as regards the syntax due to extra units which fill the colon, the explicit subject and the vocative in the case of 23a. Similar cases are scarce, but we have found 5:15ab, 6:21ab, 8:17ab and 13:26ab.

20:8cd was divided before לחרפה by all the consulted commentators except Duhm (1901, 165) and Giesebrecht (1905, 35), both of whom divided after לחרפה and replaced דבר־יהוה with דברי so that 8c would not be too long. If the prophet intended 8c as an allusion to the receiving of Yahweh's word, preparing for a deliberate anticlimax in 8d, a colon boundary before לחרפה would be quite in place, although אל and not ל is the preposition more frequently used with היה דבר־יהוה in that sense (HAL, 234). Such an interpretation also seems a bit far-fetched. On syntactical grounds and in view of the repetitive nature of parallelistic verse one would expect the colon boundary to occur between חרפה and קלס. This surmise is borne out by the fact that both the other occurrences of קלס in the Old Testament, namely in Ps 44:14 and 79:4, as well as the sole occurrence of the related קלסה in Ezk 22:4, is paralleled by the word חרפה in the previous colon. On the basis of these facts we have seen fit to differ from the majority of commentators and translations by dividing 8cd after לחרפה. It may be objected that our cola 8c and 8d are too unequal in length, 8c having five units and four stresses as against the three units and two stresses of 8d. That argument on its own is not conclusive, however, in the light of the fair number of

cases in which the second of two cola has both two units and two
stresses less than the first. Cf. 2:5ab, 2:13ab, 4:17ab, 9:10cd, 10:22cd,
12:9cd, 13:16ab, 14:3ab, 14:5ab, 15:16bc, 15:18ab, 15:18de, 17:10ab.

20:9c in the Septuagint lacks an equivalent for בלבי, which we
have nevertheless retained, seeing that it corresponds with בעצמתי
in 9d. The length of the cola is within accepted limits either way.

20:9f in the MT is only one unit, which we do not accept as a colon.
It would be possible to take ולא אוכל as part of 9e. Similar cases
occur in 20:11b, 11c and 16b. In the Septuagint, however, an equivalent of לשאת occurs at the end of the verse. According to BHK it
is also represented in the Vetus Latina and the Vulgate. We have
therefore followed Duhm (1901, 165), Giesebrecht (1905, 36), JB and
NEB in including this infinitive in our 9f, which then is an acceptable
colon on its own. On the one hand there is alliteration of ל, א, and כ
across these two cola, and on the other there is a similarity in
construction with a contrast in meaning well suited to being expressed
in two successive cola.

20:14ab and *15ab* were treated as one colon each by Wambacq
(1957, 143), Thompson (1980, 462), JB, NEB and NIV, while EÜ
took 14ab as one colon but divided 15ab. Like BHK and BHS, Cornill
(1901, 27), Duhm (1901, 166), Bright (1965, 130), Rudolph (1968,
132), Weiser (1981, 167) and RSV divided 14ab before אשר. Only
Giesebrecht (1905, 36) divided 14ab after אשר. On the other hand
15ab was divided before אשר only by Cornill (1901, 27), RSV and
EÜ, a division after בשר being preferred by Duhm (1901, 167),
Giesebrecht (1905, 36), Bright (1965, 130) and Rudolph (1968, 132)
as in BHK and BHS. Curiously, perhaps by accident, 15ab was
treated as three cola by Weiser (1981, 168). Although Wambacq
(1957, 143), JB and NIV took 14cd to be one colon, there is no way
either 14cd or 15cd can be only one colon, seeing that they would be
too long in any terms of measurement. The other sources consulted
are unanimous in their division of 14cd, and in the case of 15cd the
sources just mentioned share in the unanimity. One would therefore
expect 14ab and 15ab also to be two cola each. In verse 14 the
division is corroborated by the chiastic arrangement of אשר ילד in
14b and 14c and of ארור/ברוך in 14a and 14d. In 15ab length is
again decisive. The two cola together would be too long, so that the
only question remaining is where the colon boundary was intended to

be. To our mind it is highly unlikely that the colon boundary would occur between the verb בשׂר and its direct object, especially so shortly after the occurrence of the prominent syntactic boundary between the main clause and the relative clause. Therefore we have divided 15ab before אשׁר, a division which produces another case of 2 + 3, counting either units or stresses. Our division of 14ab and 15ab accords well with our view of 17:5ab and 7ab, these four cases being very similar in formulation.

22:10ab was treated as one colon by NEB and NIV as well as by all commentators consulted, including probably Van Selms (1972, 271) since "luttele versregels" can mean either "short cola" or a "few cola". In their colon delimitation Giesebrecht (1905, 37, adding הוי אדון to 10a), Collins (1978a, 171), RSV, JB, DLB and ANV recognised two cola, delimited as we do. We should note also that Duhm (1901, 174), who did not divide 10ab, referring to our 10a-c said: "Das erste Distichon ist übrigens etwas überladen". Our cola 10a and 10b are clearly syntactically and semantically parallel and have a clause boundary between them. In terms of both stresses and units 10a-c is 2 + 2 + 3, and it is followed by a 2 + 3.

22:10de was divided after וראה by Cornill (1901, 24), Duhm (1901, 174), Wambacq (1957, 150) and Rudolph (1968, 140), the latter two indicating that they understood ישׁוב to mean "again". If that were correct, one should probably include וראה in 10d. The colon boundary would then come between the verb and its direct object. To our mind, however, ישׁוב is here constrasted directly with הלך in 10c and has its usual sense of "return". Furthermore, 10d contains the word עוד meaning "again", which makes ישׁוב in that meaning totally superfluous. The Septuagint's rendering of the two cola is correct, even recognising the double duty of לא. We therefore agree with Giesebrecht (1905, 37), Bright (1965, 136), Thompson (1980, 475), Weiser (1981, 187) and all the consulted translations - except EÜ, which treated the verse as prose - that the colon boundary coincides with the syntactic boundary before וראה.

22:14cd in the MT has the words חלוני וצפון, which we have redivided so as to have a third person masculine singular suffix. This was also done by Duhm (1901, 175), BHK, NBG, Bright (1965, 137), Van Selms (1972, 271) and Thompson (1980, 477). These two cola were treated as one by Cornill (1901, 24), Duhm (1901, 175),

Rudolph (1968, 142), Weiser (1981, 188) and NEB. In the case of
Cornill, Duhm and NEB the combination was accompanied by the
deletion of לו. In JB 14de was treated as one colon. In view of the
syntactical parallelism of 14c, 14d and 14e, as well as the clause
boundaries and the number of units and stresses we have divided
14cde into three cola. This was also done by Wambacq (1957, 150),
Bright (1965, 137), Thompson (1980, 477), RSV, NIV, EÜ and DLB.

   22:15a was subdivided by all the sources consulted. Both Cornill
(1901, 24) and Giesebrecht (1905, 38) regarded מתחרה as the last
word of 15a. In that case it does not seem possible to make sense of
the words directly following the supposed 15a. All the others seem to
have divided before כי, or as is clear in the case of Wambacq (1957,
151) and Rudolph (1968, 142) after אתה. A division before כי
creates a first colon of only one word, comprising only one unit and
having only one stress, which is extremely unlikely. Dividing after
אתה, however, is equally unlikely, since it creates a case of
enjambement, which is very scarce in Hebrew verse and for the
occurrence of which here we can find no reason. If there had been no
כי in 15a, or if it had occurred after אתה instead of before it, a
subdivision of 15a would have been possible.

   22:17ab was treated as one colon by NEB. All the other sources
consulted divided it after ולבך, producing a long-short sequence of
cola, the first having three units and the second only one. In spite of
the presence of the two particles, the preposition and the suffix in the
supposed 17b, we find this supposed colon wanting. We therefore
suggest that עיניך and לבך be regarded as corresponding terms and
that אין does double duty. In Num 15:39 עין and לב occur together
with more or less the same meaning as here. Our interpretation and
delimitation produces an increasing pattern both of units, namely
2 + 2 + 3 + 3, and of stresses, namely 2 + 2 + 2 + 3.

   22:18 has been variously delimited. Weiser (1981, 189) and NEB
distinguished only two cola, equal to our 18abc and 18def. Duhm
(1901, 176) and Giesebrecht (1905, 38) regarded 18ab and 18de as
one colon each. On the other hand Wambacq (1957, 151), Bright
(1965, 138), Collins (1978a, 85), Thompson (1980, 477), RSV, JB,
NIV and EÜ treated 18bc and 18ef as one colon each. It may be that
they simply followed BHK and BHS in this matter, both editions not
having a clear boundary dividing 18bc and 18ef. Rudolph (1968, 139,

142) and Watson (1984, 252) clearly distinguished the same six cola in this verse as we do. From Van Selms's (1972, 274) referring to the metre of the quoted dirge formulae as being 2 + 2 here, we deduce that he also distinguished these six cola. The word הוי could hardly be without a stress. Each of the six cola then has two units and two stresses. There is an intricate pattern of parallelism, namely between 18abc and 18def, but also between 18b and 18c, and again between 18e and 18f.

23:6c along with the rest of verses 5-6 was treated as prose by RSV and EÜ. Although Duhm (1901, 181) and Giesebrecht (1905, 39) did not provide colon delimitations for these verses, the other commentators and translations consulted all regarded verses 5-6 as verse and with good reason, and were unanimous in their delimitation of the cola. O'Connor's (1980a, 87) system would allow colon 6c, which has two clause predicators but according to his count only has nominal phrases dependent on one of the predicators. We differ from him in counting suffixed objects as both units and constituents. As a result we shall also have to alter his constraint on constituents. However, this is no new problem, since we have already come across it, *inter alia* in our discussion of 6:16c.

23:9ef was interpreted as a gloss by Duhm (1901, 182) and was treated as one colon by Wambacq (1957, 157), NEB and EÜ. Giesebrecht (1905, 39) divided 9ef after ומפני, which cannot be correct unless this be regarded as a case of enjambement. We have divided before ומפני like all the other sources consulted. Again we find that מפני for the purposes of verse structure is not to be regarded as simply a preposition, but rather in accordance with its morphology, as a combination of a preposition and a noun and therefore as a unit; cf. 4:26c, 13:17c and לפני in 15:9f and 18:17b.

23:10a is continued syntactically and semantically in 10d and 10e. Similarly 10b and 10c belong together, and these two cola must be regarded either as intrusive or as transposed. Bright (1965, 147) placed 10b and 10c before 10a, which makes excellent sense. We have kept them in sequence simply to facilitate easy correlation with the printed editions. Giesebrecht (1905, 40) and Rudolph (1968, 148) chose to emend the text, but the possibility of changing the order of the cola as Bright did, obviates the need of such a measure. Duhm (1901, 183) called our colon 10a "kein vollständiges Distichon". It was subdivided after מנאפים by Collins (1978a, 64), presumably because he failed to find the corresponding colon, whilst expecting pairs of cola. That length was not Collins' consideration for such division is proven by the fact that he kept 10b as one colon (1978a, 137). Colon 10a was treated as one colon by Wambacq (1957, 157), Bright (1965, 147), Thompson (1980, 492), Weiser (1981, 200) and all the translations consulted.

23:10e was unanimously regarded as a colon by all commentaries consulted. This remains correct, whether לא־כן is one concept, as claimed by Rudolph (1968, 148, cf. 58) and HAL (459), or not. In either case כן is recognised as a unit.

23:12abc was delimited in an amazing number of different ways. The same delimitation as in BHK and BHS is to be found in Rudolph (1968, 148), Weiser (1981, 201) and EÜ. One of its faults is the one word colon כחלקלקות. Wambacq (1957, 157) accepted the first and second cola of BHK, but combined the third and the fourth. NEB distinguished only two cola, the second beginning with באפלה. NIV and ANV combined the first two cola of BHS, but accepted the third and the fourth. Cornill (1901, 26) distinguished only two cola, the second beginning with ידחו. Giesebrecht (1905, 40) distinguished three cola, of which the second began with להם and the third with באפלה. JB began its second colon with להם and accepted the last two cola of BHK. Our delimitation is natural in terms of the syntax, the two prepositional phrases forming the second colon whilst the third colon describes the sudden and fatal action. One factor which seems to have led interpreters astray was the feminine suffix in בה, which was taken to refer to באפלה, thus creating a parallelism between the third and fourth cola of BHS, which the poet had never intended. The dominant word (cf. Watson, 1984, 287) on which the content of these three cola is based is דרך, which in this case is feminine as in Ex 18:20, and to which the feminine suffix refers; cf. BDB (202) and HAL (222). Our delimitation is in agreement with that of Bright (1965, 147), Thompson (1980, 493), RSV and DLB, and incidentally with the verse division of the Massoretes, which is based on their understanding of the syntax.

23:13a has its counterpart in 14a, as is indicated inter alia by the ו with which both cola begin (Duhm, 1901, 184). This fact is commonly recognised, with the result that almost all delimit 14a in the same way as 13a, the exceptions being Giesebrecht (1905, 40) and EÜ. There is another implication of the correspondence between 13a and 14a, however, which is not generally recognised, namely that the length of the cola following 13a and 14a should not be allowed to influence one's delimitation of 13a and 14a and especially one's decision whether to subdivide 13a and 14a or not. If one thus isolates 13a and 14a from the cola which follow them and instead takes 13a and 14a as each other's context, there is no reason to subdivide either of them. They are each one clause with four units and three main stresses. They are, indeed, such normal Hebrew cola that the decision by the majority of commentators and all the translations except NEB to subdivide them would seem inexplicable if the shorter cola 13b, 13c, 14b and 14c were not in the close vicinity. The commentators and translators were no doubt influenced by the printed editions on this point, but it should be noted that Rudolph, who subdivided 13a and 14a in both BHK and BHS, did not do so in his commentary (1968, 150-151). One further argument against the subdivision of these cola is the fact that in them both the subdivision would produce a first colon with only one main stress. Our decision not to subdivide 13a and 14a is in agreement with the colon delimitation of Cornill (1901, 26), Rudolph (1968, 150-151), Weiser (1981, 203) and NEB, as well as EÜ in the case of 13a.

23:13bc was treated as one colon by Cornill (1901, 26) and Rudolph (1968, 150-151), both deleting את־ישראל as a gloss, as well as Weiser (1981, 203) and NEB. All the other commentators and translations consulted divided 13b and 13c as we do. Again it is clear that interpreters were misled by the cola of a different type in the vicinity. As in the case of 13a and 14a Rudolph's commentary differs from his treatment in BHK and BHS. The two cola 13b and 13c are two separate clauses, each having at least two units and two constituents. The two clauses are not parallel in any strict sense, but as Berlin (1985, 134) pointed out, in a context of parallelistic verse the listener or reader would regard the two clauses as parallel. This subjective experience of the listener or reader enhances the role of the clause boundary as colon boundary. In the light of all these facts we take 13b and 13c to be two separate cola.

23:14a we have treated like 13a; cf. the discussion of both above.

23:14d was printed as two cola in BHS, apparently by mistake, for all other sources consulted took it as one colon.

23:15cd provides an interesting example of one clause continuing through two cola. Together the two cola have six units, which are too many for one colon. As to the number of stresses there is less certainty, and it may be argued that 15c has only one main stress, as we have argued in the case of 13a and 14a. Here, however, the possible one stress colon is the second from last in a section or strophe, whereas in 13a and 14a the supposed one stress colon would have been the first. Excepting for the very free translation of DLB, all the consulted sources divided 15cd into two cola, although Duhm (1901, 185) and Giesebrecht (1905, 40) placed the colon boundary one word later. But in that case there is no core colon, i.e. no colon which could on its own be a complete clause. Thus we regard our colon delimitation to be correct, even if 15c should prove to have only one stress, which is not certain in view of the double preposition used before the construct relation.

23:16ef we have delimited in the same way as all commentators consulted, except Duhm (1901, 186) who did not provide a colon delimitation, and Wambacq (1957, 159) who regarded verse 16 as prose. We should point out, however, that 16f is another one stress colon.

23:17 we have emended according to the Septuagint, taking למנאצי דבר יהוה to be a double construct relation, as did Duhm (1901, 186), Bright (1965, 148), Rudolph (1968, 152), Van Selms (1972, 287), Thompson (1980, 496), RSV, JB, NEB (cf. Brockington (1973, 207) and EÜ. This involves changing the vowels only of למנאצי דבר. Without changing the sense of verse 17 it would be possible to delete אמור from 17a and אמרו from 17c, and to change וכל in 17c to ולכל. Taking these possibilities into account our text and colon delimitation are essentially the same as that of Cornill (1901, 26), Bright (1965, 148), Rudolph (1968, 152), Thompson (1980, 496), Weiser (1981, 204), JB, NEB and DLB. Our cola 17a and 17c each has five units and four main stresses, whereas both 17b and 17d have three of each. If the two possible deletions were made, both 17a and 17c would have four units and three main stresses. All four our cola are complete clauses, with the result that the colon boundaries are clause boundaries. Whether the deletions are made or not, the double long-short pattern remains clear.

23:19 is commonly delimited as we have done. Cornill (1901, 26), Duhm (1901, 188) and Giesebrecht (1905, 40) did not treat this verse. The word חמה in 19a was deleted by Bright (1965, 148), Rudolph (1968, 152) and Weiser (1981, 204), while Van Selms (1972, 287) regarded it as an explanatory addition by the prophet himself during dictation. Wambacq (1957, 159) retained the word and Thompson (1980, 486, 498) gave no indication that he was aware of the problem. From the reading of 37:23 in the Septuagint one could guess that the original reading may perhaps have been חמת יהוה instead of סערת יהוה חמה, but that would remain a mere guess. Fortunately this is a case where the colon delimitation is not affected by the text critical uncertainty.

23:20ab is commonly delimited by commentators and translators as three cola, the first ending with יהוה and the second with הקימו. Of those that provided delimitations only NEB and EÜ differed, namely by taking the second and third cola of the majority view together as one colon. To our mind there is one alternative delimitation which none of the works consulted chose to employ, but which nevertheless has much in its favour. We take עד־עשתו as part of 20a and the next three units as 20b. The two cola so produced constitute a so-called "parallel terrace" (Watson, 1984, 212). This delimitation has the advantage of having הקימו and its direct object in the same colon. Then the first colon would seem to be incomplete, an incompleteness which we regard as intentional, since that would eminently suit the sense of the verse. The temporary sense of incompleteness would be cancelled by the syntactically and semantically complete 20b. Moreover, 20a and 20b rhyme, whereas according to the generally accepted delimitation the third and second cola would rhyme, leaving the first on its own. In terms of main stresses the generally accepted delimitation would be 2 + 2 + 2, whereas our delimitation produces a 3 + 3.

23:20c is another three stress colon, from which we have deleted בינה, which is not represented in the best Greek witnesses (Ziegler, 1976, 266), the Peshitta and the doublet in 30:24. The colon was subdivided by Bright (1965, 149), Rudolph (1968, 152) and NIV, producing cola of 1 + 2 main stresses. It has only one clause and there is no good reason to subdivide it. Wambacq (1957, 160), Thompson (1980, 496), Weiser (1981, 204), RSV, NEB, EÜ, DLB and ANV correctly treated 20c as one colon.

25:30e and 31a have been variously treated. There is some difference of opinion as to the relationship of 30e to either 30a-d or to 31. Wambacq (1957, 173), RSV, NIV and ANV followed the Massoretic view that 30e belongs with 30a-d, whereas the majority of commentators and translators as well as Collins (1978a, 69) agreed with the Septuagint interpretation that 30e belongs with 31. Bright (1965, 159), Rudolph (1968, 166), JB and EÜ regarded 30e and שׁאוֹן כֹּא from 31a together to be one colon. This view seems to be influenced by the assumption that in bicola the longer colon should come first. The same observation is valid as to the decision of Thompson (1980, 518) and NEB to switch the order in which 30e and 31a occur. We have repeatedly found counter-evidence to that assumption. It seems better to keep the order of the cola as it is. Moreover, there is no reason to disconnect 30e from the cola preceding it, unless one understands parallelism always to produce bicola; cf. the three successive cola 31bcd, which depict three successive stages of trial, conviction and punishment. We understand 31a as the beginning of a new section of verse, which is consciously semantically connected with the end of the preceding section by the similarity in syntax and by the use of the same noun in the colon final position. Although our view on the connection between 30e and 31a cannot claim much support from modern scholarship, our colon delimitation does have the support of the majority of both the commentaries and the translations consulted, including Weiser (1982, 221) and DLB in addition to those already mentioned.

25:32ab was treated as one colon by Wambacq (1957, 174), Weiser (1982, 222), NEB, EÜ and ANV, whilst Weiser and NEB also took 32cd to be one colon. The supposed long cola are possible in terms of the number of units and constituents. But together 32ab would have five stresses, which are too many. Therefore we take verse 32 as four cola, twice 3 + 2 units, although 32d has only one main stress. This is the view of all the other sources consulted, including Collins (1978a, 60), but excepting Cornill (1901) and Giesebrecht (1905) who did not provide delimitations of the cola in this verse. Cf. also 6:22 and our discussion of it above.

25:38c is text critically uncertain, but the possible changes will not influence the delimitation of cola.

4.3 Systematic description of the Hebrew colometric system

The cola of the verse sections in Jeremiah 2 - 25 have been delimited above in terms of units, constituents, clause predicators and main stresses. These levels of measurement each play a role in an integrated system which determines the colometry of Hebrew verse. Our description of that system will begin by defining the terms, after which their role in the system will be described. Although the description must necessarily be offered step by step in paragraphs, what is described in each paragraph is so closely bound up with the contents of the other paragraphs, that it should not be viewed in isolation. It should be noted that this is not an attempt to describe the versification system as a whole. Such a description would *inter alia* have to include specifications for the combination of cola, for the form and nature of strophic structures, and for methods of closure in Hebrew verse. We are concerned with formulating only the constraints which the ancient Hebrew poet obeyed in creating his *cola*.

4.3.1 Terms or levels of measurement

The term *unit* was used by Albright, Bright, Kosmala, Holladay (1966, 403-404) and Margalit (1975, 291-298) and there has been some difference of opinion as to which words should count as units; cf. Kosmala (1964, 426 = 1978, 87; 1966, 169 = 1978, 124) and Holladay (1966, 403, 410). We use the term like O'Connor (1980a, 68, 87, 314-315) for each semantic word, which we understand to mean the same as Ley's *Begriffswort*, i.e. each verb, noun, pronoun, adjective or adverb is counted as a unit. Words which express relation between words, like conjunctions, particles, prepositions, articles and suffixes, do not count as units. However, a word which is prepositional in meaning, but which consists of a preposition and a noun as to its origin and morphology, e.g. לפני or מפני, does count as a unit for purposes of verse structure; cf. our discussion of 15:9f. As to suffixed objects we differ from O'Connor in that we count them as units, whereas he did not; cf. 3.3.5.4.

The term *constituent* has not often been used in discussions of Hebrew verse structure, and yet the concept is implicit in most treatments of Hebrew verse. Scholars do not assume colon ends within a construct relation or between a noun and its attribute, unless it be as a case of severe enjambement, and it should be kept in mind that enjambement is very scarce in parallelistic verse. The level of constituents was the only level taken into account by Collins (1978a). We are in essential agreement with O'Connor's (1980a, 87, 308-311) statement: "A constituent is a verb, or an argument of a predicator which appears on the surface, unless it includes a prepositional phrase, in which case it is split." As to suffixed objects we again differ from O'Connor in that we count them as constituents, whereas he did not; cf. **3.3.5.4.**

The term *clause predicator* as used by O'Connor is quite acceptable to us. His definition (1980a, 86-87) of it, however, is not clear in all respects and has been misunderstood by Watson (1984, 108 n. 77). Taking into account his discussions of it elsewhere (O'Connor, 1980a, 306-307, 311-313) we reformulate his definition as follows: The major clause predicators are a finite verb; an infinitive not used absolutely and not governing only an agent; a participle governing anything not suffixed to it or in construction with it. The minor clause predicators are vocatives and focus markers.

The term *main stress* is well known in the traditional metrical approach to Hebrew verse. By it we mean only that stress which is recognised by the grammarians as the main stress of a given word or combination of words. Particles, prepositions, negations and conjunctions have no stress of their own. When two nomina are in a construct relation, they have only one main stress. Three nomina in a double construct relation have only two main stresses. Two nomina in a construct relation with a following suffix also have two stresses. It should be noted that O'Connor offered his constrictional system as an alternative for the more usual phonological approach to Hebrew "metrics". In our opinion stress is one factor in the colometric system interacting with others, namely the syntactical constraints.

4.3.2   The variety of cola

In terms of these levels of measurement a large variety of cola can be distinguished within our corpus, which will now be illustrated. In doing this we shall mainly concentrate on the longest and shortest cola, as these are most likely to be controversial.

In the following tables the figures represent the number of units (U), constituents (C), clause predicators (P) and main stresses (S) respectively.

Cola with *two units* occur in the following variety:

U	C	P	S		
2	2	2	2	ספרו והילילו	4:8b
2	2	2	2	העיזו אל־תעמדו	4:6b
2	2	1	2	ונשמו הכהנים	4:9c
2	2	1	2	הגידו ביהודה	4:5a
2	2	1	2	גדול אתה	10:6b
2	2	1	2	נחלה מכתי	10:19b
2	2	0	2	כערבי במדבר	3:2d
2	2	0	2	במשפט ובצדקה	4:2b
2	1	0	2	אהבת כלולתיך	2:2b
2	1	0	2	ושבר גדול	4:6d
2	1	0	1	מפני יהוה	4:26c
2	1	0	2	לפני איביהם	15:9f
2	1	0	1	מעון תנים	9:10b
2	1	0	1	תרועת מלחמה	4:19e
2	1	0	1	מלך הגוים	10:7b
2	2	1	1	ואכלתם	5:14e
2	2	1	1	אל־תנחנו	14:9e
2	2	1	1	ואשחיתך	15:6d
2	2	1	2	למען תושעי	4:14b

Cola with *three units* occur very frequently and in a large variety, which the following examples illustrate:

U	C	P	S		
3	3	3	3	קראו מלאו ואמרו	4:5d
3	3	2	3	ובירושלם השמיעו ואמרו	4:5b
3	3	1	3	ברקים למטר עשה	10:13c
3	2	1	2	לא־כאלה חלק יעקב	10:16a
3	1	1	2	יהוה אלהי צבאות	15:16e

3	1	0	2	לחומת נחשת בצורה	15:20b
3	3	1	2	מי ידענו	17:9c

Cola with *four units* are also relatively frequent and occur in a large
variety, of which again only a few are quoted:

U	C	P	S		
4	4	2	4	וקדר שלחו והתבוננו מאד	2:10b
4	3	2	3	לא־ישבתי בסוד־משחקים ואעלז	15:17a
4	4	1	4	היעשה־לו אדם אלהים	16:20a
4	3	1	3	היו תהיה לי כמו אכזב	15:18d
4	3	1	3	בפעם הזאת אודיעם	16:21b
4	1	1	2	וכל־משפחות בית ישראל	2:4b

Cola with *five units* are considerably less frequent, but nevertheless
show variety:

U	C	P	S		
5	4	2	4	אי־זה דרך הטוב ולכו־בה	6:16c
5	3	2	4	לכו אספו כל־חית השדה	12:9c
5	3	2	3	שמעו דבר־יהוה בית יעקב	2:4a
5	4	1	4	מה־מצאו אבותכם בי עול	2:5a
5	4	1	4	ומצח אשה זנה היה לך	3:3c
5	4	1	4	כשמרי שרי היו עליה מסביב	4:17a
5	4	1	4	הנה סערת יהוה חמה יצאה	23:19a
5	4	1	3	ועתה מה־לך לדרך מצרים	2:18a
5	3	1	4	הנה־קול שועת בת־עמי	8:19a
5	3	1	4	כי־איך אעשה מפני בת־עמי	9:6b
5	2	0	3	איש ריב ומדון לכל־הארץ *	15:10b

Cola with *one constituent* include the following:

U	C	P	S		
4	1	1	2	וכל־משפחות בית ישראל	2:4b
3	1	0	2	גם־בני־נף ותחפנס	2:16a
3	1	0	2	בחן כליות ולב	11:20b
2	1	0	2	כי־גם־נביא גם־כהן	14:18e
2	1	0	2	בכף איביה	12:7d

U	C	P	S		
2	1	0	1	מעון תנים	9:10b
2	1	0	1	בחן כליות	17:10b
2	1	0	1	לפני אויב	18:17b

Among cola with *two constituents* are found:

U	C	P	S		
2	2	2	2	ספדו והילילו	4:8b
2	2	2	2	נדרו הלכו	9:9f
2	2	1	2	ונשמו הכהנים	4:9c
2	2	0	2	כערבי במדבר	3:2d
2	2	1	1	ואשחיתך	15:6d
3	2	1	3	לאכל פריה וטובה	2:7b
3	2	1	2	לשתות מי שחור	2:18b
3	2	0	3	אל־העם הזה מכשלים	6:21b

Cola with *three constituents* include:

U	C	P	S		
5	3	2	3	שמעו דבר־יהוה בית יעקב	2:4a
4	3	2	3	כי עברו איי כתיים וראו	2:10a
3	3	2	3	ובאחת יבערו ויכסלו	10:8a
3	3	1	3	ראי דרכך בגיא	2:23c
3	3	1	2	כי־שכחני עמי	18:15a
3	3	1	2	מי ידענו	17:9c

Among cola with *four constituents* there are:

U	C	P	S		
4	4	2	4	הכהנים לא אמרו איה יהוה	2:8a
4	4	2	4	וקדר שלחו והתבוננו מאד	2:10b
4	4	2	4	כבסי מרעה לבך ירושלם	4:14a
4	4	1	4	בארץ לא־עבר בה איש	2:6f
4	4	1	4	כי רעה אנכי מביא מצפון	4:6c
4	4	1	3	התקם כצאן לטבחה	12:3c

For further cases of cola with four constituents cf. the list of cola with five units above.

The following examples illustrate the *various numbers of clause predicators* which occur in a colon:

U	C	P	S		
2	1	0	2	אהבת כלולתיך	2:2b
3	1	0	2	גם־בני־נף ותחפנס	2:16a
5	2	0	3	איש ריב ומדון לכל־הארץ *	15:10b
3	3	1	3	קדש ישראל ליהוה	2:3a
4	3	1	4	זכרתי לך חסד נעוריך	2:2a
4	1	1	2	וכל־משפחות בית ישראל	2:4b
4	3	2	3	כי עברו איי כתיים וראו	2:10a
3	3	2	2	הושיעני ואושעה	17:14b
2	2	2	2	העיזו אל־תעמדו	4:6b
5	3	2	3	שמעו דבר־יהוה בית יעקב	2:4a
3	3	3	3	קראו מלאו ואמרו	4:5d
3	3	3	3	שמעו והאזינו אל־תגבהו	13:15a
4	4	3	3	רפאני יהוה וארפא	17:14a

Among cola with *one stress* two types can be distinguished, namely the simple construct relation, which is one constituent, and the verb with suffixed object, which is two constituents:

U	C	P	S		
2	1	0	1	תשועת ישראל	3:23d
2	1	0	1	מפני יהוה	4:26c
2	1	0	1	לפני אויב	18:17b
2	2	1	1	ואכלתם	5:14e
2	2	1	1	אל־תנחנו	14:9e
2	2	1	1	ואשחיתך	15:6d

Cola with *two stresses* have a high frequency. Only a few examples are quoted to illustrate their variety of length:

U	C	P	S		
2	2	0	2	ושבר גדול	6:1f
2	1	0	2	אהבת כלולתיך	2:2b
3	1	0	2	ראה כליות ולב	20:12b
2	2	1	2	כי תהלתי אתה	17:14c

| 3 | 2 | 1 | 2 | הקשיבו לקול שופר | 6:17b |
| 4 | 2 | 1 | 2 | וכל־משפחות בית ישראל | 2:4b |

Cola with *three stresses* also have a high frequency. A few examples will suffice to illustrate their variety of length:

U	C	P	S		
3	3	3	3	שמעו והאזינו אל־תגבהו	13:15a
3	3	2	3	צדיק אתה יהוה	12:1a
3	3	1	3	להכרית עולל מחוץ	9:20c
3	2	1	3	לראות עמל ויגון	20:18b
4	2	1	3	כי עזבו מקור מים־חיים *	17:13d
4	3	2	3	כי־שמענה נשים דבר־יהוה	9:19a
4	4	1	3	מי־יתנני במדבר	9:1a
5	4	2	3	הנני צורפם ובחנתים	9:6a
5	3	2	3	שמעו דבר־יהוה בית יעקב	2:4a
5	2	0	3	איש ריב ומדון לכל־הארץ *	15:10b

Among cola with *four stresses*, which are less frequent, are found:

U	C	P	S		
4	4	2	4	וקדר שלחו והתבוננו מאד	2:10b
4	4	1	4	כי רעה אנכי מביא מצפון	4:6c
4	4	1	4	והיה כעץ שתול על־מים	17:8a
4	3	1	4	ותהיהנה נשיהם שכלות ואלמנות	18:21c
4	3	1	4	והיה האיש ההוא כערים	20:16a

For further cases of cola with four stresses cf. the list of cola with five units above.

4.3.3 Independence of the levels of measurement

A very important feature of the different levels of measurement is their *relative independence*. By this term we mean that a specific number on one level does not necessarily imply a specific number on another level.

While on the one hand the number of *constituents* in any syntactically complete expression - whether phrase, clause or colon - can never be greater than the number of *units*, the number of constituents

can be equal to, or smaller than the number of units by one or more.
Compare the following examples:

U	C	P	S		
4	4	1	4	כי רעה אנכי מביא מצפון	4:6c
4	3	1	4	והיה האיש ההוא כערים	20:16a
4	2	1	3	כי עזבו מקור מים־חיים *	17:13d
5	3	2	3	שמעו דבר־יהוה בית יעקב	2:4a
2	1	0	1	בהבלי נכר	8:19f

From these examples it is also clear that the number of *stresses* can
be equal to or smaller than the number of *units*, but the number of
stresses cannot be greater than the number of units. In both cases
there is no fixed relation between the two levels of measurement
which would make it possible to deduce the one from the other.

Similarly the number of *predicators* is never greater than the
number for any of the *other levels* of measurement. It can be equal to
or smaller than those numbers. But the number of predicators is
never deducible from the numbers of any of the other levels, as the
following examples illustrate:

U	C	P	S		
3	3	3	3	קראו מלאו ואמרו	4:5d
3	3	2	3	צדיק אתה יהוה	12:1a
3	3	1	3	להכרית עולל מחוץ	9:20c
5	3	2	3	שמעו דבר־יהוה בית יעקב	2:4a
5	2	0	3	איש ריב ומדון לכל־הארץ *	15:10b
2	2	2	2	העיזו אל־תעמדו	4:6b

The most significant fact as to the relative independence of the levels
of measurement is that the number of *stresses* can be either equal to,
or smaller than, or greater than the number of *constituents*. Compare
the following examples:

U	C	P	S		
5	2	0	3	איש ריב ומדון לכל־הארץ *	15:10b
4	3	1	4	והיה האיש ההוא כערים	20:16a
3	3	1	3	כי הנני משלח בכם	8:17a

4	4	1	3	מי־יתנני במדבר	9:1a
5	4	2	3	הנני צורפם ובחנתים	9:6a

In the relationship between these two levels of measurement, then, there is not even the possiblity of deducing from the one either the maximum or the minimum number of the other as was the case in the relationships discussed above.

The relationships between the levels of measurement as discussed in this paragraph can be summarised in the following formulae:

$$U = /> C, S$$
$$P = /< C, U, S$$
$$C = /</> S$$

Although the examples quoted in this paragraph are all complete cola, it should be noted that the relationships between the levels of measurement as summarised in the above formulae are the same for any syntactically complete expression or any combination of such expressions.

4.3.4 Colon level constraints

As to the *range* within which each of the levels of measurement occur within the colon, we agree with the range of four each established by O'Connor (1980a, 87) for units, constituents, and clause predicators. To this we add another range of four, namely 1 - 4 stresses. It may be objected that O'Connor offered his constrictional system as an alternative description of the Hebrew versification system and that it should, therefore, not be combined with an element from other descriptions such as stress. Such an objection would be misplaced in two respects.

Firstly, although O'Connor devised his system as an alternative description of the Hebrew versification system, he did not regard it as incompatible with the taking into account of stresses. O'Connor regarded the phonological patterning as concomitant to the constrictional system (1980a, 148-149) and intended to discuss it (1980a, 149). He suggested that lines (cola) would have between two and five accents (stresses) if every unit is allowed one accent, to which he immediately added: "Statements of accentual systems usually refer to the constituent level, so the range will be between one and four accents in a line" (1980a, 150). Having this oversimplified idea of the relation between constituent and stress - which he incidentally shared with Collins (1978a, 57) - O'Connor found it unnecessary to attend to stress any further (1980a, 150). As was shown in 4.3.3 the number of constituents can be equal to, or smaller than, or greater than the number of stresses.

Secondly, it is not unusual for a versification system to have what can be called two bases, whether these are both of a phonological nature or one of a phonological and the other of a syntactical nature; cf. Wimsatt and Beardsley (1959, 587-588, 597-598), Zhirmunsky (1966a, 31-32; 1966b, 232, 242), Lotz (1972, 9-10), La Drière (1974, 672-673). We, therefore, hold that a constraint on the number of stresses per colon is quite compatible with the syntactical constraints on the colon level.

Following the example of O'Connor (1980a, 75, 138) we can summarise the system of colon level constraints in a matrix as follows:

units	2	3	4	5
constituents	1	2	3	4
clause predicators	0	1	2	3
main stresses	1	2	3	4

From the examples quoted above, especially in 4.3.2, it is evident that cola fitting the description given in this matrix do indeed occur. We have found none that does not fit this description, i.e. in the words of O'Connor (1980a, 138) "there are no lines of fewer than the leftmost or more than the rightmost number on any level."

On the point of the existence of *cola with five units* O'Connor (1980a, 75, 315) was quite adamant. In his whole corpus of 1225 cola he found 22 such cola (1980a, 317-318), namely Ex 15:4c, Dt 32:32b, 33:12c, Jdg 5:6c, 5:13a, 5:31a, Ps 78:9a, 106:46, 107:5, Zph 1:4c, 1:9c, 1:18c, 2:5b, 2:12, 2:13c, 3:1, 3:8h, 3:9a, 3:11a, 3:11c, 3:11d, 3:12c. Of these Ps 78:9a probably contains a gloss (BHK; BHS; BDB, 676; HAL, 690). All the rest are either based on unacceptable delimitation of cola or can with reasonable credibility be subdivided into cola which would be quite acceptable in terms of O'Connor's description of the colon, as well as in terms of ours. O'Connor, then, did not provide any proof of the existence of cola having 5 units. From our corpus, however, the existence of such cola can be proven. The 5 unit cola Jer 2:4a and 2:18a cannot be subdivided because they are paralleled by indivisible 4 unit cola. Some other 5 unit cola cannot be subdivided because they are syntactically too integrated to admit subdivision, namely 2:5a, 3:3c, 4:17a, 6:16c, 8:19a, 9:6b, 12:9c, 15:10b. The 5 unit colon does indeed exist in Hebrew verse.

A further matter is the existence of *one word cola*. According to O'Connor (1980a, 307) "it is agreed that there are no one word lines in Hebrew verse". Some authors will differ from him on this point (Dahood, 1967, 576-577; Hauser, 1980, 29; Althann, 1983, 35 and *passim*; cf. Watson, 1984, 110, 212). To our mind O'Connor's formulation is unclear. It may be that he meant nothing else than in his previous statement (1980a, 69) "that no unit can stand alone as a line", which is in agreement with the matrix of the constriction. The latter statement is correct, but that does not mean that the former also is, since a verb plus a suffix would be one word but two units. The only one word cola we recognise are those containing a verb plus a suffixed object pronoun. We regard them as two units and two constituents. O'Connor's unclear formulation may again be due to his not recognising suffixed object pronouns as units and constituents; cf. the discussion in 3.3.5.4.

4.3.5   Validity of the levels of measurement

It has been stated that our aim is a valid and adequate description of the colometric system, not for instance a comprehensive description of Hebrew cola. For that reason we do not count either syllables or consonants, there being no indication that these are significant in Hebrew colometry. It may now be asked whether the levels on which we count elements are all valid in the sense of being necessary in our description of the colometric system.

If four *clause predicators* did in fact occur in a colon, that colon would have been allowable in terms of all the other levels, including that of stresses. But the maximum number of clause predicators that do occur per colon is three. From this fact we deduce that the number of clause predicators is constrained or restricted by a separate constraint or restriction within the colometric system. Also the fact that fewer clause predicators than any of the other measured elements may occur per colon, namely 0, indicates that predicators are subject to a separate constraint; cf. O'Connor (1980a, 307). Therefore a formulation of that constraint has to be included in our description of the colometric system.

If five *constituents* did in fact occur in a colon, that colon would have been allowable in terms of all the other levels. This again includes the level of stresses, seeing that a verb with a suffixed object counts as two constituents but carries only one main stress. As to the minimum number of constituents it is found that cola of one constituent do occùr on the condition that they have at least two units. It is clear, then, that the number of constituents is also subject to a separate constraint; cf. O'Connor (1980a, 313). A formulation of this constraint must also be included in our description of the system.

The same argument applies in the case of *units*. Both their maximum and their minimum number per colon are subject to a constraint separate from those of the other levels; cf. O'Connor (1980a, 314-315). This constraint must also be included in our description of the colometric system.

In the case of the fourth level of our description, namely the level of *stresses*, the maximum and minimum numbers per colon are equal to the maximum and minimum numbers of constituents per colon. However, although their range is the same, the number of stresses is not equal to the number of constituents in every colon. Far from it, for one constituent can have one, two or more stresses, and in the case of verbs with suffixed objects two constituents have only one stress. Neither is there any constant relationship between the number of stresses on the one hand and either the number of clause predicators or the number of units per colon. Thus it is clear that the number of stresses per colon is regulated by a separate constraint, which in its turn must be included in our description of the colometric system.

We conclude this paragraph by stating that all four levels of measurement are valid in the sense of being necessary within our description of the colometric system.

4.3.6   Interaction of the level of stresses with the level of units

We have shown that the levels of measurement are independent of one another (**4.3.3**) and that all four levels are valid in the sense of

being necessary within our description of the colometric system
(4.3.5). In this paragraph a related feature will be discussed, namely
the interaction of the level of stresses with the level of units. The two
levels should, as has already been pointed out, not be seen as two
different alternative systems between which the poet chose at will, but
as two factors within one colometric system.

On the one hand there are cases in which the number of units is
the dominant factor. In 2:10ab, for instance, the number of stresses is
increased by 1 but the number of units is unchanged. Also in the case
of one stress cola the dominant length factor is the presence of two
units, whether it is the type consisting of a verb plus a suffixed object
pronoun - of which there are four cases, namely 5:14e, 13:17a, 14:9e
and 15:6d - or the type consisting of only a construct relation, of
which there are at least 30 cases. That the presence of the two units is
indeed the dominant factor is borne out by the fact that these cola are
regularly preceded by cola of three stresses and three units, the well
established pattern of 3 + 2 thus being applicable to the level of units;
cf. 3:23d, 4:7b, 4:9b, 4:26c, 6:1b, 9:10b, 10:7b, 12:10d, 13:16d, 13:17c,
13:23d, 15:8b, 17:1b, 18:13d, 20:13d, 22:6b, 23:9e, 23:16e, 25:32d. In
the case of 14:8a, as in the case of 13:17a, the three unit colon follows
the two unit colon. Other patterns which do occur are 4 + 2 (cf.
4:19e, 6:26d, 8:19f, 9:1b, 10:22d, 13:24b, 17:10b, 18:17b), 2 + 2 (cf.
9:1f, 10:15b) and 5 + 2 (cf. 8:19b). These are clearly less frequent and
probably explicable in terms of rules of colon combination which are
beyond the scope of this study.

On the other hand there are cases where the number of stresses is
the dominant length factor. This is such a widely accepted view that it
hardly seems necessary to substantiate it. A few examples will,
however, be in place here. It would have been possible to subdivide
5:15b, but it is followed by three cola each starting with נֵזֶר and each
having three stresses, from which it is clear that these four cola
belong together and share the same length characteristic, namely
three stresses, as do also 5:15a and 15f. For the grouping together of
עַל־נִקְלָה and לֵאמֹר in 6:14b = 8:11b we have given syntactical
reasons, but when stress is taken into account the correctness of our
delimitation becomes more apparent. In the case of 6:21cd it was
pointed out above that the two cola could in all respects have been
regarded as one, had it not been for the five stresses. Our colon

16:19d would have been unacceptable within a purely syntactical system such as that of O'Connor, and we found it necessary to take into account both syntactical considerations and the number of stresses, as in the case of the somewhat similar 6:14b = 8:11b. There are also a number of cases where we have argued that a section of verse would be unlikely to begin with a one stress colon and where we have, therefore, preferred longer cola; cf. 4:17a, 23:13a and 14a.

That the two levels of measurement with which we are concerned here do not constitute two different alternative systems, but rather function together, is indicated by those cases in which the two levels provide different but mutually complementing patterns, e.g. in 10:5, 18:21 and 22:17. Their interaction can only be proven, however, by cases where both are decisive in close proximity. In our corpus there are at least two such cases.

The first is 17:1

חטאת יהודה כתובה	a
בעט ברזל	b
בצפרן שמיר חרושה	c
על־לוח לבם	d

In 1ab the number of units is the dominant factor in the pattern 3 + 2. But if only the number of units was decisive in this verse the obvious interpretation of 1cd would be that of the Massoretes, dividing after שמיר and taking חרושה as the verb of a new clause. As was pointed out above, however, such a delimitation would produce a colon 1c of only one stress, followed by 1d with three. Our delimitation produces two cola of two stresses each and of 3 + 2 units. Both units and stresses, then, interact in the colometry of these four cola.

The second case is 18:17

כרוח קדים אפיצם	a
לפני אויב	b
ערף ולא פנים אראם	c
ביום אידם	d

In 17b the dominant factor must be the presence of two units. In 17c and 17d, however, the well known 3 + 2 pattern of stresses is present, albeit with a 4 + 2 pattern of units, which latter is perhaps an indication that also in 17a the four units are dominant, and not the two stresses. Again the interaction of the two levels within the scope of four successive cola is established.

Taking these two cases into account together with those already discussed we are convinced that the interaction of the two levels over the whole of our corpus is a reasonable postulate.

4.3.7   Other constraints

As to the other constraints which O'Connor formulated, some points of criticism can now be raised, namely:

On the *integrity of cola* O'Connor stated: "If a line contains one or more clause predicators, it contains only nominal phrases dependent on them" (1980a, 87; cf. 69). This to our mind is an oversimplification of the syntactic integrity of the colon, for there are cola containing predicators but also containing nominal phrases dependent on predicators in other cola. An example from O'Connor's corpus is Dt 32:7d, where זְקֵנֶיךָ is object to שְׁאַל, which was gapped from 7d but is present in 7c. Similarly וְלִישְׂרָאֵל in Num 23:23d is dependent on יֵאָמֵר in 23c. In our corpus Jer 2:27b, 4:23b, 8:15b and 10:24b are similar. Such cola containing nominal phrases dependent on predicators in other cola, however, are not always a result of gapping. In 5:22d חָק־עוֹלָם, which is followed by a verb with suffix, i.e. by a complete clause, is an appositional phrase dependent on 22c. Similarly הֶבֶל in 16:19f is an appositional phrase and is followed by a clause of which it is not an argument. In 20:14c the word יוֹם is repeated from 14a and followed by an אֲשֶׁר clause. Other examples where the first constituent is a repetition from a previous colon are 2:6f and 5:28d, both cola containing predicators of their own. There are also cases where the first constituent of a colon simply is a prepositional phrase dependent on a predicator in the previous colon, namely 2:35d, 8:6d, 16:19d and 17:4d, in spite of the fact that these cola each have predicators of their own. In 14:17b the first constituent is an adverbial expression dependent on the predicator in 17a, and the second is another predicator. We agree with O'Connor that cola have some syntactic integrity. This usually means that a colon containing a predicator or predicators will contain no nominal phrases dependent on colon external predicators. However, seeing that there are cases where this is not true, the nature of the syntactic integrity of the colon cannot be stated in such simple terms. We suggest that it be restated to read as follows:

> The syntactic integrity of the colon means that usually a colon containing a predicator or predicators will contain no nominal phrases dependent on colon external predicators, and that where such phrases do occur, the syntactic boundary after the colon will be no less prominent than that within the colon.

O'Connor was quite convinced that *only one predicator* per colon could have *dependent nominal phrases* in that colon (1980a, 78, 87, 307, 315). There are, however, at least five clear cases of cola each having two predicators with nominal phrases dependent on each predicator, namely Jer 2:10b, 2:27a, 4:24a, 8:15a and 12:11d. There are also a number of cola having two predicators, the second of which along with its dependent nominal phrase, on a higher level function as a nominal phrase of the first predicator, namely Jer 2:6a, 2:23d, 8:8a, 17:6b, 17:8c and 18:20c. Similar cases are present in O'Connor's corpus, for example Ps 78:39a and Zph 3:7a. If suffixed object pronouns are recognised as dependent nominal phrases, which on grounds of syntax they must be, a number of further cases from our corpus can be added, e.g. 5:3c, 5:22f, 8:13e, 9:6a, 12:5a, 15:15b, 15:16a, 18:22c and 23:6c. By the inclusion of this wrong constraint, O'Connor's description of the colon is again an oversimplification.

O'Connor stated that *dependent nominal phrases* are absent in cola with *three predicators* (1980a, 87). In a later formulation the constraint was modified to apply only to cola with three major clause predicators (1980a, 315). No reason for this difference was noticed, but the latter formulation seems to be more correct. In our corpus 17:14a is a case in point if suffixed objects are recognised as units and constituents, i.e. as dependent nominal phrases. The first predicator in 17:14a is a verb with a suffixed object, the second is a vocative and the third is another verb. It seems, then, that dependent nominal phrases are present in cola with three clause predicators only in the form of suffixed objects and only when at least one of the predicators is a minor predicator. This constraint, however, will seldom influence the delimitation of cola, seeing that cola with three clause predicators occur very infrequently. With the constriction as we have modified it by adding the level of stresses, the supposed constraint may well be a *result* rather than a *part* of the constriction.

Of the three constraints discussed here only that of the syntactic integrity of the colon is of importance in the colometric sytem. As was shown it is closely related to the concept of the most prominent syntactic boundary. Both relate to the concept of the *core colon*, and ultimately to the concept of colon as a unit of metrics or colometry; cf. the discussion in 1.5.

4.4 Conclusion

In this chapter it was attempted to establish the role of syntactical constraints in the colometry of Hebrew verse. Use was made of the insights gained from the preceding surveys of systems applied to Hebrew verse and the criticisms raised against them. O'Connor's description of the Hebrew colometric system was taken as point of departure and the cola of our corpus delimited, taking into account especially the matters on which we differed from him, as set out in 3.3.5.4.

During the work on the colographic arrangement of the text and the grounds for our delimitation of the cola it was found that it was indeed possible to delimit cola reliably. The delimitation of the cola was often guided by factors not belonging to the colometric system, e.g. *parallelismus membrorum*, various kinds of repetition, clause initial particles, and semantic considerations. These factors seem to belong to the techniques used by the poets to combine cola. Some other conclusions relating to the combination of cola should be mentioned here, although these may need revision in the light of future study of the techniques for the combination of cola. These provisional conclusions are:

1.   It seems that *binarism* has been overemphasised in many studies of Hebrew verse; cf. also 2.1, 3.3.2, 3.3.4 and 3.3.5.2. Our analysis agrees rather with the views on the use of monocola, bicola, tricola and multicola expressed by Watson (1984, 168-190).

2. *Anacrusis*, strongly advocated by Robinson (1936b), could be a
    misleading concept to use in studies of Hebrew verse. No cases
    were found where such an "extra word" falls outside the
    maximum allowed by the colometric system. For that reason,
    and to avoid subjectivity (cf. Fensham, 1966, 15), it is better to
    regard the first word of a long colon as part of the colon and it
    is suggested that another name be used for the phenomenon.
3. *Enjambement* very seldom occurs in Hebrew verse; cf. the
    various views discussed in **1.5**. This is the natural result of the
    fact that the colon boundaries are syntactic boundaries, and
    usually the most prominent ones. Only one occurrence of
    enjambement was found in our corpus, namely in 5:23ab.
4. Just as a Hebrew poet apparently had the *option to replace* an
    expected bicolon with a tricolon or monocolon, it is possible that
    he sometimes for purposes of gross structure could have used
    two cola instead of one.

For the description of the colon it was found necessary to define *four
levels* of measurement. Three of these, namely the levels of units, of
constituents and of clause predicators, were taken over from
O'Connor with slight changes in the definitions. The fourth level is
that of main stresses. All four levels are relatively independent of
each other, and all four are necessary within our description of the
colometric system. There is an interaction of the level of stresses with
the level of units. In terms of these levels cola of a large variety occur
in Hebrew verse, namely a range of 2 - 5 units, 1 - 4 constituents, 0 - 3
clause predicators, and 1 - 4 main stresses. These are the colon level
constraints, of which only the latter regulates phonological rhythm,
whilst the first three are syntactical constraints.

Three additional constraints formulated by O'Connor were
examined. Of these only the *syntactic integrity* of the colon was shown
to be important to the colometric system, but O'Connor's description
of it was shown to be inadequate. It was reformulated to make
allowance for cola containing nominal phrases dependent on colon
external predicators. Together the syntactical constraints on the colon
level and the constraint of the syntactic integrity of the colon describe
the role of syntax in Hebrew colometry.

Chapter 5

Summary and Conclusions

In *chapter 1* above some *preliminary questions* basic to our views on Old Testament literature were discussed. On the question whether there is poetry in the Old Testament (1.1) it was concluded that it can and should be distinguished from prose, but should rather be referred to as verse, the distinction being one of form. The difficulty of distinguishing verse from prose in the Old Testament was then briefly discussed (1.2) and some causes of the difficulty were mentioned. It was pointed out (1.3) that verse is characterised by lineation, which is describable in terms of a versification system. On the nature of the Hebrew versification system scholars differ widely (1.4), namely whether it is a metre and what its nature is, part of the difference of opinion being due to misconceptions as to the concept of metre, which is an abstract scheme numerically regulating certain aspects of linguistic form. This was followed (1.5) by a discussion of the concepts of colon and colometry, and of the importance of the latter, referring also to enjambement and the problem of defining it. Keeping these preliminary questions in mind, the aim of the present study was set out (1.6), namely a valid and adequate description of the colometric system of Hebrew verse. It was proposed to achieve this by surveying systems presently applied, applying the insights obtained to our corpus in the practical delimitation of cola, and then formulating our description of the colometric system.

In *chapter 2* the *non-syntactical versification systems* presently applied to Hebrew verse were surveyed. The approach on the basis of parallelism (2.1) was found to be hampered by a number of factors which make it impossible to rely on parallelism alone in a search for the system of Hebrew verse. The counting of accents or stresses (2.2) was shown to be inadequate for the delimitation of cola. The survey of the word counting approach (2.3) showed that proponents of this approach had reached no concensus, neither on what they meant by word, nor on the system according to which the words should be counted. Concerning the syllable counting approach (2.4) it was shown that there often was some uncertainty as to the exact number of syllables, that the number of syllables was very unlikely to relate at all directly to the versification system, and that syllable counts could only be undertaken for already delimited cola. Similarly the counting of consonants (2.5) was found not to deal with the versification system itself, and not to be free from subjectivity. So the conclusion (2.6) was reached that none of these approaches was adequate to delimit cola reliably. With the partial exception of the approach through parallelism, the systems were all descriptions of some facet or facets of delimited cola, instead of descriptions of the colometric system itself. Whereas the role of syntax in the system was assumed throughout, it remained unspecified. The status of the syntactical boundaries which constitute colon ends still had to be determined.

In *chapter 3* the *syntactical approach* to versification systems was surveyed. A general characterisation of the approach (3.1) was followed by brief descriptions of syntactical approaches applied to some verse systems other than Hebrew (3.2), namely Russian verse, the earliest Hungarian verse, American Indian verse narrative, Bantu praise verse, Babylonian verse, Egyptian verse and Arabic verse. This led to the following conclusions (3.2.8): Various scholars from different scientific backgrounds were convinced that syntax did play a role in the versification systems which they studied. Their views indicated that serious consideration of a syntactical system of versification for Hebrew was warranted and that such a system may have different levels.

Next the syntactical approach to the versification system of Hebrew verse was examined (3.3), beginning by pointing out that many other Old Testament scholars could be regarded as precursors of this approach (3.3.1). Four syntactic descriptions proposed for Hebrew versification were subjected to a comparative evaluation.

The first of these was the system devised by Kurylowicz (3.3.2), which was found to have the following defects: failure to recognise the abstract nature of metre, failure to explain the functioning of the very irregular "mixed metre" which he found, too heavy reliance on signs added to the Hebrew text long after its origin, and refusal to take *parallelismus membrorum* into account as one of the indicators of colon length.

The second was Cooper's attempt (3.3.3), which took that of Kurylowicz as its point of departure. Cooper, however, in practice often and without reason ignored the very signs in the text which

Kurylowicz had relied on. As to parallelism he took the view which Kurylowicz had opposed. Together these factors rendered his approach to the problems of metre and colon delimitation so arbitrary as to be completely unacceptable.

The third to be examined was Collins' description of Hebrew verse-lines in terms of constituents. In spite of its obvious merits his approach suffered severely from the following defects: oversimplification of the relation between verse-line and sentence, unspecific syntactical categories, the ignoring of the status of particles, incorrect differentiation of line-types, and unsatisfactory delimitation of lines and of their component cola. It also became clear from examining Collins' description that the relation between the syntactical description of the verse-line and metre needed further investigation.

The fourth attempt at a syntactical description of Hebrew versification examined was that of O'Connor (3.3.5). Many criticisms had been raised by scholars against his study, falling into three groups, namely: criticisms regarding his method but not affecting his system for the delimitation and description of cola, criticisms regarding his choice of the colon as basic unit, and criticisms regarding his system for the delimitation and description of cola. The first group of criticisms was only listed by us. From the discussion of the second group it was concluded that no valid and adequate proof had been provided against taking the single colon as the basic structural unit to be described. The discussion of the third group revealed a degree of arbitrariness in O'Connor's colon delimitation, which indicated that his system needed further application, testing and probably adjustment. It was then shown that O'Connor was wrong in not regarding objects suffixed to verbs as units and constituents. O'Connor's description of the dominant colon form was corrected and its theoretical status was put into perspective. As in the case of Collins' work the exact nature of the relation between the syntactical description of the colon and metre was found to need more attention. However, O'Connor's description had the following decided merits: explicit definitions, the distinction of levels of syntax, no uncertainty as to his delimitation of the cola in his corpus, description of the single colon and, therefore, applicability to all combinations of cola.

In the light of these facts our survey of the syntactical approach to Hebrew versification was concluded (3.3.6), by stating that

O'Connor's description was the one to be further tested and refined, and that the system of syntactical constraints by which he described the colon, could be either the result of metre, or a component of metre, or a substitute for metre.

In *chapter 4* it was attempted to establish the *role of syntactical constraints* in the colometry of Hebrew verse. In the brief discussion of the scope and method of the chapter (4.1) it was pointed out that O'Connor's description of the colometric system served as point of departure, that use was made of insights gained from the previous surveys, and that O'Connor's description was adjusted where necessary. The limitations imposed by the material were set out and the way in which we presented the text was described. Lastly a distinction was made between our description of the system and the colometric system itself.

The colometric analysis of the verse sections in Jeremiah 2 - 25 (4.2) was presented in two parts, namely a colographic arrangement of the text (4.2.1), and the grounds for our delimitation of the cola (4.2.2). During the work on these two sections it became clear that it was indeed possible to reliably delimit the cola of our corpus, and also which changes to O'Connor's description were necessary. The delimitation of the cola was often guided by factors not belonging to the colometric system, e.g. *parallelismus membrorum*, various kinds of repetition, clause initial particles, and semantic considerations. It is our impression that these factors form part of the techniques used by the Hebrew poets to combine cola. In connection with the combination of cola the following provisional conclusions were reached:

1.   that binarism was overemphasised in many studies of Hebrew verse
2.   that the term anacrusis should be avoided
3.   that enjambement very seldom occurs in Hebrew verse
4.   that the Hebrew poet could possibly for purposes of gross structure have used two cola where one was expected.

In the description of the colometric system (4.3), firstly, the terms or levels of measurement were defined (4.3.1). Three of these, namely the levels of units, constituents and predicators, were taken over from

O'Connor, but related to other treatments of the system and adjusted where necessary. One level of measurement, namely that of main stresses, was added. The variety of cola present in the corpus was then illustrated (4.3.2), followed by a discussion of the independence of the levels of measurement, which can be expressed in three formulae (4.3.3). Next the colon level constraints were established (4.3.4), giving special attention to five unit cola and one word cola. Our findings agree with those of O'Connor, allowing a range of 2 - 5 for the level of units, a range of 1 - 4 for the level of constituents, and a range of 0 - 3 for clause predicators, but we added a range of 1 - 4 for the level of stresses. The validity of the levels of measurement was then discussed and each level was found to be necessary within our description of the colometric system (4.3.5). The interaction of the level of stresses with the level of units was discussed and illustrated (4.3.6). O'Connor had formulated three additional constraints. Only one of these, namely that concerning the syntactic integrity of the colon, was shown to be important in the colometric system (4.3.7), but it had to be reformulated as follows:

> The syntactic integrity of the colon means that usually a colon containing a predicator or predicators will contain no nominal phrases dependent on colon external predicators, and that where such phrases do occur, the syntactic boundary after the colon will be no less prominent than that within the colon.

The question should be considered here whether our description of the colometric system has any *advantages over previous descriptions*, and if so, what these advantages are. It was shown that all the systems presently applied to Hebrew verse were unable to delimit cola reliably. In the case of all the non-syntactical approaches this was at least partially due to the role of syntax being assumed but left unspecified. The approaches on the basis of parallelism, accent counting and word counting at least are based on realities in the text which are likely to be related to the colometric system, but the factors on which the syllable counting and consonant counting approaches are based are extremely unlikely to relate directly to the colometric system. The syntactical approaches of Kurylowicz, Cooper and Collins were shown to be unreliable for colon delimitation, whereas the description of the colometric system given by O'Connor has decided advantages already summarised earlier in this chapter.

Basic to O'Connor's description of the colometric system is the principle of the syntactic integrity of the colon. It was shown that his formulation of the principle was inadequate, and it was reformulated. This reformulation, especially in conjunction with the syntactical constraints, constitutes a major improvement in the description of the colometric system.

The syntactical description given by O'Connor was in our description combined with the counting of main stresses, which is a factor of phonological rhythm. The advantage of this combination vis-à-vis the non-syntactical approaches, and specifically accent counting, is that exactly the previously assumed but unspecified role of syntax in the colometric system is made explicit in the syntactical constraints. It is these constraints which describe the conditions on which, for instance, the two types of one stress cola can occur.

Only the main stresses recognised by the grammarians were taken into account in our description. This is a further advantage because it avoids the problem of having to decide which other syllables should also be regarded as stressed for metrical purposes, especially in the so-called alternating system.

On the other hand the inclusion of stress counting into our description of the system enables us to distinguish, for instance, between a five unit colon with three or four stresses and two successive cola which together have five units but also five stresses. The status of colon ends is not describable in terms of syntax alone. This is an important advantage vis-à-vis the description devised by O'Connor. It could only be formulated once the relative independence of the levels of measurement was noticed and explicated.

A further advantage of our description is its ability to account for the interaction of the level of stresses with the level of units. The cases where such interaction occurs could not be accounted for by taking into account main stresses only or the number of units only.

Most of the factors counted on the various levels, namely the units, the constituents and the clause predicators, are of the same nature as the rationale for the colon boundaries, namely of a syntactical nature. This is as an advantage of our description of the system, because it reveals the integrity of the system. The inclusion of stress counting in our description does not affect the integrity as it is a factor of phonological rhythm, which is apt to play a role in verse structure, irrespective of what other bases a versification system may have.

In the light of these advantages it is justified to claim that our description of the Hebrew colometric system is a nearer approximation of the system used by the Hebrew poets than any other known to us and is better able to delimit cola reliably.

The last question to be considered is that of the *theoretical status* of the colometric system which we have described, and thus also of our description of the system. In the discussion of O'Connor's system of syntactical constraints the three possible relations of such a system to metre have already been mentioned. The first possibility, namely that the system which has been described is the *result* of metre, is excluded for two reasons. It was shown that all the levels of our description are valid in the sense of being necessary within our description of the colometric system. It was also shown that the level of stresses interacts with the level of units. The necessity of all the levels and the interaction indicate that what we have described is not merely the result of a versification system. The system described, then, must be either a substitute for metre or a component of metre. If it were a *substitute* for metre it would be a non-metrical versification system. In view of the definition of metre as an abstract scheme that numerically regulates certain properties of the linguistic form of verse (cf. **1.4**), the colometric system which we have described could, and should, be called a metre. In comparison the system described by O'Connor, lacking the level of stresses, proves to be only a component of the metre of Hebrew verse. However, it should be kept in mind that the term metre is also applied to higher levels of verse than cola or lines (Tarlinskaya, 1980, 48-50; Pardee, 1981, 114). Because it numerically regulates certain properties of the linguistic form of verse, the colometric system which we have described is metrical, but it is part of the comprehensive versification system and thus could, perhaps in that sense, be regarded as a *component* of metre. The rest of the versification system lies beyond the scope of our study, however, and the question whether the whole of that system is metrical cannot be answered here. On that account it cannot as yet be said whether the

colometric system is a component of metre in the higher level sense
of that term, although on the colon level there is no objection to
regarding the colometric system as *metrical*.

Index of Subjects

Index of Biblical References

Italic page numbers refer to the main discussion of cola from Jeremiah 2 - 25 in 4.2.2

Index of Hebrew Words

Index of Authors

Abbreviations

The abbreviations used are limited to publications in the fields of the Old Testament and the Ancient Near East. Short titles and titles used less than 3 times are not abbreviated in the bibliography.

ANV   Afrikaans: Nuwe Vertaling, 1983
AOAT   Alter Orient und Altes Testament
BDB   Brown, Driver and Briggs, 1968
BHK   Biblia Hebraica, ed. R. Kittel, seventh edition, 1951
BHS   Biblia Hebraica Stuttgartensia, 1967-77
BZAW   Beihefte zur Zeitschrift für die alttestamentliche Wissenschaft
CBQ   Catholic Biblical Quarterly
DLB   Die Lewende Bybel, 1982
EU   Die Bibel: Einheitsübersetzung, 1980
GKC   Gesenius, Kautzsch and Cowley, 1910
HAL   Baumgartner, 1967, etc.
HSM   Harvard Semitic Monographs
HTR   Harvard Theological Review
HUCA   Hebrew Union College Annual
JB   The Jerusalem Bible, 1968
JBL   Journal of Biblical Literature
JNES   Journal of Near Eastern Studies
JSS   Journal of Semitic Studies
MT   Massoretic Text
NBG   Bijbel: Vertaling in opdracht van het Nederlands Bijbelgenootschap, 1951
NEB   The New English Bible, 1970
NIV   Holy Bible: New International Version, 1978
RSV   Revised Standard Version, 1952
SVT   Supplements to Vetus Testamentum
UF   Ugarit-Forschungen
ZAW   Zeitschrift für die alttestamentliche Wissenschaft

Bibliography

Abbott, K.M. 1974. "Enjambement" in A. Preminger *et al* (eds.): *Princeton Encyclopedia of Poetry and Poetics* (enlarged edition). Princeton: Princeton University Press 1974, 241.

Ackroyd, P.R. 1963. "Jeremiah X.1-16", *Journal of Theological Studies* 14, 385-390.

Akmajian, A. & Demers, R.A. & Harnish, R.M. 1979. *Linguistics: An Introduction to Language and Communication*. Cambridge, Massachusetts: MIT Press.

Albright, W.F. 1942. Review of R.H. Pfeiffer: *Introduction to the Old Testament*, *JBL* 61, 111-126.

Albright, W.F. 1950/1. "A Catalogue of Early Hebrew Lyric Poems (Psalm LXVIII)", *HUCA* 23, 1-39.

Albright, W.F. 1968. *Yahweh and the Gods of Canaan*. London: The Athlone Press.

Alonso-Schökel, L. 1971. *Das Alte Testament als literarisches Kunstwerk*. Köln: J.P. Bachem.

Alonso-Schökel, L. 1978. Review of Stuart (1976), *Biblica* 59, 421-423.

Alter, R. 1983. "From Line to Story in Biblical Verse", *Poetics Today* 4, 615-637.

Althann, R. 1983. *A Philological Analysis of Jeremiah 4-6 in the Light of Northwest Semitic* (Biblica et Orientalia 38). Rome: Biblical Institute Press.

Ap-Thomas, D.R. 1982. Review of O'Connor (1980a), *Journal of Theological Studies*, 33, 224-225.

Arbusow, L. 1963. *Colores Rhetorici* (second edition, ed. H. Peter). Göttingen: Vandenhoeck & Ruprecht.

Austerlitz, R. 1958. *Ob-Ugric Metrics* (Finnish Folklore Communications No. 174). Helsinki: Academia Scientiarum Fennica.

Austerlitz, R. 1961. "Parallelismus" in Davie (1961), 439-443.

Baker, A. 1973. "Parallelism: England's Contribution to Biblical Studies", *CBQ* 35, 429-440.

Baumgartner, W. *et al* 1967, etc. *Hebräisches und aramäisches Lexikon zum Alten Testament* (dritte Auflage). Leiden: E.J. Brill. I - 1967, II - 1974, III - 1983.

Beardsley, M.C. 1972. "Verse and Music" in Wimsatt (1972), 238-252.

Begrich, J. 1934. "Der Satzstil im Fünfer", *Zeitschrift für Semitistik und verwandte Gebiete* 9, 169-209. Also in J. Begrich: *Gesammelte Studien zum Alten Testament*, ed. W. Zimmerli (Theologische Bücherei 21). München: Chr. Kaiser Verlag 1964, 132-167.

Berlin, A. 1979. "Grammatical Aspects of Biblical Parallelism", *HUCA* 50, 17-43.

Berlin, A. 1982. Review of O'Connor (1980a), *Journal of the American Oriental Society* 102, 392-393.

Berlin, A. 1985. *The Dynamics of Biblical Parallelism*. Bloomington: Indiana University Press.

Bjorklund, B. 1978. *A Study in Comparative Prosody: English and German Iambic Pentameter*. Stuttgart: Verlag H.-D. Heinz.

Bloch, A. 1946. *Vers und Sprache im Altarabischen: Metrische und syntaktische Untersuchungen*. Basel: Verlag für Recht und Gesellschaft.

Blommerde, A. 1982. Review of O'Connor (1980a), *Bibliotheca Orientalis* 39, 160-169.

Böhl, F.M. 1957/8. "Bijbelse en Babylonische Dichtkunst: Een metrisch onderzoek", *Jaarbericht van het Voorziatisch-Egyptisch Genootschap Ex Oriente Lux* 15, 133-153.

Bright, J. 1965. *Jeremiah: A new translation with introduction and commentary* (The Anchor Bible). Garden City, New York: Doubleday.

Bright, W. 1981. "Literature: Written and Oral" in D. Tannen (ed.): *Analyzing Discourse: Text and Talk* (Georgetown University Round Table on Languages and Linguistics 1981). Washington: Georgetown University Press 1982, 271-283.

Broadribb, D. 1972/3. "A Historical Review of Studies of Hebrew Poetry", *Abr-Nahrain* 13, 66-87.

Brockington, L.H. 1973. *The Hebrew Text of the Old Testament: The readings adopted by the translators of the New English Bible*. Oxford: Oxford University Press.

Brown, E.J. 1973. *Mayakovsky: A Poet in the Revolution*. Princeton: Princeton University Press.

Brown, F. & Driver, S.R. & Briggs C.A. 1968. *A Hebrew and English Lexikon of the Old Testament*. Oxford: Oxford University Press.

Bruno, A. 1953. *Jesaja: Eine rhythmische und textkritische Untersuchung.* Stockholm: Almquist & Wiksell.

Bruno, A. 1954. *Jeremia: Eine rhythmische Untersuchung.* Stockholm: Almquist & Wiksell.

Buber, M. 1964. "Zum Abschluss" in M. Buber: *Werke: Zweiter Band: Schriften zur Bibel.* München: Kösel Verlag 1964, 1175-1182.

Budde, K. [C.] 1882. "Das hebräische Klagelied", *ZAW* 2, 1-52.

Budde, K. [C.] 1902. "Poetry (Hebrew)" in J. Hastings (ed.): *A Dictionary of the Bible*, Volume IV. Edinburgh: T. & T. Clark 1902, 2-13.

Burden, J.J. 1986. "Poetic texts" in F.E. Deist & W. Vorster (eds.): *Words from afar: The literature of the Old Testament*, Volume I. Cape Town: Tafelberg Publishers 1986, 39-71.

Ceresko, A.R. 1981. Review of Loretz (1979), *CBQ* 43, 279-280.

Chisholm, D. 1975. *Goethe's Knittelvers: A Prosodic Analysis.* Bonn: Bouvier Verlag.

Chisholm, D. 1977. "Generative Prosody and English Verse", *Poetics* 6, 111-153.

Collins, T. 1970/1. "The Kilamuwa Inscription - a Phoenician Poem", *Die Welt des Orients* 6, 183-188.

Collins, T. 1978a. *Line-Forms in Hebrew Poetry.* Rome: Biblical Institute Press.

Collins, T. 1978b. "Line-Forms in Hebrew Poetry", *JSS* 23, 228-224.

Cooper, A.M. 1976. *Biblical Poetics: A Linguistic Approach.* Ann Arbor: University Microfilms.

Cooper, A.M. 1979. Review of Stuart (1976), *Bulletin of the American Schools of Oriental Research* 233, 75-76.

Cornill, C.H. 1901. *Die metrischen Stücke des Buches Jeremia reconstruiert.* Leipzig: J.C. Hinrichs.

Cross, F.M. 1974. "Prose and Poetry in the Mythic and Epic Texts from Ugarit", *Harvard Theological Review* 67, 1-15.

Cross, F.M. 1980. "Foreword" in D.N. Freedman (1980), vii-viii.

Cross, F.M. 1983a. "Studies in the Structure of Hebrew Verse: The Prosody of Lamentations 1:1-22" in C.L. Meyers and M. O'Connor (eds.): *The Word of the Lord shall go forth: Essays in honor of David Noel Freedman.* Winona Lake, Indiana: Eisenbrauns 1983, 129-155.

Cross, F.M. 1983b. "Studies in the Structure of Hebrew Verse: The Prosody of the Psalm of Jonah" in H.B. Huffmon (ed.): *The Quest for the Kingdom of God: Studies in honor of George E. Mendenhall*. Winona Lake, Indiana: Eisenbrauns 1983, 159-167.

Culley, R.C. 1967. *Oral Formulaic Language in the Biblical Psalms*. Toronto: University of Toronto Press.

Culley, R.C. 1970. "Metrical Analysis of Classical Hebrew Poetry" in J.W. Wevers and D.B. Redford (eds.): *Essays on the Ancient Semitic World*. Toronto: University of Toronto Press 1970, 12-28.

Culley, R.C. 1978. Review of Stuart (1976), *CBQ* 40, 255-256.

Cunningham, J.V. 1976. "How shall the poem be written?" in *The Collected Essays of J.V. Cunningham*. Chicago: Swallow Press 1976, 256-271. Originally published in *Denver Quarterly* 2, 1967.

Dahood, M. 1967. "A New Metrical Pattern in Biblical Poetry", *CBQ* 29, 574-579.

Dahood, M. 1968. *Psalms II: A new translation with introduction and commentary*. (The Anchor Bible). Garden City, New York: Doubleday.

Dahood, M. 1976. "Poetry, Hebrew" in K. Crim (ed.): *Interpreter's Dictionary of the Bible*, Supplementary Volume. Nashville: Abingdon Press 1976, 669-672.

Davidson, A.B. 1901. *Introductory Hebrew Grammar: Hebrew Syntax* (third edition, reprint 1976). Edinburgh: T. & T. Clark.

Davie, D. (ed.) 1961. *Poetics I* (Congress 1960). Warszawa: Polish Scientific Publishers.

De Groot, A.W. 1964. "The Description of a Poem" in H.G. Lunt (ed.): *Proceedings of the Ninth International Congress of Linguistics*. The Hague: Mouton 1964, 294-300.

De Moor, J.C. 1978a. "The Art of Versification in Ugarit and Israel, I: The Rhythmical Structure" in Y. Avishur & J. Blau (eds.): *Studies in Bible and the Ancient Near East presented to S.E. Loewenstamm*. Jerusalem: Rubenstein's 1978, 119-139.

De Moor, J.C. 1978b. "The Art of Versification in Ugarit and Israel, II: The Formal Structure", *UF* 10, 187-217.

Denis, A.-M. 1982. Review of O'Connor (1980a), *Le Muséon* 95, 220-221.

Duhm, B. 1901. *Das Buch Jeremia* (Kurzer Handcommentar zum Alten Testament). Tübingen: J.C.B. Mohr.

Eaton, J. 1980/81. "What is Hebrew Poetry?", *Expository Times* 92, 316-317.

Eissfeldt, O. 1964. *Einleitung in das Alte Testament* (dritte, neubearbeitete Auflage). Tübingen: J.C.B. Mohr.

Erlich, V. 1955. "Verse Structure: Sound and Meaning" in *Russian Formalism*. 's Gravenhage: Mouton 1955, 182-198.

Fensham, F.C. 1966. *'n Ondersoek na die Geskiedenis van die Interpretasie van die Hebreeuse Poësie*. Annale van die Universiteit van Stellenbosch 30B1.

Fensham, F.C. 1981. Review of O'Connor (1980a), *Journal of Northwest Semitic Languages* 9, 160.

Finnegan, R. 1970. *Oral Literature in Africa*. Nairobi: Oxford University Press.

Finnegan, R. 1977. *Oral Poetry: Its Nature, Significance and Social Context*. London: Cambridge University Press.

Fohrer, G. 1962. "Zehn Jahre Literatur zur altestamentlichen Prophetie (1951-1960)", *Theologische Rundschau* 28, 1-75.

Fohrer, G. 1967. "Über den Kurzvers" in *Studien zur altestamentlichen Prophetie (1949-1965)* (BZAW 99). Berlin: Töpelmann 1967, 59-91. Revision of *ZAW* 66, 1954, 199-236.

Foster, J.L. 1975. "Thought Couplets in Khety's 'Hymn to the Inundation' ", *JNES* 34, 1-29.

Foster, J.L. 1977. *Thought Couplets and Clause Sequences in a Literary Text: The Maxims of Ptah-hotep* (Society for the Study of Egyptian Antiquities Publications, Volume 5). Toronto.

Foster, J.L. 1980. "*Sinuhe*: The Ancient Egyptian Genre of Narrative Verse", *JNES* 39, 89-117.

Fraser, G.S. 1970. *Metre, Rhyme and Free Verse*. London: Methuen & Co.

Freedman, D.N. 1960. "Archaic Forms in Hebrew Poetry", *ZAW* 72, 101-107.

Freedman, D.N. 1971. "The Structure of Psalm 137" in H. Goedicke (ed.): *Near Eastern Studies in Honor of W.F. Albright*. Baltimore: Johns Hopkins University Press 1971, 187-205. Also in Freedman (1980), 303-321.

Freedman, D.N. 1972. "Prolegomenon" to reprint of G.B. Gray: *The Forms of Hebrew Poetry*. New York: Ktav Publishing House 1972, vii-lvi. Also in Freedman (1980), 23-50.

Freedman, D.N. 1974. "Strophe and Meter in Exodus 15" in H.N. Bream (ed.): *A Light unto My Path: Old Testament Studies in Honor of Jacob M. Myers*. Philadelphia: Temple University Press 1974, 163-202. Also in Freedman (1980), 187-227.

Freedman, D.N. 1977. "Pottery, Poetry, and Prophecy: An esssay on Biblical Poetry", *JBL* 96, 5-26. Also in Freedman (1980), 1-22. Also in J.L. Maier and V.L. Tollers (eds.): *The Bible in its Literary Milieu*. Grand Rapids, Michigan: Eerdmans 1979, 77-100.

Freedman, D.N. 1980. *Pottery, Poetry, and Prophecy: Studies in Early Hebrew Poetry*. Winona Lake, Indiana: Eisenbrauns.

Freeman, D.C. (ed.) 1970. *Linguistics and Literary Style*. New York: Holt, Rhinehart and Winston.

Galbraith, J.A. 1983. Review of O'Connor (1980a), *CBQ* 45, 464-466.

Garr, W.R. 1983. "The Qinah: A Study of Poetic Meter, Syntax and Style", *ZAW* 95, 54-75.

Gasparov, M.L. 1980. "Quantitative Methods in Russian Metrics: Achievements and Prospects", *Russian Poetics in Translation* 7, 1-19.

Geller, S.A. 1979. *Parallelism in early Biblical Poetry* (HSM 20). Missoula, Montana: Scholars Press.

Geller, S.A. 1982a. "Theory and Method in the Study of Biblical Poetry", *Jewish Quarterly Review* 73, 65-77.

Geller, S.A. 1982b. "The Dynamics of Parallel Verse: A Poetic Analysis of Deut 32:6-12", *Harvard Theological Review* 75, 35-56.

Gesenius, W. & Kautzsch, E. & Cowley, A.E. 1910. *Gesenius' Hebrew Grammar* (second edition, reprint 1976). Oxford: Oxford University Press.

Giesebrecht, F. 1905. *Jeremias Metrik am Texte dargestellt*. Göttingen: Vandenhoeck & Ruprecht.

Good, E.M. 1978. Review of Stuart (1976), *JBL* 97, 273-274.

Good, E.M. 1982. Review of O'Connor (1980a), *Journal of the American Academy of Religion* 50, 111-112.

Gordis, R. 1971. "The Structure of Biblical Poetry" in *Poets, Prophets and Sages: Essays in Biblical Interpretation*. Bloomington: Indiana University Press 1971, 61-94. Revision of Hebrew article from 1944/5.

Gordis, R. 1974. *The Song of Songs and Lamentations*. New York: Ktav Publishing House.

Gordon, C.H. 1965. *Ugaritic Textbook* (Analecta Orientalia 38). Rome: Pontificium Institutum Biblicum.

Gordon, C.H. 1981. "Ugarit in Retrospect and Prospect" in G.D. Young (ed.): *Ugarit in Retrospect: Fifty Years of Ugarit and Ugaritic* (Symposium 1979). Winona Lake: Eisenbrauns 1981, 183-200.

Gray, G.B. 1915. *The Forms of Hebrew Poetry*. Reprinted: New York: Ktav Publishing House 1972.

Gross, W. 1974. *Bileam. Literar- und formkritische Untersuchung der Prosa in Num 22-24* (Studien zum Alten und Neuen Testament 38). München: Kösel Verlag.

Gross, W. 1976. *Verbform und Funktion: wayyiqtol für die Gegenwart? Ein Beitrag zur Syntax poetischer althebräischer Texte* (Arbeiten zu Text und Sprache im Alten Testament 1). St. Ottilien: EOS Verlag.

Gross, W. 1982. "Otto Rössler und die Diskussion um das althebräische Verbalsystem", *Biblische Notizen* 18, 28-78.

Greenstein, E.L. 1983. Review of O'Connor (1980a), *Religious Studies Review* 9, 267.

Hagstrom, D.G. 1982. Review of O'Connor (1980a), *Interpretation* 36, 84-85.

Halle, M. & McCarthy, J.J. 1981. "The Metrical Structure of Psalm 137", *JBL* 100, 161-167.

Hammond, M. 1961. "Poetic Syntax" in Davie (1961), 475-482.

Hartman, C.O. 1980. *Free Verse: An Essay on Prosody*. Princeton: Princeton University Press.

Hauser, A.J. 1980. "Judges 5: Parataxis in Hebrew Poetry", *JBL* 99, 23-41.

Heller, J.R. 1977. "Enjambment as a Metrical Force in Romantic Conversation Poems", *Poetics* 6, 15-26.

Hoftijzer, J. 1981. *A Search for Method: A study in the syntactic use of the H-locale in Classical Hebrew*. Leiden: E.J. Brill.

Holladay, W.L. 1966. "The Recovery of Poetic Passages of Jeremiah", *JBL* 85, 401-435.

Horst, F. 1953. "Die Kennzeichen der hebräischen Poesie", *Theologische Rundschau* 21, 97-121.

Hrushovski, B. 1960. "On Free Rhythms in Modern Poetry" in T.A. Sebeok (ed.): *Style in Language*. Cambridge, Massachusetts: MIT Press 1960, 173-190.

Hrushovski, B. 1965. "A Note on Hebrew Prosody: I. Biblical Verse" in S. Burnshaw (ed.): *The Modern Hebrew Poem Itself*. New York: Schocken Books 1965, 211-212.

Hrushovski, B. 1981. "Note on the Systems of Hebrew Versification" in T. Carmi (ed.): *The Penguin Book of Hebrew Verse*. New York: Viking Press 1981, 57-72.

Hymes, D.H. 1976. "Louis Simpson's 'The Deserted Boy' ", *Poetics* 5, 119-155.

Hymes, D.H. 1977. "Discovering Oral performance and Measured Verse in Indian Narrative", *New Literary History* 8, 431-457.

Hymes, D.H. 1980. "Tonkawa Poetics: John Rush Buffalo's 'Coyote and Eagle's Daughter' " in Jacques Maquet (ed.): *On Linguistic Anthropology: Essays in honor of Harry Hoijer 1979.* Malibu: Undena Publications 1980, 33-87.

Jakobson, R. 1966. "Grammatical Parallelism and its Russian Facet", *Language* 42, 399-429.

Jakobson, R. 1972. "Der grammatische Bau des Gedichtes von B. Brecht 'Wir sind sie' " in H. Blumensath (ed.): *Strukturalismus in der Literaturwissenschaft.* Köln: Kiepenheuer & Witsch 1972, 169-183. Revision of *Festschrift Wolfgang Steinitz*, 1965, 175-189.

Kayser, W. 1948. *Das sprachliche Kunstwerk: Eine Einführung in die Literaturwissenschaft* (siebzehnte Auflage 1976). Bern: Franke Verlag.

Kecskés, A. & Kerek, A. 1980. "Directions in Hungarian Metric Research" in J. Odmark (ed.): *Linguistic and Literary Studies in Eastern Europe*, Volume 2. Amsterdam: John Benjamins 1980, 319-359.

Kiparsky, P. 1975. "Stress, Syntax, and Meter", *Language* 51, 576-616.

Kirk, G.S. 1976. "Verse-structure and sentence-structure in Homer" in *Homer and the Oral Tradition.* Cambridge: Cambridge University Press 1976, 146-182. Shortened version of *Yale Classical Studies* 20, 1966, 105-152.

Kosmala, H. 1964. "Form and Structure of Ancient Hebrew Poetry, I (A New Approach)", *Vetus Testamentum* 14, 423-445. Also in Kosmala (1978), 84-106.

Kosmala, H. 1966. "Form and Structure of Ancient Hebrew Poetry, II (Continued)", *Vetus Testamentum* 16, 152-180. Also in Kosmala (1978), 107-135.

Kosmala, H. 1967. "Form and Structure of Isaiah 58", *Annual of the Swedish Theological Institute* 5, 69-81. Also in Kosmala (1978), 136-148.

Kosmala, H. 1978. *Studies, Essays and Reviews*, Volume I: Old Testament. Leiden: E.J. Brill.

Krahmalkov, C.R. 1975. "Two Neo-Punic Poems in Rhymed Verse", *Rivista di studi fenici* 3, 169-205.

Krenkow, F. 1934. "Sadj'" in M.T. Houtsma (ed.): *The Encyclopedia of Islam*, Volume 4. Leiden: E.J. Brill 1934, 43-44.

Kugel, J.L. 1981. *The Idea of Biblical Poetry: Parallelism and its History*. New Haven: Yale University Press.

Kurylowicz, J. 1972. *Studies in Semitic Grammar and Metrics*. Warszawa: Polska Akademia Nauk.

Kurylowicz, J. 1975. *Metrik und Sprachgeschichte*. Warszawa: Polska Akademia Nauk.

La Drière, J.C. 1974. "Prosody" in A. Preminger *et al* (eds.): *Princeton Encyclopedia of Poetry and Poetics* (enlarged edition). Princeton: Princeton University Press 1974, 669-677.

LaSor, W.S. 1979. "An Approach to Hebrew Poetry through the Masoretic Accents" in A.I. Katsh and L. Nemoy (eds.): *Essays on the Occasion of the Seventieth Anniversary of the Dropsie University (1909-1979)*. Philadelphia: Dropsie University 1979, 327-353.

Leech, G.N. 1969. *A Linguistic Guide to English Poetry*. London: Longman.

Link, J. 1979. *Literaturwissenschaftliche Grundbegriffe* (zweite Auflage). München: Fink.

Loewenstamm, S.E. 1980. "The Expanded Colon in Ugaritic and Biblical Verse" in S.E. Loewenstamm: *Comparative Studies in Biblical and Ancient Oriental Literatures* (AOAT 204). Kevelaer: Butzon & Bercker 1980, 281-309. Revision of *JSS* 14, 1969, 176-196.

Longman, T. 1982. "A Critique of Two Recent Metrical Systems", *Biblica* 63, 230-254.

Loretz, O. 1970. "Die Sprüche Jeremias in Jer 1,17 - 9,25", *UF* 2, 109-130.

Loretz, O. 1975. "Die Analyse der ugaritischen und hebräischen Poesie mittels Stichometrie und Konsonantenzählung", *UF* 7, 265-269.

Loretz, O. 1979. *Die Psalmen: Teil II: Beitrag der Ugarit-Texte zum Verständnis von Kolometrie und Textologie der Psalmen: Psalm 90-150* (AOAT 207/2). Kevelaer: Butzon & Bercker.

Lotman, M.Y. 1980. "The Natural Language / Metre Interrelationship in the Mechanism of Verse", *Russian Poetics in Translation* 7, 86-89.

Lotz, J. 1972. "Elements of Versification" in Wimsatt (1972), 1-21.

Lowth, R. 1787. *Lectures on the Sacred Poetry of the Hebrews*, Volume I and II (translated by G. Gregory). Reprinted: Hildesheim: Georg Olms 1969.

Lowth, R. 1848. "The Preliminary Dissertation" in *Isaiah: A New Translation* (14th edition, corrected). London: William Tegg 1848, i-lii.

March, W.E. 1980. Review of Collins (1978a), *JBL* 99, 301.

Margalit, B. 1975. "Studia Ugaritica I: 'Introduction to Ugaritic Prosody' ", *UF* 7, 289-313.

Margalit, B. 1980. *A Matter of 'Life' and 'Death': A Study of the Baal-Mot Epic (CTA 4-5-6)* (AOAT 206). Kevelaer: Butzon & Bercker.

Matthews, P.H. 1981. *Syntax.* Cambridge: Cambridge University Press.

McLendon, S. 1981. "Meaning, Rhetorical Structure and Discourse Organization in Myth" in D. Tannen (ed.): *Analyzing Discourse: Text and Talk* (Georgetown University Round Table on Languages and Linguistics 1981). Washington: Georgetown University Press 1982, 284-305.

Michel, D. 1960. *Tempora und Satzstellung in den Psalmen* (Abhandlungen zur evangelischen Theologie 1). Bonn: Bouvier Verlag.

Mowinckel, S. 1950. "Zum Problem der hebräischen Metrik" in W. Baumgartner *et al* (eds.): *Festschrift für Alfred Bertholet zum 80. Geburtstag.* Tübingen: J.C.B. Mohr 1950, 379-394.

Mowinckel, S. 1956. "Marginalien zur hebräischen Metrik", *ZAW* 68, 97-123.

Mowinckel, S. 1967. *The Psalms in Israel's Worship,* Volume I (translated by D.R. Ap-Thomas). Oxford: Blackwell.

Muilenburg, J. 1953. "A Study in Hebrew Rhetoric: Repetition and Style", *Congress Volume Copenhagen 1953* (SVT 1). Leiden: E.J. Brill 1953, 97-111.

Mukarovsky, J. 1964. "Standard Language and Poetic Language" in P.L. Garvin (ed.): *A Prague School Reader on Esthetics, Literary Structure, and Style.* Washington: Georgetown University Press 1964, 17-30. Also in Freeman (1970), 40-56.

Mukarovsky, J. 1977. *The Word and Verbal Art.* New Haven: Yale University Press.

Nelis, J. 1982. "Poesie" in H. Haag (ed.): *Bibel-Lexikon* (dritte Auflage). Zürich: Benziger Verlag 1982, 1393-1398.

Neuwirth, A. 1981. *Studien zur Komposition der mekkanischen Suren.* Berlin: De Gruyter.

O'Connor, M.P. 1977. "The Rhetoric of the Kilamuwa Inscription", *Bulletin of the American Schools of Oriental Research* 226, 15-29.

O'Connor, M.P. 1980a. *Hebrew Verse Structure.* Winona Lake: Eisenbrauns.

O'Connor, M.P. 1980b. Review of Collins (1978a), *CBQ* 42, 91-92.

Ohmann, R. 1970. "Modes of Order" in Freeman (1970), 209-242.

Opland, J. 1975. *"Imbongi Nezibongo*: The Xhosa Tribal Poet and the Contemporary Poetic Tradition", *Publications of the Modern Languages Association of America* 90, 185-208.

Opland, J. 1976. "Huso and Mqhayi: Notes on the Southslavic and Xhosa Traditions of Oral Poetry" in B.A. Stolz and R.S. Shannon (eds.): *Oral Literature and the Formula*. Ann Arbor: University of Michigan 1976, 120-124.

Opland, J. 1983. *Xhosa Oral Poetry: Aspects of a Black South African Tradition*. Johannesburg: Ravan Press.

Pardee, D. 1981. "Ugaritic and Hebrew Metrics" in G.D. Young (ed.): *Ugarit in Retrospect: Fifty Years of Ugarit and Ugaritic* (Symposium 1979). Winona Lake: Eisenbrauns 1981, 113-130.

Parker, S.B. 1974. "Parallelism and Prosody in Ugaritic Narrative Verse", *UF* 6, 283-294.

Peabody, B. 1975. *The Winged Word*. Albany: State University of New York Press.

Polzin, R. 1976. *Late Biblical Hebrew: Toward an historical typology of Biblical Hebrew Prose* (HSM 12). Missoula, Montana: Scholars Press.

Pope, M.H. 1966. Review of J. Gray: *The Legacy of Canaan*, 1965. *JSS* 11, 228-241.

Popper, W. 1925. "Notes on Parallelism", *HUCA* 2, 63-85.

Powell, T.M. 1982. *The Oracles of Balaam: A Metrical Analysis and Exegesis*. Ann Arbor: University Microfilms.

Richter, W. 1980. *Grundlagen einer althebräischen Grammatik. B. Die Beschreibungsebenen. III. Der Satz (Satztheorie)* (Arbeiten zu Text und Sprache im Alten Testament 13). St. Ottilien: EOS Verlag.

Ridderbos, N.H. 1972. *Die Psalmen: Stilistische Verfahren und Aufbau* (BZAW 117). Berlin: De Gruyter.

Robinson, T.H. 1936a. "Some Principles of Hebrew Metrics", *ZAW* 54, 28-43.

Robinson, T.H. 1936b. "Anacrusis in Hebrew Poetry" in *Werden und Wesen des Alten Testaments* (BZAW 66), 1936, 37-40.

Robinson, T.H. 1947. *The Poetry of the Old Testament*. London: Duckworth.

Robinson, T.H. 1950. "Basic Principles of Hebrew Poetic Form" in W. Baumgartner *et al* (eds.): *Festschrift für Alfred Bertholet zum 80. Geburtstag*. Tübingen: J.C.B. Mohr 1950, 438-450.

Robinson, T.H. 1953. "Hebrew Poetic Form: The English Tradition" in *Congress Volume Copenhagen 1953* (SVT 1). Leiden: E.J. Brill 1953, 128-149.

Rycroft, D.K. 1980. "The Question of Metre in Southern African Praise Poetry" in P.J. Wentzel (ed.): *Third African Languages Congress of Unisa*. Pretoria: Unisa 1980, 289-312.

Ross, H. 1981. "Robert Frost's 'Out, out - '; A way in" in W. Klein & W. Levelt (eds.): *Crossing the Boundaries in Linguistics* (Festschrift M. Bierwisch). Dordrecht: Dorothy Reidel Publishing Company 1981, 265-282.

Rudolph, W. 1968. *Jeremia* (Handbuch zum Alten Testament) (dritte, verbesserte Auflage). Tübingen: J.C.B. Mohr.

Sappan, R. 1981. *The Typical Features of the Syntax of Biblical Poetry in its Classical Period*. Jerusalem: Kiryat-Sefer.

Sawyer, J.F.A. 1981. Review of Collins (1978a), *JSS* 26, 123-125.

Schmitt, H.-C. 1982. Review of O'Connor (1980a), *ZAW* 94, 179.

Schramm, G.M. 1976. "Poetic Patterning in Biblical Hebrew" in L.L. Orlin (ed.): *Michigan Oriental Studies in honor of George G. Cameron*. Ann Arbor: University of Michigan 1976, 167-191.

Segert, S. 1953. "Vorarbeiten zur hebräischen Metrik: I und II", *Archiv Orientalni* 21, 481-542.

Segert, S. 1958. "Die Methoden der althebräischen Metrik", *Communio Viatorum* 1, 233-241.

Segert, S. 1960. "Problems of Hebrew Prosody" in *Congress Volume Oxford 1959* (SVT 7). Leiden: E.J. Brill 1960, 283-291.

Segert, S. 1969. "Versbau und Sprachbau in der althebräischen Poesie", *Mitteilungen des Instituts für Orientforschung* 15, 312-321.

Segert, S. 1979. "Ugaritic Poetry and Poetics: Some Preliminary Observations", *UF* 11, 729-738.

Smend, R. 1981. Review of Collins (1978a), *Die Welt des Orients* 12, 190-193.

Smith, G.A. 1912. *The Early Poetry of Israel in its Physical and Social Origins*. London: Oxford University Press.

Stankiewicz, E. 1960. "Linguistics and the Study of Poetic Language" in T.A. Sebeok (ed.): *Style in Language*. Cambridge, Massachusetts: MIT Press 1960, 69-81.

Stek, J.H. 1974. "The Stylistics of Hebrew Poetry", *Calvin Theological Journal* 9, 15-31.

Stuart, D.K. 1976. *Studies in early Hebrew Meter* (HSM 13). Missoula, Montana: Scholars Press.

Stutterheim, C.F.P. 1961. "Poetry and Prose, their interrelations and transitional forms" in Davie (1961), 225-237.

Talstra, E. 1984. Review of Collins (1978a), *Bibliotheca Orientalis* 41, 453-457.

Tarlinskaja, M.G. & Teterina, L.M. 1974. "Verse - Prose - Metre", *Linguistics* 129, 63-86.

Tarlinskaya, M.G. 1980. "The Problem of English Versification: A Re-Examination", *Russian Poetics in Translation* 7, 45-60.

Tedlock, D. 1977. "Toward an Oral Poetics", *New Literary History* 8, 507-519.

Thompson, D.L. 1973. *The Order of Adverbial Modifiers in Genesis and Proverbs: A Study in the Syntax of Hebrew Poetry*. Ann Arbor: University Microfilms.

Thompson, J. 1961. "Linguistic Structures and the Poetic Line" in Davie (1961), 167-175. Also in Freeman (1970), 336-346.

Thompson, J.A. 1980. *The Book of Jeremiah* (The New International Commentary on the Old Testament). Grand Rapids, Michigan: W.B. Eerdmans.

Todorov, T. 1972. "Die Kategorien der literarischen Erzählung" in H. Blumensath (ed.): *Strukturalismus in der Literaturwissenschaft*. Köln: Kiepenheuer & Witsch 1972, 263-294. Originally published in *Communications* 8, 1966, 125-151.

Van der Lugt, P. 1980. *Strofische Structuren in de Bijbels-Hebreeuwse Poëzie*. Kampen: J.H. Kok.

Van der Westhuizen, J.P. 1973. *Literary Devices in Biblical Hymns of Praise*. Unpublished Dissertation for D. Litt. et Phil. University of South Africa.

Van Rensburg, J.F.J. 1983. *Die Tipering van Reëls in 'n Babiloniese Gedig*. Unpublished Dissertation for D. Litt. University of Pretoria.

Van Selms, A. 1972. *Jeremia*, deel I (De Prediking van het Oude Testament). Nijkerk: G.F. Callenbach.

Von Herder, J.G. 1833. *The Spirit of Hebrew Poetry*, Volumes I & II (translated by J. Marsh). Reprint: Naperville, Illinois: Aleph Press 1971.

Von Soden, W. 1952. *Grundriss der akkadischen Grammatik* (Analecta Orientalia 33). Rome: Pontificium Institutum Biblicum.

Von Soden, W. 1982. "Untersuchungen zur babylonischen Metrik, Teil I", *Zeitschrift für Assyriologie und vorderasiatische Archäologie* 71/2, 161-204.

Wahl, T.P. 1976. *Strophic Structure of Individual Laments in Psalms Books I and II*. Ann Arbor: University Microfilms.

Wambacq, B.N. 1957. *Jeremias, Klaagliederen, Baruch, Brief van Jeremias* (De Boeken van het Oude Testament). Roermond en Maaseik: J.J. Romen.

Watson, W.G.E. 1975. "Verse-Patterns in Ugaritic, Akkadian and Hebrew Poetry", *UF* 7, 483-492.

Watson, W.G.E. 1980. Review of Collins (1978a), *Biblica* 61, 581-583.

Watson, W.G.E. 1983. Review of O'Connor (1980a), *Biblica* 64, 131-134.

Watson, W.G.E. 1984. *Classical Hebrew Poetry: A Guide to its Techniques* (Journal for the Study of the Old Testament Supplement 26). Sheffield: JSOT Press.

Watters, W.R. 1976. *Formula Criticism and the Poetry of the Old Testament* (BZAW 138). Berlin: De Gruyter.

Weiser, A. 1981. *Das Buch Jeremia: Kapitel 1 - 25,14* (Das Alte Testament Deutsch) (achte Auflage). Göttingen: Vandenhoeck & Ruprecht.

Weiser, A. 1982. *Das Buch Jeremia: Kapitel 25,15 - 52,34* (Das Alte Testament Deutsch) (siebte, unveränderte Auflage). Göttingen: Vandenhoeck & Ruprecht.

Williams, R.J. 1976. *Hebrew Syntax: An Outline* (Second edition). Toronto: University of Toronto Press.

Wilson, G.H. 1982. "Ugaritic Word Order and Sentence Structure in Krt", *JSS* 27, 17-32.

Wimsatt, W.K. 1971. "The Rule and the Norm: Halle and Keyser on Chaucer's Meter" in S. Chatman (ed.): *Literary Style: A Simposium*. London: Oxford University Press 1971, 197-215 and discussion on 215-220.

Wimsatt, W.K. (ed.) 1972. *Versification: Major Language Types*. New York: New York University Press.

Wimsatt, W.K. & Beardsley, M.C. 1959. "The Concept of Meter: An Exercise in Abstraction", *Publications of the Modern Language Association of America* 74, 585-598.

Winograd, T. 1983. *Language as a Cognitive Process, Volume I: Syntax*. Reading, Massachusetts: Addison-Wesley.

Wohlenberg, D. 1967. *Kultmusik in Israel: Eine forschungsgeschichtliche Untersuchung.* Dissertation, University of Hamburg.

Würthwein, E. 1957. *The Text of the Old Testament* (translated by P.R. Ackroyd). Oxford: Blackwell.

Yoder, P.B. 1972. "Biblical Hebrew" in Wimsatt (1972), 52-65.

Young, G.D. 1950. "Ugaritic Prosody", *JNES* 9, 124-133.

Zhirmunsky [Zirmunski(j)], V.M. 1966a. *Introduction to Metrics* (translated from the Russian of 1925 by C.F. Brown). The Hague: Mouton.

Zhirmunsky [Zirmunski(j)], V.M. 1966b. "The Versification of Majakovski" in R. Jakobson (ed.): *Poetics II* (Congress 1964). Warszawa: Polish Scientific Publishers 1966, 211-242.

Ziegler, J. (ed.) 1976. *Jeremias, Baruch, Threni, Epistula Jeremiae* (Septuaginta: Vetus Testamentum Graecum Auctoritate Academiae Scientiarum Gottingensis editum, vol. XV) (zweite, durchgesehene Auflage). Göttingen: Vandenhoeck & Ruprecht.